CLARENDON LAW LECTURES

THE PRACTICE OF PRINCIPLE

THE PRACTICE OF PRINCIPLE

In Defence of a Pragmatist Approach
to Legal Theory

JULES L. COLEMAN

OXFORD
UNIVERSITY PRESS

OXFORD

UNIVERSITY PRESS

Great Clarendon Street, Oxford OX2 6DP

Oxford University Press is a department of the University of Oxford.
It furthers the University's objective of excellence in research, scholarship,
and education by publishing worldwide in

Oxford New York

Athens Auckland Bangkok Bogotá Buenos Aires Calcutta
Cape Town Chennai Dar es Salaam Delhi Florence Hong Kong Istanbul
Karachi Kuala Lumpur Madrid Melbourne Mexico City Mumbai
Nairobi Paris São Paulo Shanghai Singapore Taipei Tokyo Toronto Warsaw

and associated companies in Berlin Ibadan

Oxford is a registered trade mark of Oxford University Press
in the UK and certain other countries

Published in the United States
by Oxford University Press Inc., New York

© Jules L. Coleman 2001

The moral rights of the author have been asserted
Database right Oxford University Press (maker)

First published 2001

British Library Cataloguing in Publication Data

Data available

Library of Congress Cataloging-in-Publication Data
Coleman, Jules L.
The practice of principle: in defense of a pragmatist approach to legal theory / Jules L. Coleman.
p. cm.
Includes bibliographical references and index.
1. Law—Philosophy. 2. Jurisprudence. 3. Principle (Philosophy). I. Title.
K230.C64 A2 2001
340'.1—dc21 00–068685
ISBN 0–19–829814–5

1 3 5 7 9 10 8 6 4 2

Typeset by Graphicraft Limited, Hong Kong
Printed in Great Britain
on acid-free paper by
Biddles Ltd., Guildford and King's Lynn

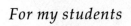

For my students

Preface

This book expands the argument introduced in the Clarendon Lectures in Law presented at Oxford University in the fall of 1998. Being invited to present these lectures represents the greatest honor I have experienced in my professional life. I hope this book justifies the confidence the Clarendon committee displayed in me. I presented three lectures at Oxford: the first on tort theory; the second on jurisprudence; the third on certain methodological issues in jurisprudence. This book follows the outline of the lectures, but expands on the argument in each case considerably. Somehow three one-hour lectures have been transformed into twelve.

Raised on Hart's *The Concept of Law*, cutting my teeth on Dworkin's *Taking Rights Seriously* and Raz's *Practical Reason and Norms*, being a student of Joel Feinberg's—clearly I have been blessed with the great good fortune of becoming interested in legal philosophy during an extraordinary period in its history. H. L. A. Hart has left a mark on us all, and his influence on me is all over this book. Obvious too is the impact of Feinberg, Raz, and Dworkin. The philosophically trained reader will detect other influences as well: especially those of Wilfrid Sellars, W. V. O. Quine, Isaac Levi, and Donald Davidson. For this book is an effort not just to defend a range of substantive views in legal philosophy, but also to vindicate a certain philosophical approach to legal theory that I label pragmatist. It is a pragmatism that has almost nothing to do with the way that term has been employed in contemporary legal scholarship; its roots are, however, deep in this distinctly American approach to analytic philosophy.

My entire professional life has been an extended educational experience. I write not so much to solve problems as to satisfy myself that I understand what they are. Many people have played significant roles in helping me grasp the problems in philosophy that have consumed me; no one, however, has been more influential on me than have been my students. I take great pride in their accomplishments and smile as they pass me by. The least I could do is thank them for what I have learned from them, and so I dedicate this book to them as a way of expressing my gratitude.

Several people have read part or all of the manuscript in earlier drafts, and I have benefited from their comments. I am especially indebted to Scott Shapiro, Mark Greenberg, Kenneth Himma, Arthur Ripstein, Ben Zipursky, Andrei Marmor, Wil Waluchow, George Fletcher, Charles Sabel, and Brian Bix for their comments on earlier drafts. Chuck Sabel had a depth of understanding of the project and of its interest that exceeded my own and that inspired me especially at those moments when my own interest and confidence in it flagged. Scott Shapiro has influenced nearly every argument in the second part of the book; and Mark Greenberg's detailed and subtle comments on the first part deepened the argument considerably. Neither Chuck, Scott, nor Mark agree fully with the argument, but their critical reflections on it were essential to my development of it.

In dedicating the book to my students, it is hard to single out former students and friends for their particular contributions to this project, so much have I benefited from so many of them. It is fitting, however, that I emphasize the contribution of Stephen Perry and Scott Shapiro. Though I take issue in this book with Stephen's claims about the nature of methodology in legal philosophy, no one has done more to bring attention to the subject than has Stephen. No one has done more to stimulate my work in tort theory either. We share more common ground there, but our differences have forced me to rethink and at times to abandon some of my views, and at other times in response to his objections to deepen them. His friendship is more important still; and I cannot thank him enough for the strength he has provided during trying times. Since I wrote "Negative and Positive Positivism," I have continued dabbling in jurisprudence and thinking about it while teaching it pretty regularly once coming to Yale, but I had lost some interest in the subject. Scott not only rekindled my interest in it, but in the past five or six years he has taught me more about it and more about what my own views on it are than I had learned in all my studies until then. Scott has a distinctive voice, with an understanding and maturity that belies his youth: an openness to argument and a thirst for knowledge that is not merely refreshing, but nearly unrivaled. In addition, he has the great virtue of having his head screwed on correctly, which makes him reliable as a friend and colleague in ways in which many of our academic "friends" often prove not to be. I have had great teachers: Donald Davidson, Joel Feinberg, Guido Calabresi, Wilfrid Sellars, among them. No one has taught me more than Scott, nor helped me understand better what I apparently already knew. So influential has Scott been that it is hard to know where his contributions end and mine begin. Certainly it should be clear to anyone who reads this book that only H. L. A. Hart has more substantially influenced me.

I consider myself a good writer, especially clear on difficult and technical material. For the first time in my academic career, however, I have turned my work over to a professional editor, Eric Cavallero. Working with Eric was a revelation, a pleasure, and extremely educational. I learned more about my own positions as we went over his edits than I thought was there, and I am convinced this process significantly deepened the argument. In addition, if the book, which is dense and demanding at points, is readable, even occasionally enjoyable, Eric should get the credit. If the argument remains unpersuasive, blame it on the bossa nova.

My wife, Mimsie, accompanied me to Oxford for the lectures and held me together as I prepared for the first, as she has held me and our family together from the start. The only demand she has ever made on me is that I turn down the stereo when I listen to music and the amplifier when I play guitar; she has also begged me not to sing when doing either. A tough but fair deal all around.

I also owe a special debt of gratitude to my assistant Alieta-Marie Levesque, to the support staff and Dean's Office at Yale Law School, and especially to Dean Anthony Kronman, who has been a loyal and unfailing friend, and a generous supporter of my scholarly efforts.

I wish as well that I could find a way to thank Sidney Morgenbesser for his contribution to this project, but the truth is he hasn't read a word of it. Nevertheless, whenever I think about why I do philosophy—why doing it is a passion and an obligation and way too much fun, and why philosophers are the source of so much humor and pathos—I think of Sidney. Everybody who knows him no doubt thinks of him the same way. Even if he hasn't read a word of this book, his inspiration is all over it.

My family, friends, and many of my peers know I love rock, jazz, and blues music. I even author a little-read, occasional music column. At this point I am trying to convince Oxford University Press to publish some of these columns along with several more serious, but perhaps less enjoyable, academically respectable articles in an edited collection of my work. To this point Oxford has resisted in spite of my willingness to pay the additional printing costs. For some reason, the Press keeps claiming they have something of a professional reputation to maintain. Something about the inappropriateness of columns extolling the virtues of "Acid Jazz" mavens Isotope 217 and Liquid Soul or blues unknowns like Honeybee Edwards, and rockers like the Chills and Yo La Tango in a serious scholarly work. I am sure it's all part of the Britney Spears Conspiracy (now there's a promising name for a group).

I am an avid, if by no means accomplished, blues guitarist. One of the great things about the blues is that songs are constructed around a very few basic formats and progressions. Moreover, there are several blues tunes one has to play in order to play the blues. Everybody learns these tunes; no one is embarrassed about playing them, or making a certain interpretation of them part of one's repertoire. Students of the blues just do not go out riffing on their own, inventing new song structures, running aimlessly through scales in the hopes of hitting on an interesting "idea". I conceive of being a philosopher in the same way. The legal academy puzzles and troubles me just because so many people riff randomly without understanding the foundation of the disciplines they draw upon. To quote one of my favorite rock singers, Graham Parker, "they make a lot of noise, but they got nothing to say". Real philosophers not only learn the history of their discipline; they internalize it. They are not embarrassed by the fact that there is an important sense in which nothing is new in philosophy. They are not embarrassed working and reworking familiar themes. What distinguishes good philosophers from others is not that they invent new paradigms. By that standard, in the history of Western civilization there would be only about a dozen good philosophers—at most. Good philosophy is like good blues. Great blues players first make it clear to us that they are playing a blues—the references to the familiar are all there, the chord progression is outlined—then they go off, play around and through the familiar, connect the dots in unusual, sometimes awe-inspiring ways, then bring us back to the familiar again, thus deepening our understanding and showing us the extraordinary possibilities inherent in what we already know. In this way, they expand the form while all the time working within it. Philosophy is similar. It does not educate us by mystifying our experience. It illuminates the practices in which we are engaged. It clarifies our understanding of what we are doing. If that enables us to do better, so much the better. If it enables us to understand ourselves better, that is better still. Like the blues, good philosophy penetrates the heart, touches the soul, turns pain into a form of pleasure; alas, played too loudly, or by someone with no ear or heart for it, it can leave one's ears ringing and one's head shaking.

I could not have completed this project without the help of a number of good friends and excellent philosophers who shared their ideas and their time with me. And I would not have wanted to without the love and support of my wife, Mimsie, and our children, Jesse, Jeremy, and Laura. I love my work, but I cherish my family.

Jules L. Coleman

New Haven, Connecticut

Contents

Introduction

In this book I introduce and attempt to sustain two different kinds of argument; the aim is not only to defend a range of views on substantive issues in legal theory, but also to vindicate by example a certain methodological approach to such issues—an approach whose fundamental commitments are those of philosophical pragmatism. In so characterizing the method, I do not mean to align myself with the fashionable "pragmatism" of today's American legal academy; nor do I mean to suggest—as common usage might have it—that the method I employ is "pragmatic" in the sense of eschewing theory. On the contrary, the pragmatism I embrace is, in the first instance, a set of commitments about the semantic contents of theories and about the criteria of theory justification. While one could defend any of the main substantive views about legal theory that I endorse in this book without being a pragmatist (and while one could be a pragmatist and reject the lot of those views as well), pragmatism has nonetheless left a distinctive mark on the positions I defend, and I hope it will prove valuable to expose the method to critical scrutiny. The basic elements of the methodology are introduced in Lecture 1.

On the substantive side of things, the book advances three main theses. In Part I, I defend the view that the core of tort law is best understood as embodying the principle of corrective justice. In Part II, I defend a version of inclusive legal positivism. In Part III, I defend what has been called (quite misleadingly, by both Hart and his critics) "descriptive jurisprudence". In each case, I have found it helpful to contrast the view I defend with familiar alternative accounts. Thus, in the first part my foil is the economic analysis of law. In the second part the contrasting position is exclusive legal positivism. And in the third part the enemies of the good and the noble are Dworkin's interpretivism and both normative and naturalized jurisprudence. I have a great deal of respect for each of the bodies of theory that I take on, and I certainly offer no knockdown arguments against any of them. Indeed, I am drawn in ways to each, and regard them as valuable contributions to a dialogue that I hope this book advances further.

The argument presented in Part I presupposes, and occasionally draws on, the argument of my earlier book *Risks and Wrongs*. I do not attempt here a detailed development of a particular conception of corrective justice.[1] The

---

[1] For that the reader is directed to several essays I have written since *Risks and Wrongs* (Cambridge: Cambridge University Press, 1992). In particular, "Mischief and Misfortune" (with A. Ripstein) *McGill Law Journal* 41 (Dec. 1995) 91–130 and "The Practice of Corrective Justice" in David G. Owen (ed.), *Philosophical Foundations of Tort Law* (Oxford: Clarendon Press, 1995) present my substantive views about the nature of corrective justice as a moral ideal, its relationship to distributive justice, and its role in our social lives.

focus in Part I is instead the more general question of what is to count as an explanation of a part of the law—in this case, tort law. I distinguish among three different kinds of explanations one might offer: conceptual explanation, causal–functional explanation, and constructive interpretation. I raise the critical question, what kind of explanation is the economic analysis supposed to be? And I seek to make clear what kind of an explanation the corrective justice account is. In *Risks and Wrongs* I was not explicit about the kind of explanation of tort law that I was providing, but it would not have been unfair to read it as a kind of constructive interpretation in the Dworkinian sense. In this book I explicitly advance the different view that the corrective justice account is a specific kind of conceptual explanation of tort law.

Consider a common claim about tort law—that it is a social practice designed by humans, presumably in order to serve human interests. This claim often invites a kind of instrumentalist or functionalist account of the institution. If among the key elements of tort law are the concepts that are central to it—concepts such as action, duty, breach, causation, and harm—then one kind of conceptual explanation of tort law would explain the content of these concepts in terms of the putative function that the institution serves.[2] Economic analysis often seeks to explain tort law in this way, by reducing its concepts to terms that reflect the function of producing economically efficient outcomes. Thus, it is a staple of the economic analysis that once we understand the concept of negligence or unreasonable risk in terms of "cost-justified precautions", there is nothing else left in the concept for us to understand. The content of the concept of negligence is exhausted by its relationship to a certain economic theory of the law's function. I argue that this reductive conceptual analysis of tort law fails. The reductive accounts of concepts like negligence do not exhaust their legal content; and, moreover, these accounts leave altogether unexplained some concepts— like that of duty—that are central to tort law.

However, there are other kinds of conceptual explanations, and corrective justice is an example of one. It purports to explain tort law in a non-reductive way, by identifying the principle that ties together its central concepts and explains the practical inferences they warrant. Tort law is itself a scheme of practical reason. Typically, the plaintiff has the burden of presenting evidence and argument to support various allegations—among them, typically, that she was harmed in a way the law ordinarily protects; that the defendant breached a duty that he had toward the plaintiff; and

---

[2] Such an explanation would also display why these elements are present in the law in terms of the function the law serves. We can, of course, divide up the institution in a variety of different ways—in terms, for example, of its structure and its substantive and procedural rules. Such an explanation would also display why these elements are present in the law in terms of the function the law serves.

that in breaching the duty, the defendant caused the plaintiff's harm in a way that makes the harm attributable to the defendant as his doing. If the plaintiff makes out her case, then a certain practical inference is thought to be warranted—namely, that the defendant owes the plaintiff compensation for the loss she has suffered. Notice the concepts that are prominent in this practice—wrong, harm, responsibility, and repair among them. These are the concepts that organize our tort practice. What the principle of corrective justice does, I maintain, is to make transparent their relationships to one another and to the inference of liability. In this sense, the principle of corrective justice is embodied in tort law in a way in which the principle of efficiency clearly is not—or so I argue in Lecture 2. In other words, economic analysis fails both as a reductive account of the content of the concepts central to tort law, and as an account of the scheme of practical inference that is reflected in the relationship among them. Where corrective justice makes that relationship transparent, economic analysis mystifies it.

In Lecture 3 I return to the idea that tort law is a human practice that, broadly speaking, serves certain functions. If the economic account fails both as a reductive conceptual analysis and as a device for illuminating the scheme of practical reason embodied in tort law, perhaps we should regard the economic account as a social-scientific or causal–functional explanation of tort law, and not as a conceptual analysis of any sort. We are familiar with causal–functional explanations from evolutionary biology. For example, the function of the heart is to pump blood, and this explains certain characteristic features of that organ; similarly, the fact that leopards have spots is to be explained by their serving the function of making the leopard a more effective hunter. In a standard explanation of this kind, the function may be said to explain the existence, persistence, and shape of a system only in so far as there is an appropriate causal mechanism that links the explanans to the explanandum. Without the causal mechanism, a putative functional explanation of this sort is merely a "Just So Story". I argue that if it is to be understood as a causal–functional account, the economic analysis of tort law has not risen beyond being a "Just So Story". It does not defend its claim that tort law actually produces optimal deterrence (there is no persuasive empirical data to this effect), and, more importantly, it proposes no causal mechanism that might explain how this putative fact about the outcome or effect of tort law might explain tort law's existence, persistence, and shape.

Perhaps the most plausible way to understand economic analysis is to regard it as an explanation of the sort that Ronald Dworkin calls "constructive interpretation". Understood this way, the claim is that the alleged function or point of tort law—optimal risk reduction—is the hermeneutic glue that holds the elements of tort law together so as to display it in its best light. However, I argue that economic analysis does not fare particularly well as constructive interpretation either, since rather than holding the disparate elements of tort law together, economic efficiency mystifies those elements and renders their connection to one another opaque. To make matters worse, efficiency is not the sort of point or purpose whose moral defensibility or attractiveness is obvious—and so we are owed an argument for that element of the interpretation as well. An argument, by the way, that the literature on the subject suggests is not available.

Also in Lecture 3 I respond to an important set of objections. The corrective justice account may seem to be unsatisfactory as an account of tort law in at least two different ways. First, while corrective justice may explain why tort law imposes liability for certain kinds of wrongful conduct when harm is caused as a result, the account does not pick out the specific wrongs that warrant the imposition of liability. It is in this sense formalistic and empty; its content has to be filled in by some other theory. Or if it is not entirely empty, it is at least incomplete in a way that renders it inadequate. This putative emptiness of corrective justice might even suggest that the economic analysis of law could provide a supplemental account of the first-order duties that are enforced in tort law as a matter of corrective justice. I respond to each of these objections, explaining why the corrective justice account is neither empty nor in need of a supplemental account in order to be an adequate explanation of tort law.

One thing that could be said about economic analysis is that even if does not explain anything convincingly, it explains a lot of things not altogether implausibly. It displays a certain consilience. In contrast, the corrective justice account might seem to explain or to shed light on nothing more than our tort practice—if indeed it sheds light on anything at all. Were that the case, it would be odd and problematic for the theory. After all, the concepts that figure in tort law—responsibility, harm, wrongdoing, compensation, and so on—are familiar in other areas of our legal and moral life. Shouldn't we expect the principles that govern the relationships among these concepts in the context of tort law also to yield some insight into the range of other practices in which the concepts figure? In Lecture 4 I allay this worry by arguing that the corrective justice account of tort law illuminates not only tort law, but also the connection between our institutions of corrective and distributive justice, and helps us to understand the requirements of fairness in keeping track of the costs of life's misfortunes more generally.

Corrective justice governs the scheme of practical reasoning found in tort law, and in that sense explains it. At the same time, I maintain, the practice of tort law itself helps to fill out the content of our concept of corrective justice.[3] In Lecture 5 I respond to an obvious challenge—namely, that this two-way relationship between practice and principle is objectionably circular. I conclude the first part with some very provisional remarks on the

---

[3] I first introduced this idea in "The Practice of Corrective Justice".

relationship of corrective justice to fairness and of fairness to a certain liberal ideal of the person as the author of her own life.

Part II is devoted to the ongoing debate among jurisprudential theorists about the nature of law, and about how we are to understand its purported normativity. In Lecture 6 I formulate several distinctions that are to figure in the discussion that follows. One of the most crucial of these is a distinction among three related sets of questions: (1) What are the existence conditions of legal authority? How can we explain the concept of legal authority without presupposing it? (2) What kind of authority is legal authority? (3) Under what conditions, if any, is law's claim to legitimate authority true?

In Lecture 7 I answer the first of these questions. I defend there what I have called the "conventionality thesis", the claim that legal authority is made possible by a specific kind of conventional social practice. The conventionality thesis is my version of the familiar positivist thesis that the criteria of legality are in a sense conventional. In explicating this thesis, I put critical pressure on a number of familiar claims about the positivist conception of the rule of recognition: first, that the content of the rule is determined by the practice that supports it; second, that the scope of the obligation it imposes is limited to the scope of the convergent behavior of officials; third, that the conventionality of the rule of recognition is incompatible with all but the most peripheral disagreements about its content; and fourth, that such disagreement cannot be resolved by substantive moral argument. Readers familiar with the current state of jurisprudence will quickly see that these are all claims that Ronald Dworkin imputes to positivism as entailments of its commitment to the conventionality of the rule of recognition. I argue that the rule's conventionality entails none of these four claims, and moreover that each is mistaken. Lecture 7 is, by my lights, the most important in this part of the book.

If what unites positivists is a commitment to the conventionality of the criteria of legality, the main issue that divides us is the question of whether other commitments of positivism, or any conceptual truths about law, impose constraints on the content of those criteria. Exclusive legal positivists, most notably Joseph Raz, maintain that all criteria of legality must be social sources. Inclusive legal positivists, myself among them, deny that. In particular, inclusive legal positivists maintain that the substantive morality of a norm can be a condition of its legality—provided that is specified in the conventionally accepted and practiced rule of recognition. In Lecture 8 these differences between inclusive and exclusive legal positivism are laid out; and I take some pains to distinguish my version of inclusive legal positivism from other accounts. In general, I do not believe that other inclusive legal positivists have always grasped, as well as they might, just what it is about our thesis that is objectionable from the exclusive legal positivist point of view.

In Lecture 9 I consider what Raz in particular finds objectionable in it. He believes it is a conceptual truth that law necessarily claims to be a legitimate authority. That claim can, as an empirical matter, always turn out to be false; however, it is not necessarily or analytically false, and therefore it could be true. If it could be true, then law must be the sort of thing that this claim could be true of. Raz believes that law's claim to legitimate authority could be true only if it is possible to identify legal norms and their content by appealing to social sources alone—for example, by consulting the form and manner of a law's enactment; thus, he concludes, the criteria of a norm's legality must be social sources, and cannot, for example, make reference to the norm's substantive moral merits. Raz calls this conclusion the "sources thesis". It is strictly incompatible with the inclusive legal positivist claim that, under certain circumstances, the legality of a norm may be a matter of its substantive moral merit, and not a matter of its social source. Drawing on several distinctions—most especially, that between validity and identification conditions of legal norms—I argue that even if Raz is right about law's conceptually necessary claim to authority, the sources thesis as a theory of legal validity does not follow from it. My strategy in Lecture 9 is thus to grant all of Raz's claims about authority—even the most controversial of them—but to deny that they have all of the implications he claims they do.

Law is a normative practice—everyone agrees on that much. Raz explicates law's normativity in terms of a putative claim to legitimate authority, buttressed by a particular account of what it means to be a practical authority. His account is powerful but controversial, and thus his attack on inclusive legal positivism turns on potentially vulnerable premises. Recently, Scott Shapiro has characterized legal normativity in more general terms, propounding what has come to be called the "practical difference thesis". One polemical advantage of the practical difference thesis is that it captures the essence of Raz's attack on inclusive legal positivism without the controversial aspects of his full-blown theory of authority. Shapiro has argued powerfully that the practical difference thesis is incompatible with inclusive legal positivism. Thus, he aims to vindicate a conclusion similar to Raz's, but to do so on the basis of weaker premises. In Lecture 10 I lay out Shapiro's argument and explain why various responses to him have failed. I then present a general argument against both Shapiro and Raz to the effect that even if it is true of law that it must make a practical difference, or that it must be the sort of thing that could be a legitimate authority, it does not follow that the same must be true of each and every law. To think otherwise appears to be an instance of the fallacy of composition. Thus, the fact—if it is one—that rules valid under "inclusive clauses" of a rule of recognition can neither be legitimate authorities nor make a practical difference is not decisive against inclusive legal positivism.

That said, it may nonetheless have to be granted that Shapiro's critique is decisive against Hart, who is its proper target. For Shapiro makes a strong case that Hart is committed to the view that all laws must be capable of making a practical difference. This seems to follow from what is arguably Hart's commitment to a certain kind of functionalism about law.[4] Shapiro's somewhat speculative suggestion that Hart's view about law's guidance function is connected to his general functionalism about law has led me to reconceptualize an important part of *The Concept of Law*. Some of the results of this rethinking are discussed at the end of Lecture 10.

Some readers of drafts of the manuscript have wondered about the relationship between my corrective justice account of tort law and my legal positivism. Two related questions in particular have arisen. Some have wondered how I could defend a corrective justice account of tort law—one in which tort law is said to embody a moral ideal—while at the same time advancing a positivist theory of the concept of law. Others have wondered whether my tort theory is supposed to fall out of my general theory of the concept of law. Both worries betray serious misunderstandings of the relationship between a general jurisprudence and a philosophical theory of a substantive area or body of the law. Legal positivism is a general jurisprudence that asserts that morality is not a necessary condition of legality or that wherever there is law, the criteria of legality are conventional. Legal positivism does not deny that the law of a community, in part or in general, can be morally defensible or otherwise express or embody moral ideals. One might hope this is often the case; even positivists are entitled to do so. Legal positivism denies only that areas of the law *must* embody or express the demands of morality as a condition of their legality; and the argument of the first part of the book is that Anglo-American tort law is best understood as articulating a conception of corrective justice. Moreover, whereas I defend the view that corrective justice is a morally attractive ideal, my argument that Anglo-American tort law embodies it does not depend on this fact about it. Nor should one expect a particular theory of tort law to fall out of a general jurisprudence. A theory of the nature of law or of the concept of it is a theory about what it is to have a certain kind of social practice. It is not a theory about what particular substantive bodies of the law should look like, or whether indeed we must have a tort, contract, or criminal law.

The literature contains two important challenges to conceptual analysis. The first maintains that we should just give up on a priori conceptual analysis altogether, abandoning philosophical jurisprudence in favor of a naturalized or scientific jurisprudence. A weaker version of the claim is that conceptual analysis of law can do little more than the preliminary

---

[4] Thus, while I would like to believe that my view represents the true legacy of Hart's positivism, Hart may actually be driven by a kind of functionalist picture of law that I reject.

spadework necessary to an overall naturalistic project. Conceptual analysis is incapable on its own terms of providing insight into legal practice or
resolving the theoretical debates that divide legal theorists. A thoughtful
version of this position is advanced by Brian Leiter. The other response—
that of normative jurisprudence—is more philosophically conservative; it
holds that we cannot get at truths about law by reflection on the concept,
but only by engaging in substantive moral and political debate about
why and when law is a desirable form of governance. To identify what
law *is* requires arguing about why it is in some sense good or desirable.
Conceptual analysis or philosophical inquiry into the nature of law is
from beginning to end an exercise in substantive political theory.

In Part III, I defend conceptual analysis against this two-pronged attack.
In Lecture 11 I outline my views on the three fundamental substantive
issues in jurisprudence regarding the relationship between law and political morality. These are: (1) What are the existence conditions of the criteria
of legality in any community? (2) What are the constraints, if any, on the
content of those criteria? (3) How do we construct the content of the law of
any community? I argue that conceptual analysis reveals that the existence
conditions of the criteria of legality are social, not moral, facts; that morality can be, but need not be, a criterion of legality; and that determining the
content of law in any community is not an exercise in political morality. In
defending these claims, I display the tools available to conceptual analysis,
tools that are underestimated, misunderstood, or mischaracterized by its
critics. I also draw out the difference between these *substantive* claims about
the relationship between law and morality, and the very different *methodological* claim that providing a theory of the concept of law of the sort that I
have provided in the book is itself an exercise in first-order moral and political theory.

Having illustrated the richness of the resources available to conceptual
analysis, I take up in Lecture 12 the full range of arguments designed to
show that the philosophical investigation of law and of the concepts that
figure in it must be an activity of moral or political philosophy. I find the
standard formulations of the debate between so-called descriptive and
normative jurisprudence misleading and unhelpful. The task of finding a
satisfactory formulation of the dispute occupies much of the lecture; a
good deal of the rest is devoted to resolving the dispute. In the end, I believe
that we can accommodate what is true and insightful in these critical perspectives without giving up the distinctively philosophic activity of conceptual analysis. This final section of the book is my effort to sketch how that
might be done, and in doing so to reveal how rich in resources conceptual
analysis really is.

Part One

Tort Law and Corrective Justice

Part One
Tort Law and Corrective Justice

Lecture One—
The Pragmatic Method

There is an important and familiar distinction between theoretical explanations and theoretical justifications. While both can illuminate or deepen our understanding, explanations do so by telling us what the nature of a thing is, or by telling us why things are as they are; by contrast, justifications seek to defend or legitimate certain kinds of things—for example, actions, rules, courses of conduct, practices, institutions, and the like.[1] This distinction can lead to the mistaken view that explanation is a descriptive activity, whereas justification is a normative one. In fact, both are norm-governed. Explanations are regulated by norms of descriptive and/or predictive accuracy, while justifications are regulated by the appropriate moral norms—justice, virtue, goodness, fairness, and so on. In addition, both explanation and justification are subject to a range of formal norms that govern all theories— norms like simplicity, coherence, elegance, and consilience.

Philosophical explanations of practices typically take the form of analyses of the concepts that figure prominently in those practices. Some legal philosophers believe that at least in the case of law, the projects of explanation and justification are deeply interdependent in the sense that a philosophical explanation of the concept of law cannot even begin without invoking some moral norms.[2] While I disagree, I do not mean to assert that a philosophical explanation of our concept of law answers to no norms. In fact, an explanation of our concept of law answers to a range of theoretical norms.

In general, it is important to distinguish claims of the type "Our concept of X depends on what *that concept* ought to be", from claims of the very different type, "Our concept of X depends on what *X* ought to be." In the case of law, the first type of claim would imply that our concept of law answers to norms governing concept formation and theory construction—to theoretical or epistemic norms—and is thus revisable in the light of normative considerations of that sort. By contrast, the second type of claim would imply that our concept of law answers to moral or political norms in a way that makes the analysis of that concept primarily a matter of substantive moral or political argument. I wish to affirm the first and deny the second kind of claim about law. Our concept of law certainly depends in part on

---

[1] For brevity, I will use "justification" to mean moral justification. There are of course other kinds: the justification of an inference by the rules of logic; the justification of an empirical belief by the appropriate evidential criteria; the justification of a course of treatment by the standards of medicine, etc.   [2] I take up this argument in Part III.

what *our concept* of law ought to be; but our concept of law does not, in any theoretically interesting way, depend on what *the law* ought to be.[3]

The distinction between these two views about the ways in which an explanation of law might answer to norms is important to the overall argument of the book. The distinction is especially important in this, the first part, because a failure adequately to attend to it invites a natural, but dangerous, confusion. The argument in this section of the book develops the claim that tort law is best understood in terms of a conception of corrective justice. The mistake would be to think that the argument for this claim rests on the moral attractiveness of corrective justice. It does not. The considerations that support the account are epistemic or theoretical, not moral or political.[4]

---

[3] In other words, I deny that conceptual analysis of normative predicates—including law—is itself primarily a kind of substantive moral–political philosophy. There is an important distinction between the claim that conceptual analysis will reveal that our concept of law is of something that is itself essentially moral or political in character, and the claim that "pure" conceptual analysis is itself impossible—that, in other words, conceptual analysis is itself a part of moral or political philosophy. The first, a claim usually associated with the natural law tradition, is a substantive thesis about law—a thesis whose truth is presumably revealed to us through ordinary conceptual analysis. The second is a thesis about the methodology of jurisprudence, and is often referred to (somewhat misleadingly) as "normative jurisprudence". In Part II of this book I defend a form of legal positivism, and thus reject the first of these claims. In Part III, I consider several arguments in support of normative jurisprudence and find each wanting. In the process, I defend a form of conceptual analysis—one, however, that is in an appropriate sense normative, and that explains the role of moral and political principles in conceptual analysis. As a holist and a pragmatist (commitments to be discussed more fully below) I cannot and do not deny that moral norms may in some way enter into the sphere of considerations that govern concept revision—they may do so whether the issue is our concept of law or our concept of laundry. What I deny is that our concept of law answers to moral or political norms in a way that makes the analysis of that concept primarily a matter of substantive moral or political argument.

[4] I would like to take this opportunity to discourage two ways in which my project has been misread. Some have thought that I seek to do a kind of "value-free" descriptive legal philosophy. They may mean by this either that no values are to enter into or to govern the description of law, or that the description cannot reveal law as embodying values, or that the description cannot reveal law as valuable; or perhaps all three are meant. In any case, none of this could be further from the truth about my project. In so far as description figures as part of an explanatory project, description as I understand it is normative from beginning to end. To be sure, the relevant values or norms are not, in the first instance, moral ones; rather, they are the norms that govern explanation. Nonetheless, moral norms too have their place in my project. For example, in the first part of the book I explicitly maintain that corrective justice is an aspect of justice, and that to understand what corrective justice is entails understanding at least in part why it could make sense for individuals to want corrective justice to be realized in public practices and institutions. I also state explicitly that tort law is a valuable social institution. To be sure, my argument that tort law embodies and is explained by corrective justice (in a sense that I seek to make clear) does not depend on the value of either. That is a crucial claim and one that I stand by. But it certainly does not entail that I am engaged in anything that could reasonably be characterized as "value-free" philosophy of law.

Ironically, while some have been inclined to think the book is an exercise in a value-free jurisprudence, others have worried that my position is so far from being value-free that it amounts to a kind of Dworkinian interpretivism. As regards the first part of the book, I try explicitly to show how my account differs from Dworkin's. Briefly, in a Dworkinian

The defensibility of corrective justice as a moral ideal is thus independent of its role in explaining tort law; and in arguing that tort law is best explained by corrective justice I do not mean to be defending tort law thereby. As it happens, the conception of corrective justice embodied in tort law expresses important moral values, and in what follows I will say something about these values and the ways in which corrective justice expresses them. Still, even if tort law is best explained by corrective justice *and* corrective justice is an important and independent moral ideal, it does not yet follow that tort law represents a justified—let alone a morally required—institution. Its desirability or defensibility depends on the place we wish to accord in our public life to the values implicated in corrective justice; on whether or not those values can be expressed better in other institutional arrangements; and on other, similar considerations.[5]

Because the goal of Part I is not only to explore certain explanatory claims about the law of torts, but also to illustrate and thematize a particular methodological approach, I wish to make clear at the outset the relationship between the moral or justificatory questions and the explanatory project. Political philosophy often proceeds, as it were deductively, from a set of political–moral principles that are believed to have a claim on us, to a set of justified institutional structures. The goal is to develop a standard against which actual institutions can be evaluated. While much good theory takes this "top down" form, it is noteworthy that the practical standards that issue from such accounts are generally at a level of abstraction that hovers above, and is consistent with, a broad range of different and non-compossible legal institutions.

There are limits to the extent to which this approach can be brought to bear systematically on the concrete particulars of law. I prefer to begin not at the top, but in the middle, by asking what principles, if any, are embodied in the legal practices we are presently engaged in. This form of inquiry does not ask how our existing legal practice might be derived from *justified* principles. We do not begin with any presupposition about the moral status of the principles we will find. Rather, we simply seek to identify the normatively

interpretive argument part of a claim that tort law is best explained by corrective justice would depend on the value of corrective justice as a moral ideal; and, as I have just noted, the value of corrective justice as a moral ideal is no part of the argument that tort law embodies and is explained by it. As for the second and third parts of the book, no one who reads them can seriously entertain the proposition that my project is a Dworkinian one. While we share similar views on some issues, and while we are trying to explain roughly the same phenomenon, I explicitly articulate the differences between our views on a range of important matters, both methodological and substantive.

[5] The principle of corrective justice expresses a particular conception of fairness, of responsibility for the outcomes of one's choice, and of the importance of certain interests to human welfare or well-being; tort law embodies this conception of corrective justice. It may nevertheless be true that these values are not of paramount importance in our public institutional life, or that they might be given more appropriate expression in public institutions other than tort law.

significant elements of the practice and to explain them as embodiments of principle. Having once identified those principles and understood them not only in the abstract, but also in light of their concrete embodiment in practice, we are then in a position to ask not only to what extent they are embodied, but also how attractive the principles themselves are. The key point is that the moral or justificatory questions are not prior to the explanatory ones, but can grow out of the explanatory project as it reveals the abstract principles in greater specificity and concreteness.

The analytic strategy of starting in the middle, with the actual practices of law, is one of the broadly pragmatic features of the method exemplified here, and the deeper motivations of this strategy are to be found in the fuller development of the pragmatic method. Pragmatism, a term with a long and illustrious history in American philosophy, has had the great misfortune of falling into favor among the American legal academy, where it is too often reduced to a series of slogans providing cover for a flourishing philosophy-made-easy school of legal theory.[6] Despite—or because of—this fashionable interest, the relevance of pragmatism for legal theory has not yet been properly appreciated. Many of the substantive views I have developed over the years represent an effort to bring this relevance to light.

The method of pragmatism that I develop here can be characterized in terms of five basic characteristics. These are: (1) a commitment to semantic non-atomism; (2) the view that the content of concepts is to be explicated in terms of their inferential role in the practices in which they figure (practical inferential role semantics); (3) the view that sometimes a philosophical explanation of a practice takes the form of showing how certain principles are embodied in it (explanation by embodiment); (4) the view that the way in which a concept figures in one practice influences its proper application in all others, and that, in this sense, practices are to be viewed holistically; and (5) a commitment to the in-principle revisability of all beliefs, categories of thought, etc. The argument of this book is dense and philosophically demanding, and so I want to say something by way of preliminary introduction about each of these tenets, if only to flag some of the issues that will arise in what follows. I recognize that anything I might say by way of explication at this point is bound to be, at best, rough and incomplete. Still, we have to begin somewhere, and this as good a place as any.

Semantic non-atomism covers a range of views about the meanings of concepts and of the words that express them; the meanings of propositions and

---

[6] Legal academics typically draw, for their understanding of philosophical pragmatism, upon the work of Richard Rorty, John Dewey, and William James (and the latter two are themselves often seen through Rorty's interpretation of them). These are not my roots or my sources. The sources I draw from include, most prominently, Wilfrid Sellars (especially his view of semantic content as inferential role), W. V. O. Quine (especially his semantic holism and doctrine of revisability), Donald Davidson, and Hilary Putnam.

of the sentences that express them; and the contents of beliefs and other mental states that we may characterize as attitudes to propositions. Semantic non-atomists deny that any single semantic element has a determinate meaning independent of at least some of the other elements of the semantic system (that is, the language, conceptual scheme, or belief set of which the element is a part).[7] Thus, the semantic non-atomist claims that the conditions of application of a concept (or of the word that expresses it)—and the truth-value of a belief in which that concept figures (or of the proposition that expresses such a belief)—depend on at least some of the relations between that concept or word and other concepts or words.

Closely related to semantic non-atomism, *inferential role semantics* is the claim that the content of a concept can be analyzed in terms of the inferential role it plays in the variety of practices in which it figures. The inferential roles our concepts play reveal the holistic (or semi-holistic) web of relations in which they stand to one another, and it is this web that determines a concept's content. Suppose, for example, that I say to Smith, "I promise to meet you for lunch today." Understanding this as a *promise* means knowing that it warrants a variety of inferences—for example, that I predict I will show up for lunch; that I have a duty to show up; that Smith has a right that I show up; and so on. The content of the concept "promise" is revealed in the range of inferences warranted by the belief that a promise has been made; and to grasp the concept of a promise is to be able to project the inferences it warrants.

Two features of the example are noteworthy. First, while some of the noted inferences are theoretical, others are practical. Some state predictions; others state responsibilities and rights, and thus prescribe or prohibit courses of action. The second noteworthy feature is that the inferences in question are not formally valid. A formally valid inference is one whose conclusion follows from its antecedent (or premises) according to rules governing the logical operators. For example, from "I promise to do X", we may infer formally "I promise to do X, or snow is white". That inference is warranted by the rules governing the logical operator "or". The inferences in the example, however, are not formally valid in this sense; they are grounded not in the rules of logic, but in our grasp of a concept. Some would say that this grasp takes the form of knowing a large set of formal rules for applying the concept, but this raises daunting philosophical

---

[7] Semantic non-atomism covers a range of possible views between a very narrow molecularism (according to which the meaning of an element depends on only a small part of the semantic whole) and absolute holism (according to which the meaning of an element depends on an entire language or set of beliefs). Views that identify meaning with rather large parts of the semantic whole are often called "holistic"; and in referring to my view as holistic, I intend at least this moderate sense. However, I leave it open whether the whole semantic system enters into the meaning of every concept, proposition, and belief.

problems. What we know, in the first instance, is not a set of rules, but simply *how* to engage in a variety of practices in which promises are made. This kind of "knowing how" is not necessarily reducible to "knowing that".[8]

In saying that pragmatism recognizes *explanation by embodiment* as a legitimate form of philosophical explanation of a practice, I mean that in certain kinds of practices, the inferential roles of concepts may be seen to hang together in a way that reflects a general principle. The principle can then be said to be *embodied in the practice* and, at the same time, to explain it.[9] In arguing that tort law embodies a principle of corrective justice, for example, I will be arguing that the principle identifies certain elements of the practice as normatively significant and tells us what that significance is. The injurer–victim relationship is one such element. It is normatively significant in a way that is spelled out by corrective justice, and understanding the relationship in light of that principle is the best way to make sense of the role the relationship plays in tort practice.[10]

To return to my earlier example, the concept of a promise also provides a useful illustration of the fourth tenet noted above, which asserts that the practices in which our concepts are embedded must themselves be viewed holistically: that is, we must see them as acting together to articulate, realize, or make explicit the content of the concepts and principles they embody. Promises figure in a range of practices—some are personal, some political, and some legal. The content of the concept "promise" as it figures in, say, our legal practices is not given simply by the inferences that concept warrants in legal contexts. Rather, its content depends on all of the practices that involve promising. This is true in general: the meaning of a concept in any one practice influences its proper meaning in all the others.

Finally, a commitment to the *revisability* of all beliefs is (if anything is) the hallmark of the pragmatic attitude. Everyone agrees that empirical beliefs are revisable, and should be revised, in the light of recalcitrant experience. If I believe I have a full tank of gas, but then see that my fuel

---

[8] This "knowing how" element of inferential competence represents a second, and deeper, sense in which an inferential role semantics can be said to be "practical". In the first sense, it is practical in so far as some meaning-constitutive inferences prescribe or prohibit courses of action. In this second sense, however, even our "theoretical" inferences are practical, because the concept mastery that constitutes inferential competence—knowing how to go on—is grounded ultimately in the totality of our practical involvements in the world, or what Wittgenstein calls "a way of life".

[9] When the knowledge expressed in such a principle is (in the sense just noted) irreducibly practical, the actual practices themselves are needed to *realize, articulate,* or *make explicit* the principle or principles they embody.

[10] It is natural to suppose that we cannot explain a set of concepts in terms that employ any of the same concepts. Part of the view that explanation can take the form of revealing a kind of embodiment relationship is a denial of this. Indeed, the pragmatic–holist picture denies a great deal of this kind of conventional wisdom, and I will have occasion to draw attention to these differences many times in the argument that follows.

gauge indicates an empty tank, I thereby have reason to revise my original belief set. Traditionally, however, it was thought that some beliefs were true in virtue of their meaning, and thus immune to revision. "All bachelors are unmarried" and "All criminals are lawbreakers" are examples of these so-called "analytic" truths. In the tradition of an important current of twentieth-century pragmatism, I maintain that no belief is immune to revision.

It is a further question whether all are revisable in light of the same kinds of considerations. We may draw a distinction between pragmatic and empirical criteria of revision. The former include such theoretical concerns as coherence, simplicity, and consilience, together with considerations of practical usefulness. Those committed to the analytic–synthetic distinction might hold that while synthetic statements are revisable in the light of recalcitrant experience, analytic statements (because they are immune to disconfirmation by experience) are revisable only the light of pragmatic concerns. By contrast, Quineans and others who reject the analytic–synthetic distinction maintain that all statements are revisable in light of both empirical and pragmatic concerns. I accept that all statements are in principle revisable in light of both of these kinds of concerns.[11]

In this work the notion of revisability is extended beyond its familiar application to the "web of belief" to include the categories and concepts we employ to organize our thinking about various areas of the law as well as the categories we employ to divide one area of the law from another. All are, in principle, revisable.

As I have said, the main argument of the first part of the book is that tort law is best explained by corrective justice. The central concepts of tort law—harm, cause, repair, fault, and the like—hang together in a set of

[11] The doctrine of universal revisability is most closely associated with the work of W. V. O. Quine, whose view is driven by his confirmation holism: the same empirical evidence is consistent, for any statement, with that statement's being either true or false—depending on which other statements are held to be true and which false; or to put it differently, any statement can be held true (or held false) in a way that is consistent with experience, so long as the necessary adjustments are made in the web of beliefs. The decision to hold a statement true (or false) is thus always a matter of pragmatic considerations. We may and should revise any belief if doing so yields an overall improvement in our capacities for prediction and control.

This is a doctrine, in the first instance, about *empirical* claims. While I am sympathetic to it, my own concerns are primarily with the revisability of *evaluative*—and, specifically, moral—claims. In so far as these do not come before the "tribunal of experience", evaluative claims, on Quine's view, are noncognitive; there is no fact of the matter about their truth or falsehood. It would follow trivially that evaluative claims are "revisable"—we can just revise them to suit ourselves; they are, at bottom, a matter of taste.

I reject the view that evaluative claims are noncognitive, however; and can therefore maintain that they are revisable in a more interesting sense: there are objective criteria of revision. Many of these criteria—simplicity, consilience, and the like—are the same as those that govern the revision of empirical claims. However, the ultimate pragmatic ends that inform the criteria of revision for evaluative claims are not the ends of prediction and control. I leave open what the relevant ends might be.

inferential relations that reflect a principle of corrective justice.[12] This principle is thus embodied in and explains tort law, and tort law, in turn, articulates that principle and makes its requirements explicit.

Tort law is (in part) a system of practical reasoning. Litigants bring evidence in support of some set of assertions (for example, that the defendant acted negligently, that the defendant had a duty to forbear from imposing certain risks on the plaintiff, that the plaintiff was injured, and so on) from which certain practical inferences are thought to follow (either that the defendant should be held liable to the plaintiff or not). Corrective justice enables us to understand why this kind of evidence is introduced, and why other evidence—for example, evidence of the relative capacity of the litigants to reduce accidents at various costs—is not; and it displays how the inference to a judgment of liability (or freedom from liability) is warranted. Corrective justice captures the structure and nature of this scheme of practical reasoning, and in doing so constitutes an explanation of it. However, the content of corrective justice must be explicated not only in terms of the inferences that it warrants in the context of the law of torts, but also in every other context—moral, political, and so on—in which corrective justice figures.[13]

---

[12] Benjamin Zipursky usefully refers to this line of argument as "pragmatic conceptualism" in a wonderfully illuminating essay in which he criticizes my version of it and defends his own. See "Pragmatic Conceptualism" *Legal Theory* 6/4 (Dec. 2000).

[13] The form of analysis that I defend in this part of the book differs from a Dworkinian interpretation in a number of important ways. I maintain that tort law embodies corrective justice, in a sense that licenses the claim that corrective justice explains tort law. The argument does not depend on the moral value of corrective justice, but, rather, builds on the way in which corrective justice reveals the actual structure of practical reasoning displayed in the relationships among the concepts central to tort practice. Thus, whereas a Dworkinian interpretation is committed to displaying the law in its "best light", the method employed here is not; it is committed only to identifying what principles, if any, reveal the actual structure and content of practical inference in the law. Moreover, because a Dworkinian interpretation is committed to seeing law in its best light, part of any claim such an interpretation might make to explain tort law in terms of corrective justice would presumably have to rely on the moral value of corrective justice. The argument presented here nowhere relies on such a claim about corrective justice. A third contrast between my method and Dworkin's is more difficult to draw, because it is not clear exactly how we are supposed to understand Dworkin's interpretive project— whether as a purely epistemic enterprise, or as one that also entails metaphysical claims about the law. Understood in a strictly epistemic sense, constructive interpretation is put forth as a way of identifying or coming to know what the content of the law is, and says nothing particularly interesting about its ontological status. Understood metaphysically, on the other hand, constructive interpretation is put forth as actually *constitutive* of the law; the very nature of legal content is that it is constructed via our interpretive practice (in this sense, Dworkin's project would have many features of a standard internal realist metaphysics). The conceptualist account that I am presenting here is different from both the epistemological and the metaphysical understanding of Dworkin. My account is, in a sense, a metaphysical theory about the content of legal concepts; but its metaphysical commitments are different from those we might impute to Dworkin. I maintain that legal concepts are constituted by practice—but not by specifically *interpretive* practice and certainly not, in any privileged way, by practice that gives special significance to substantive moral inquiry. Rather, conceptual content takes its

No philosopher of tort law would deny that it is a human institution—a social construct in an obvious and unproblematic sense of the term—and that it responds to or serves a variety of human interests. One way of expressing the thought that tort law serves human interests is to say that it serves a function (or a variety of functions). For the economic analyst of law, the human interests to which tort law responds (the functions it serves, if you will) are expressed in the concept of economic efficiency. In particular, the economic analyst maintains that tort law serves the function of minimizing the sum of accident costs and accident avoidance costs.

A general lack of methodological reflectiveness in the economic accounts of tort law makes them difficult to criticize: since it is seldom clear exactly what kind of explanation is being offered, the criteria of adequacy for the economic accounts are not immediately apparent. The project of economic analysis might be explicated in at least three different ways, giving rise to three different sorts of "function-based" economic explanations of tort law. In what follows, I try to show that none of these ways of understanding the economic explanation yields an adequate analysis of tort law.

On one understanding, the economic explanation purports to be a kind of reductive conceptual analysis. It seeks to explain tort law by showing that its central concepts can be reduced to the concept of economic efficiency. A good example of this reductionist strategy is the widespread effort among economists of law to explain the concept of negligence in terms of the well-known Learned Hand formula. On the economists' understanding of it, the Learned Hand test asserts that "reasonableness" is just a matter of making socially optimal investments in accident avoidance. Similar efforts have been made by economists to explicate the relevant concept of responsibility in economic terms.

Reductive analyses are sometimes illuminating, other times not. Such analyses are typically motivated by the desire to substitute for a concept that is mysterious or unfamiliar other concepts that are more familiar or whose content is less mysterious. For the economist, concepts like welfare or well-being—themselves reducible to the concept of preference satisfaction—are more familiar and less mysterious than concepts like duty, justice, fairness, and the like. The problem with regarding the economic account of tort law as a conceptual analysis, however, is that by the economic analysts' own acknowledgement the content of many of the concepts of tort law cannot be reduced to any economic function. As a

broad outlines, and much of its detail, from the whole system of our conceptually mediated practical lives; legal concepts are then further refined, articulated, or worked out in specifically legal practice. Because my view of the relationship between legal content and practice does not assign special significance to substantive moral inquiry, I can and do reject the claim that what the law is depends in any interesting way on what the law ought to be. This is just another way of marking the difference between a Dworkinian holism and the kind of holism that is consistent with the positivist project.

consequence, there is a tendency simply to ignore or abandon these recalcit-rant concepts. For example, their inability to provide a reductive account of duty in tort law has led most economists of law to follow Richard Posner in denying that the concept of duty plays any role in tort law at all. But the expedient of abandoning concepts that play an important role in our tort practices is difficult to reconcile with a project of conceptual analysis.

The view that tort law has a function might also figure in a different kind of explanation. Rather than seeking to reduce to economic terms the con-cepts that figure in tort law, this approach appeals to its supposed economic function as part of a causal explanation of the existence and shape of tort law. The best-known successful examples of functional explanations of this sort are found in evolutionary biology, in which natural selection and other evolutionary pressures are proposed as mechanisms that provide a causal link between a purpose or function and a biological trait that is said to serve that function. The problem here, as we shall see, is that economic analysis fails to satisfy the requirements of a formally adequate functional explana-tion of this kind.

Finally, the claim that tort law promotes economic efficiency may be con-strued as an interpretive, rather than a conceptual or causal, explanation. The notion of interpretation I have in mind is the familiar Dworkinian one, and the argument for an efficiency interpretation of tort law is that by posit-ing optimal deterrence as the goal of tort law, its component parts are seen to hang together coherently in a way that reveals the institution in its best light. The problem with viewing an economic explanation of tort law as an interpretive explanation of the Dworkinian kind, though, is that it fails on the dimensions of both fit and value. The economic account makes the bilateral structure of tort law mysterious, while at the same time failing to provide anything like an adequate moral or political defense of it. Thus, while economic analysis may be a formally adequate constructive inter-pretation of tort law, it is substantively inadequate.

It is ironic, from where I stand, that even critics of economic analysis gen-erally credit it with a fair degree of explanatory accuracy, and direct their critical energies at the moral defensibility of efficiency as a goal of law; while corrective justice is usually defended as a moral ideal, rather than as an explanation of the law as it is. The view that I articulate here is precisely the reverse of this common wisdom. Whether or not it fails as a moral ideal, economic analysis certainly fails as an explanation. And whether or not cor-rective justice is an ideal to which the law should aspire, it is the principle that best explains what tort law is.

Lecture Two—
Bilateralism

As I have suggested, there are several ways in which one might construe the general project of explaining tort law in terms of its purported economic function: we might regard such an explanation as a conceptual analysis, as a causal explanation, or as an interpretive reconstruction in the Dworkinian sense. These different kinds of explanation are sometimes combined (and sometimes confused) in particular economic accounts. My approach in this and the next lecture will be to consider each type of explanation in turn, and to argue that none of these ways of understanding economic analysis is satisfactory as an explanation of the law of torts. In this lecture I argue that economic analysis is unsatisfactory as conceptual analysis.

To provide a conceptual analysis of a social institution is to identify the central concepts that figure in it, and to explicate their content and their relationships with one another: we identify the criteria for the proper application of each key concept in the domain and, to the extent possible, show what these various criteria have in common. Conceptual analysis is essentially a philosophical enterprise: its aim is to help us to think more clearly.

Conceptual analysis of a social practice can take a variety of forms, depending on the kind of criteria that the analysis appeals to, and the kinds of relationships it discovers among the concepts. The analysis is *functional* if it appeals to the function of the practice in order to explicate its concepts. It is *reductive* in so far as the content of some or all the key concepts of the practice can be specified in terms of a smaller number of more basic concepts. One familiar feature of economic analyses of law—and in particular, of tort law—is that such analyses seem to offer a functional, reductive conceptual analysis.

According to the economic analysis of tort law, its function is to optimally reduce accident costs. How well tort law serves that function depends on two factors: the degree to which it reduces the costs of accidents, and the cost of its doing so. The standard to which tort law should aspire, on this view, is the optimal reduction of overall accident costs, or in other words, the minimization of the sum of the costs of accidents and the costs of avoiding them.

Having identified the function of tort law as the optimization of accident costs, economic analysis then purports to explain key concepts of tort law by showing how they reflect this economic function. The concepts of responsibility, causation, duty, wrong, harm, loss, foreseeability, compensation, and so on are among the central concepts that figure in tort. Some of these concepts are explicitly contained in others: but-for cause is a component of causation, which is itself an element of responsibility; the concept of a wrong can be analyzed as a failure to satisfy the relevant duty of care; the duty of care in turn can be explicated in terms of the scope of foreseeable risk; and so on. Taking into account these sorts of containment relations among the concepts, we can think of them metaphorically as arrayed along a dimension of size: but-for cause is a micro-concept, whereas liability for loss is a macro-concept. Between them lies the range of what we might think of as mid-size concepts, such as negligence, proximate cause, and (perhaps) duty of care. In the typical case, an economic analysis of tort law will offer an economic–functionalist reduction of these mid-size concepts. The most familiar example of such a reduction is the economic analysis of the concept of negligence.

Under the negligence rule someone can be liable for the upshots of his doings only if they result from his negligence. The economic analysis explicates negligence in terms of the Learned Hand formula. This formula asks us to compare two quantities: first, the value of the expected harm some individual's conduct may impose on others; and second, the costs to that individual of taking precautions that would reduce the risk of the harm. When the costs of the harm (to others) discounted by the probability of its occurrence exceeds the costs of added precautions, then a failure to take those precautions would be negligent. Negligence is the imposition of unreasonable risks, and the criteria for the proper application of the concept of a reasonable risk are given by the Learned Hand test. The Learned Hand test is itself simply an expression of the economic goal of tort law, namely, the optimal reduction of accident costs. Thus, the concept of negligence has been reduced to the economic terms of cost and risk. The analysis is reductive because it purports to exhaust the content of the concept that is explained: once we understand its analysis in economic terms, there is nothing more to be understood about how the concept is to be applied. Similar reductive analyses are proposed for other central concepts of tort law.

In what follows, I will myself defend a certain form of conceptual explanation of tort law. The explanation I offer is, however, neither reductive nor functionalist; instead, it takes the form of showing how a certain principle —the principle of corrective justice—is embodied in tort law, in the sense of "embodied" that was briefly sketched in the previous lecture. I will also offer a variety of reasons for rejecting the economic analysis. In doing so, however, I do not mean to suggest that tort law serves no function, or that it serves no economic function. I do, however, want to insist that there is a significant gap between, on the one hand, the goals or functions that a social practice may happen to serve, and, on the other hand, the goals, functions, and other features that constitute the nature of that practice and tell us what it *is*.

Here is a simple, homey example. Recently, I received an invitation to attend a tribute in honor of a colleague. I engaged my colleague in the hall to congratulate him for an honor well deserved. He responded, sardonically, that it was merely a fundraiser. One goal of the event—one of its functions, if you like—may well have been connected to a desire to raise money for the organization honoring my colleague. But that does not tell us what the event is. It is a tribute. To analyze the concept of a tribute in terms of the goal of fundraising is to miss something about what tributes are.

The idea is not that inquiry into the economic effects of tort law cannot be illuminating or otherwise worth while. It is natural to suppose that tort law, a social institution developed and maintained by humans, serves a variety of human interests, among them economic ones, and may in some sense have the "function" of doing so. If it serves the interests well—if it functions well—then we may conclude that it is a valuable and desirable institution. If, on the other hand, it serves our interests poorly, then it should perhaps be replaced by an institutional arrangement that works better. For reasons like these, it is worth while to inquire into the ways in which tort law serves our interests, and to consider how it might serve them better. But such an investigation will not necessarily yield an analysis of the central concepts of tort law or bring us closer to an understanding of what tort law is.

This lecture argues that the kind of conceptual explanation of tort law that economic analysis offers is deeply inadequate, in a way that becomes clear when we consider the sort of explanation offered by the principle of corrective justice, which forms the core of the account presented here. That principle states that *individuals who are responsible for the wrongful losses of others have a duty to repair the losses.* While I do not mount a thorough defense of the corrective justice account, I do aim to articulate its main elements in a way that I hope is also persuasive. Corrective justice can provide an account of what tort law is, in a way that economic analysis fails to do.[1] That is the argument of this lecture, to which I now turn.

Anyone who claims that tort law embodies certain ideals or principles must provide a conception of tort law and of the relevant principles or ideals, as well as an argument to the effect that tort law, so conceived, is best understood in the light of those principles or ideals. The core of tort law is composed of structural and substantive elements. The substantive core is represented by its basic liability rules: fault and strict liability.[2] Any plausible theory of tort law should explain both—and the difference between them—and should if possible provide a defense of each, and an

---

[1] In this lecture my aim is to illustrate the philosophically important features of my methodological position, and not to repeat a defense that I have offered elsewhere of the corrective justice account of tort law. For my substantive views on torts, see *Risks and Wrongs*; see also "Second Thoughts and Other First Impressions" in Brian Bix (ed.), *Analyzing Law: New Essays in Legal Theory* (Oxford: Oxford University Press, 1988); and Coleman and Ripstein, "Mischief and Misfortune".

[2] By a core of tort law I mean a set of features (expressed at a certain level of generality) that form part of our pretheoretic conception of the central elements of the practice, especially those that have normative significance.

explanation of why fault liability provides the appropriate standard of liability and recovery in some cases, while liability in other cases is appropriately strict.[3]

Tort law's structural core is represented by case-by-case adjudication in which particular victims seek redress for certain losses from those whom they claim are responsible. In the event a victim's claim to recovery is vindicated, her right to recover takes the form of a judgment against the defendant (a judgment which the defendant can discharge either directly or by some contractual relation, e.g. insurance). The victim is not, in contrast, awarded a claim against society as a whole or against a "pool"; and, in the event a defendant is judged liable, she is not required to pay into a general pool, or to compensate some randomly chosen victim, but must instead make good her "own" victim's compensable losses. Any plausible account of tort law must explain why claims are taken up in this case-by-case fashion. A plausible account must also explain the bilateral nature of litigation.[4]

Economic analysis provides a "forward-looking" account of tort law.[5] The costs of any particular tort are sunk. There is nothing to be done about them, no way of annulling or annihilating them. All that is left is to determine their incidence. Should the loss be left the burden of the victim or shifted to someone else, such as the injurer? Since the past cannot be undone, the decision to shift the loss or to leave it where it lies must be taken in light of the consequences of that decision. Thus, we should ask what social good can be secured by imposing the costs on one person rather than another. In the part of tort law devoted to accidents and their costs, for example, the natural consequences to which one ought to attend are the effects of loss-shifting rules on the costs of accidents. The relevant social good is thus the reduction of accident costs, and the economic analyst concludes that the correct liability rules governing accidents are those likely to lead to the optimal reduction in the costs of accidents.

---

[3] It is possible, of course, that the best theory of tort law will tell us that one of the two principles of liability lacks rationale or justification—or that the two represent conflicting principles or ideals. In that case, it is possible that existing tort law would need to be reformed in a particular way—for example, by abandoning one principle of liability in favor of the other.

[4] Even if it is controversial whether the elements of tort law I have identified constitute its core, it is not controversial that someone purporting to explain the fundamentals of tort law would miss something important were she to leave out these structural and substantive features. Any claim about the core of tort is bound to be controversial; tort scholars (and others familiar with the law) may plausibly disagree with one another regarding its essentials.

[5] I use the terms "economic analysis", "law and economics", and "economic analysis of law" interchangeably to refer to a range of theories that share a commitment to efficiency as a criterion of assessment of legal practices and institutions. There are also many different conceptions of efficiency. For a discussion of the defining characteristics and conceptual foundations of economic analysis, see Jules Coleman "Efficiency, Utility and Wealth Maximization" *Hofstra Law Review* 8/3 (Spring 1980) 509–51.

Of course, any theory of tort law that ignores the costs of accidents and the need to reduce those costs would miss something both obvious and important. Showing that this important feature of our accident law is also an explanation of its existence, endurance, and shape is the burden of the economic explanation. The problem that confronts economic analysis, or any entirely forward-looking theory of tort law, is that it seems to ignore the point that litigants are brought together in a case because one alleges that the other has harmed her in a way she had no right to do. Litigants do not come to court in order to provide the judge with an opportunity to pursue or refine his vision of optimal risk reduction policy. Rather, they seek to have their claims vindicated: to secure an official pronouncement concerning who had the right to do what to whom. The judge is there, in some sense to serve them—to do justice between them; they are not there to serve the judge in his policy-making capacity. Or so one might think prior to theorizing about tort law.

Under economic analysis the litigants to a tort suit bear no normatively significant relationship to one another, or in any case, do not do so in any fundamental way.[6] What is important is the relationship of each to the goals of tort law, in particular, optimal risk reduction. From that point of view, the important questions include: how good is the injurer (or injurer class) at reducing accidents of this type, and at what cost? How good is the victim (or victim class) at reducing risk, and at what cost? Need incentives be placed on both of them to achieve optimal deterrence? If so, how should that be done? In contrast with these kinds of considerations, our actual institution of tort law is structured so that the important questions it asks are ones about the relationship between the injurer and victim—not questions about the relationship of either or both to the goals of tort law.

There is simply no principled reason, on the economic analysis, to limit the defendant or plaintiff classes to injurers and their respective victims. The classes of victims and injurers are identified entirely by backward-looking features (the harmful event); yet those best able to reduce the costs of accidents are identified by their relationship to the forward-looking goal of cost reduction. The class of optimal cost reducers is not selectable by any event in which *either* participated, much less by an event in which *both* participated—and certainly not by an event in which they both participated *in a particular way* (namely, as victim and injurer). There may be some

---

[6] On the economic analysis, any normative significance the victim–injurer relationship has must derive from a more fundamental set of relations. The primary normative relationships are between the injurer and the economic goals of tort law on the one hand, and the victim and those same goals on the other. Thus, the normative significance of the victim–injurer relationship depends on a range of search and other transaction costs, and is in this sense derivative or superficial.

overlap between the class of injurers and that of optimal cost reducers, but any such overlap can only be accidental. To put it quite simply: in any case in which A hits B, it is an open question whether A, B, C, D, E ... is in the best position to reduce the future risks at the lowest cost.[7]

How then does the economist account for the fact that in the typical tort suit the victim sues the alleged injurer and not the alleged cheapest cost avoider? How does one square the forward-looking goal of tort law (on the economic model) with the backward-looking structure of tort law? The economist cannot appeal to the obvious answer that the victim believes the injurer harmed him wrongfully and in doing so incurred a duty to make good the victim's losses. In the economist's account, the victim sues the injurer because the costs of searching for those in the best position to reduce the costs of future accidents is too high.

Next, how does the economist explain the fact that if the victim makes out his case against the injurer, he is entitled to compensation for damages *from the injurer?* Again, the economist cannot call upon the fact that the injurer incurs a duty to repair the victim's loss because he has wrongfully harmed him. It is one thing to ask whether there are good economic reasons for holding the injurer liable to certain costs. It is another question whether similar economic considerations require that *the victim* be compensated for his loss. It is yet another question—assuming that the injurer should be liable and the victim compensated—whether the victim should be compensated *by the injurer.*

The economic explanation cannot avail itself of the natural answer; instead, matters of liability and compensation are to be resolved in the light of their expected impact on the precautions that potential injurers and potential victims—considered separately—will be induced to take. Thus, the injurer should be made to bear costs sufficient to induce potential injurers to take cost-effective precautions. These costs may turn out to be more or less than the damages the victim actually suffers. Moreover, producing this incentive for potential injurers does not require that the injurer pay the victim—only that he pay someone an amount sufficient to induce his compliance with the optimal risk-reducing strategy.

It is an open question in every case whether the victim should be encouraged to take precautions and if so, which ones. The answer to that question

---

[7] The so-called "bilateralism critique" of economic analysis was set out first in Jules Coleman, "The Economic Structure of Tort Law" *Yale Law Journal* 97 (May 1988) 1233–53. Since then several others have argued along similar lines and in doing so have deepened the critique significantly. Among the most important of these are Ernest Weinrib, *The Idea of Private Law* (Cambridge, Mass.: Harvard University Press, 1995); Benjamin Zipursky, "Rights, Wrongs and Recourse in the Law of Torts" *Vanderbilt Law Review* 51/1 (Jan. 1998) 1–100; and Martin Stone, "On the Idea of Private Law" *Canadian Journal of Law and Jurisprudence* 9 (July 1996) 235–77. I have further developed the argument in *Risks and Wrongs* and "Second Thoughts and Other First Impressions".

will determine whether, on the economic account, he should be compensated; and if so, how much. Therefore, whether the victim is entitled to
recover, and how much he should recover, does not depend on whether
he was injured wrongfully or the extent of his injury, but on whether
compensating him is necessary to avoid over-deterrence (that is, to
avoid giving the victim and those in the victim's circumstances incentive to take overly costly precautions), or whether fully compensating
him leads to too little deterrence (that is, fails to incite the most effective level of precaution-taking by the victim and those in the victim's
circumstances).

There are other, more general, economic reasons for compensating
victims—or at least for holding out the prospect of doing so. In any torts
case, the victim acts as a private prosecutor bringing an action not only on
his own behalf but also as an "agent" of the state. The state has an interest
in discouraging economically inefficient behavior, but has only limited
resources for doing so. By providing an avenue through which victims can
secure recourse for harm done to them, the state creates an institution of
"private enforcement". The expectation (or hope) of compensation induces
private prosecutions, necessary to secure the optimal mix of private and
public enforcement. However, on the economic analysis, it is no part of the
victim's case for compensation that he has absorbed a loss as a result of
another's wrongdoing. Rather, compensating him is to be explained as the
result of the mix of the goals of inducing victims to litigate, and inducing
both victims and injurers to take optimal precautions.

Consider, further, the economic explanation of the fact that in the typical
case the victim sues the person she alleges wronged her. Because the point
of tort law is (forward-looking) cost avoidance, we need to explain why the
victim sues the injurer rather than seeking out the person who is in fact in
the best position to reduce accidents at the lowest cost. It is always an open
question whether that person is the injurer or someone else. The standard
economic explanation is that the costs of searching on a case-by-case basis
for the person who might be the better cost avoider is too high; and so,
to follow a familiar strategy, a general rule in which the victim sues the
alleged injurer is the second-best alternative.

This explanation has bizarre consequences, however. The claim that
victims sue injurers only because search costs require them to do so as a
second-best alternative seems to imply that, in the absence of search costs,
victims who wish to sue would have the responsibility of seeking out the
cheapest cost avoiders. In other words, were it costless or very cheap to
locate the person in the best position to reduce costs, then it would be the
duty of the victim who wishes to sue to find that person.

Moreover, it appears to follow that were search costs trivial, and the goal
of tort law to provide incentives to those in the best position to reduce costs,

then not only should the victims who want to sue have a duty to seek out the cheapest cost avoiders, but victims in general should have those duties—whether or not they are personally disposed to litigate. This is in startling contrast to the fact that tort law provides victims with a right of recourse, an opportunity and a power to seek redress if they are so inclined— not a duty to do so. The point of conferring a power rather than imposing a duty is, of course, that powers are left to the control of those who have them.[8]

To generalize about these features of the economic account: every core feature of the structure of tort law is explained by first (so to speak) disconnecting the injurer from the victim. The injurer and the victim are brought together for no reason having to do with an event that allegedly occurred between them. That is merely *accidental* to the structure of litigation. The victim is involved for reasons having to do with the various goals of tort law (understood from an economic perspective); and the same is true of the injurer. The importance of the fact (if it is one) that the injurer wrongly harmed the victim is epistemic, not normative. It may provide grounds for thinking that the injurer is a good cost avoider, but it is irrelevant beyond that. The economic account has the overall effect of making tort law appear mysterious.[9]

Consider some basic facts about our existing tort institutions: (1) The plaintiff sues the person he alleges to have injured him, and not somebody else. (2) The plaintiff presents arguments and evidence to the effect that the defendant acted wrongfully towards him and that, as a result, he (the plaintiff) suffered harm. (3) The wrongfulness of the act, the fact of the harm, and the causal relation between the two are all pertinent to the outcome of the lawsuit. (4) The jury decides—in accordance with instruction by the judge as to what duties, if any, the defendant owed the plaintiff and the relevant standard of compliance with those duties—whether the plaintiff has made out the relevant case in the light of the evidence introduced. (5) If the plaintiff is found to have made out his case successfully, he is awarded a

---

[8] Moreover, the power in question is a power to seek out not the cheapest cost avoider, but rather the person the victim believes wrongfully harmed him. Nor is there any reason why the victim is in the best position to find the cheapest cost avoider (he is, of course, in a relatively good position to locate his alleged injurer).

[9] If search costs were low enough, it is hard to understand why we would even wait for a tort to occur. In economic analysis the significance of the tort itself is only epistemic, and not justificatory. This is because the tort concerns something that has already occurred, whereas the point of the practice is to secure some future-oriented goal. The fact that the injurer harmed the victim only matters if that fact gives us some reason for believing that either the injurer or the victim is in a good position to reduce accidents of this sort in the future. What happened between the injurer and the victim provides no reason that justifies liability or recovery, both of which are justified by their impact on future agents. When search costs are low enough, the epistemic value of the tort is lost. Without that value, the tort has no significance at all.

claim against his injurer, who is in turn required to make good the victim's losses.[10]

These features of tort law are plain to anyone without the benefit of theory, and the purpose of these features seems transparently evident in the light of our ordinary intuitions about corrective justice. It is a notably unattractive feature of economic analysis that it renders these obvious and intuitively transparent features of tort law mysterious and opaque. In the absence of any explanatory theory, our intuition is that a victim is entitled to sue *because* he makes a cognizable claim that the injurer has wrongfully harmed him; that the victim must present arguments in support of that claim *because* the harm and the wrong are recognized by the law as pertinent to the outcome of the lawsuit; and that if the victim's claims are vindicated, he recovers against his injurer *because* the law recognizes wrongful harm as grounds for such recovery. The economic theory tells us, however, that each of these intuitions is wrong; that the apparently transparent purpose of the tort law in each case is not the real purpose; and that the real purpose, efficiency, has nothing at all do with the fact that the injurer may have wrongfully harmed the victim. If the fact of the harm has any significance at all, it is epistemic. Thus, while the corrective justice account of tort law seeks to show how the structural components of tort law are independently intelligible and mutually coherent in the light of a familiar and widely accepted principle of justice, the economic analysis asserts that in the absence of search, administrative, and other transaction costs, these structural features of tort law would be incomprehensible.[11]

[10] In saying that the plaintiff typically has to show that the defendant acted wrongly toward him, I should not be read as claiming that all of tort liability is based on fault. The notion of wrong to which I am referring is more general than that, and refers simply to a breach of duty. So, for example, I can have a duty not to harm you negligently or, under certain circumstances, I can have a duty simply not to harm you. In the latter case, I breach my duty if I harm you, whether or not I do so negligently or am otherwise at fault. To breach a duty to someone is, in the relevant sense, to wrong her. Thus, there is no liability in the absence of a wrong, though of course there can be liability in the absence of fault. By the same token, I do not wrong you in the relevant sense if I act negligently toward you but no harm results—though arguably my negligence is a moral defect of my action or character, and thus constitutes a wrong in some other sense. The notion of wrong that I am emphasizing throughout this discussion is the breach of the duty, not the defect in the character of the action or of the actor. I am not emphasizing fault to the exclusion of other ways of wronging. For a nice discussion of these distinctions in the context of so-called "outcome-responsibility", see John Gardner's "Obligation and Outcome in the Law of Torts" in John Gardner and Peter Cane (eds.), *Relating to Responsibility* (Oxford: Hart, 2000).

[11] Perhaps some proponents of corrective justice have wanted to claim that the relationship between the victim and injurer reflected in its bilateral structure is necessary or essential to tort law because it reflects the underlying moral structure of the world, and that the problem with economic analysis, therefore, is that it renders the relationship contingent. The problem with economic analysis, then, is that it renders a metaphysically essential component of tort law contingent. That is not my objection, however. I make no metaphysical claim about the essence of tort law in order to argue that a certain view about the normative significance of the relationship between victim and injurer is part of the best explanation of our tort institutions.

Let me recast all of these points in the light of the kind of explanation that was briefly sketched in Lecture 1. I claimed there that the content of concepts is to be understood in terms of the role that they play in warranting inferences in the practices in which they figure. Now, whatever else it may be, tort law is a system of practical reason. Evidence is introduced and arguments are made on behalf of various claims, and inferences are drawn regarding the truth of those claims and the practical consequences they might license. Typically, the plaintiff has the burden of establishing that he was harmed in a way that the law finds potentially compensable; that the defendant had, with respect to the plaintiff, a duty of care that the defendant failed adequately to discharge; that the defendant's failure adequately to discharge the duty of care was both a but-for and a proximate cause of the plaintiff's misfortune; that, as a result, his loss is the defendant's doing, and so on. If the jury accepts the plaintiff's claims as true (or as more probable than not), then in conjunction with the relevant instructions from the judge, those claims are thought to warrant a judgment of liability against the defendant. This judgment, in other words, is an inference warranted by the acceptance of certain claims, many of which employ concepts such as harm, wrong, duty of care, but-for and proximate cause, and so on.

The principle of corrective justice accounts for this scheme of practical inference. The principle states that those who are responsible for the wrongful losses imposed on others have a duty to repair those losses. Thus, the relevance of the propositions for which evidence is introduced in court is made clear by the principle of corrective justice. Corrective justice not only explains when and why an inference to a judgment of liability is warranted, but it shows how the various features of the structure of tort law hang together in a coherent, mutually supportive whole.

By contrast, economic analysis (if it is really to be understood as conceptual analysis) requires that we assign to the central concepts of tort law contents that bear no immediate relationship to the actual structure of inferences those concepts warrant in the practices of tort law. In effect, the economists tell us that the process of reasoning in which participants in our tort institutions engage is a kind of ideological illusion. Whatever reasons there might be for believing that (and the bar of demonstration for such a claim is high), we can no longer maintain that the economic account is tenable as a conceptual analysis.

Consider what tort law would be like if economic analysis did provide an adequate conceptual analysis—if, in other words, the principle of efficiency was embodied in our practice and reflected in its practical reasoning. The plaintiff would bring evidence to support the claim that the defendant is a better risk reducer than he is. He would offer no evidence about what he alleges occurred in the past, but rather, only evidence about who is in the best position to reduce accident costs in the future. He would not seek to establish a failure to discharge a duty, the occurrence of a harm, and a causal connection between the two. For her part, the judge would instruct the jury to find against the party who is in the best position to reduce harm in the future, and so on. In other words, were the concept of efficiency embedded in tort law, we should expect to have an entirely different structure and content to the practice of reasoning. The inferences warranted by efficiency would be different and the grounds on which those inferences would be made would also be very different from those we find in tort law.

Aside from its failure to account for the relation between the content of the concepts central to tort law and their inferential roles, the reductive economic approach cannot, even on its own terms, provide an explanation of some of the concepts that figure prominently within tort law. A good example is the concept of a duty of care. In tort law it is not enough to show that the defendant imposed unreasonable risks which led (causally) to the loss of which the plaintiff complains. The plaintiff must also establish that the defendant owed her a duty of care. Failure to establish that is a bar to recovery.

Since on the economic analysis the goal is to provide the economically optimal incentives for potential injurers, there is no reason to exclude from the ambit of liability those victims to whom the defendant owed no specific duty of care. If the law is to provide the desired incentives, then injurers must face the full social costs of their conduct, not just the costs that might befall those to whom the injurers had a specific duty of care.[12]

Thus, understood as a conceptual analysis, the economic account is a failure. It renders the structure of tort law mysterious; it suggests a scheme of practical inference altogether different from the one actually in place; and its reductionist impulse leads the economist to jettison concepts that are in fact central to our legal practice. On the other hand, the principle of corrective justice succeeds as an explanation exactly where economic analysis fails. Corrective justice illuminates the structure of practical reasoning in tort law and deepens our understanding of its structure by displaying the coherence and mutual support of its component elements. The relations among the central concepts of tort law—wrong, duty, responsibility, and repair—are best understood as expressing the fundamental normative significance of the victim–injurer relationship as it is expressed in the principle of corrective justice. To understand tort law is precisely to understand the way in which the principle of corrective justice is embodied in it.

Though the economic account clearly fails as a conceptual analysis of tort law, that does not mean it necessarily fails to explain tort law. After all, the

---

[12] For a fuller development of this line of argument, see Zipursky, "Rights, Wrongs and Recourse in the Law of Torts". See also John C. P. Goldberg and Benjamin C. Zipursky, "The Moral of MacPherson" *University of Pennsylvania Law Review* 146/6 (Aug. 1998) 1733.

relationship between the world and the concepts that enable us to organize our experience of it, and to make it rationally intelligible, is among the most profound issues that philosophy engages. It remains an important question whether our conceptual apparatus maps onto or represents the way the world really is—whether our concepts "carve the world at its joints". As long as this question remains open, we must mark a distinction between *conceptual inquiry* and *metaphysics*. Conceptual inquiry seeks to illuminate our understanding of the world in so far as our concepts can give us rational access to it. Metaphysics seeks to illuminate the way the world really *is*.

It might be thought that when the part of the world we seek to describe is a human practice or institution, the gap between metaphysics and conceptual inquiry must narrow or close entirely. Certainly this is a natural attitude to adopt when the practice in question appears—as does tort law— to be an exercise of practical reason. Here the central elements—actions, agents, rules, responsibility—all have an intentional component; the conceptual is already implicated in the phenomenon we seek to describe.[13] Still, there are ways of driving a wedge between concept and reality, even when the reality in question is an exercise of reason. It is not incoherent to claim that the self-understanding of participants in tort law, as reflected in the content of the concepts they employ, may be mistaken.

There is ample reason to think that economists indeed seek to drive a wedge between the concepts employed in tort law and what tort law actually is. On the standard economic view, the role played by the concept of duty, for example, is supposed to be misleading, or even to falsify what the actual practice of tort law is about. The metaphysical facts about tort law and the content of its key concepts come apart. So perhaps we should disregard the parts of the economic account that appear to be conceptual analysis; we have seen that those parts are mistaken and confused, but they may not undo the entire enterprise. It is possible that the strongest claims of the economic analysis of torts are in fact metaphysical claims.[14]

---

[13] Thus, even if idealism is not a generally plausible metaphysical stance, it may nevertheless prove more promising as a metaphysics of social practices. That is at least one reason why a conceptual explanation of our social practices—including law—may be especially apt.

[14] However, if the law and economics theorist wishes to maintain that what the law *is* does not correspond to the way we conceptualize it, then he takes on a special burden. For surely he must now owe us an explanation of how it is that we have come to conceptualize our legal practices in a way that so poorly tracks their actual organizing concepts.

Lecture Three—
Function and Explanation

We have seen that the economic analysis of tort law cannot succeed as a conceptual analysis. It is not and cannot be that kind of explanation. The charitable critic must then consider whether economic analysis might succeed as a different kind of explanation. One alternative is suggested by the very way in which the economic model fails as conceptual analysis: it fails because it ignores, as it must, the actual inferential practices of participants in tort institutions.[1] What they think they are doing and what they are "really" doing come apart on the economic analysis, and their self-understanding is portrayed as a kind of ideological illusion. This feature of the economic account is reminiscent of certain Marxian explanations of law in capitalist societies, as well as of certain functional accounts in cultural anthropology.[2] Such accounts seek to establish that the reason why an institution or practice exists is not to be found in anyone's intentions, but rather in the fact that the practice produces a certain outcome. The outcome is said to explain the existence and the shape of the practice, and in this sense the outcome is said to be the *function* of the practice. Perhaps the economic analysis of tort law is a functional explanation of this kind.

Of course, the simple fact that some practice P has outcome X cannot warrant the claim that X is the reason why P exists, explains P, or is P's purpose or function. The most straightforward sense in which an outcome can be called the function of practice is in the case where the practice is intended by its designers or participants to produce the outcome. This kind of explanation is not "functional" in the sense we are now considering, because the function enters into the explanation only in so far as it is the aim or goal of some *intentional agent*. Clearly this cannot be the nature of the economic explanation, since no one wishes to claim that the many individuals who contributed over the centuries to the development of our tort institutions

---

[1] I do not mean to suggest that each actual inference made by a participant is necessarily part of the content of a concept. Inference is a norm-governed activity, and participants can make wrong inferences. Here I simply assume that it is possible to specify some appropriate sense in which certain inferences are warranted and others not. It should be clear that however the details are filled in, the economic model will fare poorly in capturing even the most ideal or canonical inferences that figure in tort practice.

[2] A basic tenet of historical materialism, for example, states that the relations of production (including the entire property regime) serve the function of enabling the further development of the forces of production (and are replaced by new relations of production when they fail of that function). I am indebted to Eric Cavallero for this point and for the general line of argument in these passages.

were aiming at economic efficiency.[3] By contrast, the kind of explanation we are now considering is one that asserts that the outcome of economic efficiency is the function of tort law, and explains it, even though efficiency was not part of the intentions of the developers, and remains alien to the intentions of the bulk of its contemporary participants.

If a practice or institution really is to be explained by an outcome that lies outside the intentions of those who have developed and maintained it, then a particular kind of causal relationship must be shown. The kind of causal relationship that must figure in a formally adequate functional explanation should support a range of theoretically interesting counterfactuals. It must be the case that were the outcome substantially different, the practice would not exist, or its central elements would be different. Barring some appeal to the intentions or goals of an agent, only a causal relation can support such counterfactuals, and thus warrant the claim that the outcome is the practice's purpose or function.[4]

The idea is usefully illustrated by the familiar example of the leopard's spots. Here what is to be explained is, of course, a genetic trait and not a social practice; but the formal features of the functional evolutionary explanation provide an analogy to the kind of explanation we are considering. The leopard's spots, we know, have the effect, or produce the outcome, of camouflaging the leopard, thereby increasing its success as a hunter. We might then conjecture that the existence and—quite literally—the shape of the leopard's spots are explained by reference to this effect or outcome; that is, we might regard "camouflage efficiency" as the purpose or function of the spots. But so far, this conjecture remains a just so story and not a genuine functional explanation. Missing is the causal mechanism that would support the counterfactual, "Were they not camouflage-efficient, the leopard's spots would not be" (or, ". . . would not be the shape they are"). Random mutation and natural selection (jointly) suffice as a plausible causal mechanism supporting that counterfactual, and thus suffice to turn our Just So Story into a formally adequate functional explanation.[5]

---

[3] There is, of course, an element of the American bench today—notably, Posner, Easterbrook, and (perhaps) Calabresi—who consciously and explicitly embrace the aim of economic efficiency. But this is a relatively late development, and no one means to suggest that it explains the basic institutions of tort.

[4] Some of the best critiques of functional explanations in the social sciences are developed in Jon Elster, *Making Sense of Marx* (Cambridge: Cambridge University Press, 1985). Whatever the strengths of the economic analysis of the law may be, its proponents are not particularly reflective about the methodology of the social sciences.

[5] To say that such an explanation is 'formally adequate' is not to say that it succeeds in explaining the phenomenon; it is simply to say that the explanation is well formed, or, in other words, that it has the right parts in the right order to count as a possible explanation. If it is actually to succeed in explaining the phenomenon, then other conditions must also be met. For example, its factual assertions must be true.

The challenge to economic analysis should now be apparent. It begins by rejecting the self-understandings of the developers and participants in the practice, and in doing so it rejects the strategy of offering an intentional explanation. Yet the typical economic analysis of tort law (or of any other body of law, for that matter) offers no causal mechanism either—no analogue of random mutation and natural selection. It thus appears to remain at the level of a Just So Story.

The claim is not that there can be no functional economic explanation of the law that would satisfy the causal mechanism requirement. A good example of functional economic explanations of the law is found in the evolutionarily based litigation-and-settlement models offered by Priest and Klein, among others.[6] Their idea is that the efficiency of the common law is an unintended by-product of rational litigation strategies. The litigation-settlement factors are said to constitute a causal mechanism (albeit one that affects intentional behavior) that could support the relevant range of counterfactual claims. If this account were true in its particulars, the outcome of efficiency could thus explain at least some aspects of the law, even if no involved individual's actions have ever aimed at efficiency.

But while these accounts might explain some parts of the law, they cannot serve as a functional explanation of the core of tort law. The litigation-and-settlement models purport to work by emphasizing the way principles of rational choice guide litigants to adopt strategies of litigation and settlement that lead, ultimately, to an *efficient* common law. This might (if factually supported) explain the behavior of litigants *confronted with the institutions of the common law*. But this cannot even purport to explain the existence or shape of those institutions, or of the concepts embodied within them. The litigation and settlement models are predicated on the existence of the kinds of tort institutions we have, and thus cannot explain them. These models cannot explain why tort law is distinct from the other parts of the private law, nor why any of these parts have the characteristic features and central concepts that they have. The litigation and settlement models start from the assumption that tort law has its characteristic bilateral structure, and make no pretense of explaining this structure.[7]

---

[6] See George L. Priest and Benjamin Klein, "The Selection of Disputes for Litigation" *Journal of Legal Studies* 13 (Jan. 1984) 1–55.

[7] Many of the structural features of tort law—including aspects of its bilateral structure—are common to all parts of the common law. An explanation of these features of tort law, then, might take the form of a general explanation of why the common law has such features. Indeed, for reasons of explanatory economy, such an explanation might, *ceteris paribus*, be preferable. However, the evolutionary or Darwinian accounts—such as the settlement–litigation models—presuppose the structural features that tort law shares with, for example, contract and property law, and thus leave those features unexplained.

Until this point I have not challenged the economic analyst's contention that tort law tends to produce an optimal reduction in accident costs. My focus has been on the conditions under which such a tendency could figure in a functional explanation of tort law. It is not obvious, however, that our tort law produces anything like optimal deterrence. We can, no doubt, safely assume that on balance tort law reduces accident costs, as compared to a situation in which there is no legal recourse to recover for harms. But lower costs than might exist in the absence of our tort law need hardly be optimal costs, nor even approach them. Economic analysis needs an argument to show that tort law has developed over time in a way that approximates an efficient reduction in accident costs. Only then is there even prima-facie reason to look for a causal mechanism that would show how efficiency explains the shape of the legal institutions. In short, without both a prima-facie demonstration of efficiency, and a plausible causal mechanism, it is hard to credit economic analysis with providing even a formally adequate functional explanation of tort law, let alone a convincing or persuasive one.[8]

I have been focusing on the explanatory claims of economic analysis; but in addition to explaining, economic analysis also seeks to recommend ways in which the law of torts might be improved. On the economic analysis, the existence, endurance, and shape of tort law are all to be understood *instrumentally* in terms of an economic goal. As with any instrument, we may evaluate tort law by its *effectiveness*, that is, how well or poorly it serves its function. Herein lies the great attraction of economic analysis for the reform-minded legal academic. It allows us not merely to understand and assess the law, but also to prescribe changes to our legal institutions. It gives us a purchase on every question we might ever ask about any rule of tort law—substantive, structural, or procedural. All are measured by their economic efficiency, and endorsed or criticized depending on how well they serve that goal. Law review article after law review article is then published suggesting reforms—large and small, important and trivial.

Of course, it is no mean question what institutions would most effectively reduce accidents and their costs, or how, given our existing system of tort law, we might tinker with it in order optimally to serve that end. Such questions are worth asking. But claiming that the Anglo-American common law of torts should produce a certain outcome—or even that it tends to do so—is altogether different from claiming that this outcome is the best or

---

[8] In contrast, the corrective justice account of tort law invokes no opaque or hidden goal like efficiency. Indeed, the relationship between tort law and corrective justice is not instrumental in any interesting sense; corrective justice itself may be a goal of the practice, but it is not a goal external to it and at which the practices of tort law are aimed. Rather, Anglo-American tort law *expresses*, *embodies*, or *articulates* corrective justice. Tort law is an institutional realization of principle, not an instrument in the pursuit of an external and hidden goal.

most plausible explanation of the law's existence and shape.[9] I believe I have shown that the economic account cannot succeed in explaining these things either as a conceptual analysis or as a causal–functional explanation. Still, it would be premature to conclude that the law and economics account is therefore nothing more than a set of straightforward policy prescriptions that have somehow mistaken themselves for an explanation.

Indeed, the idea that a certain kind of functional explanation of law (or of a body of law) can have prescriptive implications is characteristic of a well-known approach in legal theory. This approach, which Ronald Dworkin has labeled "constructive interpretation", employs the concept of a function differently from the way in which that concept figures in a causal–functional form of explanation. In the Dworkinian picture explanations of social practices and of bodies of the law (or of the whole of the law) are arrayed and assessed along two dimensions: fit and value. The interpretation must make sense of enough of the practice by showing how its component parts fit together (the fit requirement). However, many putative interpretations can satisfy this requirement. The best explanation is the one which not only fits the shape of the institutions or practice, but also reveals it "in its best light", as the best version of the sort of thing it purports to be—this is the value component of the assessment. [10]

In offering an interpretation in this sense, one must posit a point, purpose, or function of the institution or practice. The component parts must then be shown to hang together in a way that this function or point makes perspicuous. Thus, the function provides a lens through which the component aspects of the practice are seen to cohere and to be mutually

---

[9] This is not to say that a descriptive or explanatory account cannot have prescriptive implications; but if it is to succeed as an explanation, it must meet the adequacy conditions of an explanation; this is something that, as we have seen, the economic analysis appears not to do.

[10] In what follows, I will take at face value the distinction between fit and value as Dworkin has articulated it. However, Mark Greenberg has convinced me that Dworkin, as a holist, cannot in fact draw the distinction between fit and value in the way he does. He cannot, in other words, posit a threshold level of fit beyond which value or justificatory force becomes the only criterion of a good interpretation. Greenberg suggests that Dworkin's separation of fit and justification is an unfortunate expository device intended to simplify presentation of the account. Fit is better understood as one aspect of justification. To borrow one of Dworkin's own examples, if we interpret an Agatha Christie murder mystery as the story of Hamlet, we do not thus construe it as a good literary work at all, but rather as a very bad one. The fact that the story of Hamlet is, independently, a richer or more profound subject for literature does not make it a good interpretation of Agatha Christie. The reason is because, on any plausible theory of literary value, a work whose theme is utterly unconnected with its text is a poor work. So the question we must ask is, what interpretation would make a work of literature the best work it could be, *given the actual text*? Similarly, when we interpret a statutory text or a legal system, we do not first see which candidate interpretations meet a threshold of fit, and then ask which of the remaining candidates yields a rule that is morally best. Rather, we just ask which interpretation, given the actual text or practices, would be most justified. It should be clear, however, that the economic analysis of torts is hardly redeemed by this more sophisticated understanding of constructive interpretation.

supporting. At the same time the posited purpose or function should allow us to see the practice or institution as the best of its kind. In other words, the posited function must be assessed both in terms of its capacity to shed light by unifying the practice, and in terms of its independent moral defensibility.

Rather than conceiving of economic analysis as a functional explanation in the standard sense that characterized our earlier discussion, we might most charitably think of it in Dworkin's sense, as a constructive interpretation of tort law: what we might refer to as a functional explanation in the hermeneutic sense. In this way, positing the function of producing efficient accident cost avoidance reveals to us the way in which the disparate components of the structure and substance of tort law hang together in a way that is, at the same time, normatively attractive: in a way, in other words, that allows us to see tort law in its best light.

Thus, in the typical economic explanation, various parts of the law of torts—the rule of negligence, the definition of reasonableness, the but-for causation requirement, or the like—are each shown to further efficiency; and so efficiency is said to be the best interpretation of them, individually and collectively. No causal claim need be involved. Efficiency provides an interpretive scheme that holds together the elements of tort law, and this coherence—along with the independent moral attractiveness of the goal of efficiency—is what grounds or justifies the interpretation. If this interpretation requires some procrustean modifications, they are justified by an attractive goal, since it is obviously preferable to have fewer accidents than to have more, and (other things equal) it is most preferable to have the fewest at the lowest possible cost.

The hermeneutic interpretation of the project may be the most charitable we can provide. After all, economic analysis has yet to provide the two essential components of a standard functional explanation: a demonstration that the outcome of tort law really is efficient cost reduction, and a causal mechanism that feeds back that outcome into an explanation of tort law's existence and shape. Moreover, while in the typical economic explanation of tort law the descriptive and prescriptive aims are combined in a way that would be indefensible for a social-scientific functional account, this combination of descriptive and prescriptive elements is the very hallmark of an interpretive reconstruction.

Should economic analysis turn out to be an interpretive theory rather than a traditional functionalist theory, that would in itself be nothing to be embarrassed about. While it might offend the positivistic social science scruples of some of its proponents, that would be something to get over, not fret over. There would be some things to fret over, though, and perhaps even to be embarrassed about. Two of these are especially important. First, if economic analysis is an interpretive theory in the Dworkinian sense, then it is a particularly bad one on the dimension of fit. Where an interpretation is supposed to help us see the way the parts of an institution hang together, fit, or cohere with one another, economic analysis appears to do just the opposite with respect to the structural features of tort law. It treats the key roles of victim and injurer as things that are not deeply normatively related to one another, and accords only epistemic significance to the existence of the tort itself. [11] The dimension of fit has, it appears, been sacrificed altogether for the sake of the posited function, which now takes on the role of cementing together the disjointed parts. The result is less an interpretation of an actual institution than it is the imposition on it of a completely external goal. It is as though we sought to explain Christmas by interpreting it as a yearly boost for the retail industry.

Nor is the economic interpretation successful on the dimension of value, where an argument is still required. Typically, economists of law shy away from defending the normative attractiveness of efficiency as the primary or exclusive aim of law generally, or of tort law in particular. They have little to say on the subject, and what they have said has not been particularly persuasive. But if the economic analysis of tort law (or of any body of law for that matter) is to be an interpretation in the Dworkinian sense, then the argument for efficiency as the best explanation of tort law requires an argument for the moral attractiveness of efficiency as the exclusive or paramount aim of tort law, and indeed requires an argument that the exclusive aim of efficiency is more attractive morally than the set of values embodied in corrective justice.

The foregoing discussion may have uncovered problems for economic analysis deeper than the ones with which the discussion began. Some progress has been made, though. For with the project reinterpreted as a form of normative reconstruction or interpretation, the economist has been freed of the burden of demonstrating a causal connection between efficiency and the existence of tort law, and moreover sense has been made of the otherwise inexplicable combination of descriptive and prescriptive elements in the economic account. For the interpretive reconstruction to be a plausible one, however, the economist needs to provide a better argument than he has so far to establish a "fit" between efficiency and the structure and substance of tort law, and a much better defense of the moral value of efficiency than has been offered to this point.

Before going further, I would like to consider an objection that seeks to turn the tables on the corrective justice account, arguing that it fails to meet certain standards of explanatory adequacy where the economic analysis succeeds. The corrective justice theory does not adequately explain tort law because

---

[11] This is among the claims of Lecture 2.

it does not provide a theory of what counts as a wrong of the sort that gives rise to a duty of repair; nor, relatedly, does corrective justice tell us what the primary or first-order duties are that corrective justice enforces by imposing a second-order duty of repair. The corrective justice theorist cannot tell us why Jones ought to exercise a certain degree of care toward Smith; at best he can only tell us why, if Jones fails to do so and Smith is injured as a result, Jones has a duty of repair. In contrast, the efficiency theorist tells us not only why Jones must exercise reasonable care toward Smith, but also what reasonable care consists in. So, at best, the corrective justice theory is an incomplete explanation, while the economic account is a complete one. I take this to be a serious and thoughtful objection, but I do not find it persuasive. Let me explain why.

Corrective justice claims that when someone has wronged another to whom he owes a duty of care, he thereby incurs a duty of repair. This means that corrective justice is an account of the second-order duty of repair. *Someone* does not incur a second-order duty of repair unless he has failed to discharge some first-order duty. However, the relevant first-order duties are not themselves duties of corrective justice. Thus, while corrective justice presupposes some account of what the relevant first-order duties are, it does not pretend to provide an account of them.

At the same time corrective justice is not compatible with just any set of first-order duties. We cannot even make corrective justice intelligible as a principle of justice without identifying at least some first-order duties that might plausibly be said to give rise to duty of repair as a matter of corrective justice. It is only in the light of such paradigm cases that we can understand how corrective justice might express a principle of justice in the first place.[12] This is a burden that is readily met, however, and I would suggest that assault and battery against the person provides a suitable paradigm. If I batter or assault another person who is injured as a result, it should be perfectly clear in what sense I might be said to have incurred a duty of repair as a matter of corrective justice. Thus, the paradigm of assault—together, perhaps, with some other, equally accessible paradigm cases—is sufficient to make clear the way in which corrective justice purports to be a principle of justice. This is not a matter of providing a theory from which all and only the duties that are protected or enforced by a practice of corrective justice might be derived. A set of paradigms suffices to make corrective justice an appropriately complete account of what it purports to explain.

It may be helpful to consider this response in light of an analogy with retributive justice and the criminal law.[13] Retributivism is standardly viewed

[12] Stephen Perry also emphasizes this point, and I believe it is recognized by every noteworthy advocate of a corrective justice account.
[13] I am no defender of retributivism as a theory of punishment and I employ the example for purposes of exposition only, not in order to defend corrective justice by analogy.

as a justificatory theory, in the sense that it purports to explain why a legal practice involving punishment is justified. It can, however, be viewed as an explanatory theory—that is, as an explanation of our actual punitive practices, in much the same way that I maintain corrective justice to be an explanation of our liability practices. Yet no one regards it as an objection to retributivism that it fails to provide a theory or a list of the kinds of conduct that ought to be criminalized. Retributivism is not a theory of criminality; it is a theory about what ought to be, or of what may legitimately be done by the state in those cases where a criminal misdeed has been committed. Of course retributivism thereby presupposes that there will be some means of picking out the relevant class of misdeeds. It presupposes an account of criminality, or at least a list of what the crimes are. But that does not mean that retributivism is therefore inadequate as an explanation of our practices of punishment (though of course it may be deemed inadequate on other grounds).[14] At the same time, in order to make intelligible the claim that retributivism is a specific sort of moral principle, we need to appeal to some—possibly revisable—set of paradigm cases of the sort of conduct that might plausibly call for hard treatment by the state as something morally deserved, and not merely as a matter of instrumental value to society.

Once retributivism has thus been made intelligible by paradigm examples, we can see that it imposes certain constraints on criminality. If punishment is to be understood on retributive grounds, then the kind of wrongdoing that we punish must be the kind that could plausibly warrant hard treatment as a matter of desert. Retributivism is not compatible, for example, with the abandonment of the various mental elements of a crime in favor of general strict liability. Something similar is true of corrective justice. The principle of corrective justice does not entail a list or a theory of tortious acts; but it nonetheless imposes constraints on the kinds of interests that can be protected by tort law, and on the conditions of agency and responsibility that tort law requires for liability.

For example, as I have argued elsewhere, while the set of holdings that can be secured by a practice of corrective justice need not coincide exactly with the holdings that should exist according to the best theory of distributive justice, holdings must nonetheless satisfy certain minimal conditions of moral legitimacy in order for it to make sense for us to speak of protecting them by a practice of corrective justice.[15] The principle of corrective justice

---

[14] Conversely, the great twentieth-century work on criminality Joel Feinberg's *The Moral Limits of the Criminal Law* (New York: Oxford University Press, 1984) is not, nor does it purport to be, an account of the grounds or justification for punishing those who fail to live by the criminal law's demands.

[15] See *Risks and Wrongs*. This position has been further developed by Stephen Perry. See "On the Relationship between Corrective and Distributive Justice" in Jeremy Horder (ed.), *Oxford Essays in Jurisprudence*, 4th ser. (Oxford: Oxford University Press, 2000).

similarly imposes constraints on the conditions of responsibility—for example, it is inconsistent with corrective justice that someone could be held liable for another's costs just because the former is in a better position to reduce or spread risks.

To summarize, even though corrective justice operates on a scheme of first-order duties that are not themselves derivable from corrective justice, there must nonetheless be certain paradigm cases of the relevant first-order duties if we are to be able to understand their enforcement by tort law as a matter of corrective justice. That is sufficient, however, to make the theory a complete account of what it purports to explain. Moreover, even though corrective justice does not generate an exhaustive list of the relevant duties, it does impose constraints on what those duties can be and on what the conditions of responsibility for failing to conform to them must be. All of this is closely analogous to the situation with respect to a retributive theory of punishment.

Still, this leaves us with a largely unspecified conception of the duties that tort law enforces, and it might be thought that this is just not a satisfactory situation. Whether or not the corrective justice account owes us a theory of first-order duties, one might suppose that we still need such a theory—that is, one from which the duties enforced by tort law might be systematically derived—before we can claim to have provided an adequate account of our tort institutions and practices. Indeed, it might be thought that here is precisely where the principle of efficiency enters the picture. Efficiency can go beyond the paradigm cases and tell us, systematically and as it were deductively, what duties ought to be enforced. In this way it might be thought that the corrective justice account and the economic analysis are not only compatible, but actually complementary, theories of tort law.

I reject the suggestion that an adequate account of tort practices requires that there be a general theory of first-order duties from which we can derive them all systematically. Indeed, I am dubious about the prospects for such a theory. On my view, much of the content of the first-order duties that are protected in tort law is created and formed piecemeal in the course of our manifold social and economic interactions.[16] These generate conventions that give rise to expectations among individuals regarding the kind and level of care they—we—can reasonably demand of one another. The content of these duties is then *further* specified in the practice of tort law itself—in the process of litigation, in the development of case law, in the writing of restatements, and the like.[17] If I am right about this, then it seems unlikely that we could ever have a general theory from which we might derive the

---

[16] See *Risks and Wrongs.*

[17] No other corrective justice theorist need be committed to this view about the relationship between the principle of corrective view and the duties that are enforced by it. However, I believe that many would be drawn to a similar account.

first-order duties protected by tort law. Whether or not I am right about the way these duties are created, however, there is no reason to *suppose* that they must be derivable from some theory, nor that providing such a theory is a condition for an adequate explanation of our tort practices.[18]

But while I thus have my doubts about the prospects for a general comprehensive theory of enforceable private duties, I certainly haven't proved that such an account could not succeed. It is even conceivable that an economic account could provide the right theory of the underlying duties that our tort institutions protect as a matter of corrective justice. I do not believe that a hybrid theory of this sort could be supported by what we find in our actual institutions of tort law, but I do not mean to say it is an *inconceivable* arrangement.

Still, it is important to bear in mind that the sorts of "duties" that fall out of a standard economic account could not play this hybrid role. These accounts do not use efficiency to discover an independent class of duties that are analytically prior to our liability practices. In the standard economic analysis, there is no boundary, as it were, between what the duties are and what the liability practices should be. What counts as a "duty" or a "wrong" in a standard economic account depends on an assessment of what the consequences are of imposing liability in a given case. Duty and wrong, as independent categories, are doing no work in the story.[19] So while in principle we could have an efficiency theory of duties, what

[18] Nor is there any reason to suppose that duties cannot justifiably be enforced by a practice of corrective justice unless they can be derived from some general theory.

[19] In claiming that the category of duty does no work in the law and economics accounts of tort law, I do not mean to suggest that such accounts make no reference to the concept of duty or that they see no role for it in tort law. Rather, the point I am emphasizing is that duty provides no independent grounds for judgements of liability. Let me explain. In tort law, the duty to compensate is a second-order duty that is imposed, in part, as a result of the defendant's failure to discharge a first-order duty of care. Failure to discharge the first-order duty is what makes an individual liable to a second-order duty of repair. The concept of a duty in tort law is central both to strict and fault liability. In strict liability, the generic form of the first-order duty is a "duty not to harm someone", while in fault, the generic form of the duty is a "duty not to harm someone negligently or carelessly". In order for the first-order duty to be a ground of liability, the specific first-order duties of care that one has must be defensible as standards of conduct. This means that the duties articulated in the law of torts purport to express genuine reasons for acting, or standards with which one ought to comply. Tort law recognizes that failure to comply with such duties legitimately exposes one to a certain kind of legal responsibility or liability. The duties, in this sense, come first—normatively, as well as logically. If they are to come first normatively, then they must express reasons for acting quite apart from the imposition of liability.

In the economic analysis, the fundamental question is how to allocate costs between defendant and plaintiff. Rather than being logically prior to the liability as the ground of it, the duty not to harm is construed in the economic analysis as a *consequence* of the liability. Thus, the "primary" duty simply falls out of the economic grounds for imposing a duty to compensate, and is not a duty that is independently defensible as a standard of conduct apart from the role it plays in warranting or explaining a liability judgment. In that sense, economic analysis eliminates the concept of duty in tort law—that is, it eliminates the concept of something that can be defended as a standard of conduct and not merely as a condition of liability.

economists offer is not an efficiency theory of duties at all, but an efficiency theory of liability or of cost allocation.

Moreover, it is for good reason that the economists proceed this way. If they were to deny that the overall practice of enforcing private duties is itself subject to a principle of efficiency, there would be nothing particularly attractive about the principle of efficiency as an explanation of the duties that are enforced. So aside from being improbable, a hybrid account that uses efficiency to explain the underlying duties would also be unmotivated.[20]

Finally, I would like to consider the suggestion that the corrective justice theory must be supplemented by some other theory that explains those features of tort law that it does not explain—for example, vicarious liability, or perhaps products liability. It is not my view that all of tort law must be explained by corrective justice. What corrective justice purports to do is to explain the core of tort law. Some parts of the law of torts, like vicarious liability, make sense only in the light of whatever account we have of the core of liability. Vicarious liability is defensible as a principled extension of the core case; and there can be no vicarious liability if the core claim of liability is not itself satisfied. So if corrective justice explains the core, it is essential to our understanding instances of liability that are parasitic on the core. The same could be said for a range of cases and doctrines that extend the core or paradigm cases explained by corrective justice.

Now, I have no doubt that there will be other cases that cannot be accounted for in terms of principled extensions of the core of tort law. These doctrines and cases may well have nothing at all to do with corrective justice.[21] But I do not think that such cases show the need for another explanatory theory. They simply show that sometimes there are very good reasons of an instrumental type for imposing liability without regard for whether or not the normally required conditions of responsibility or wrong are met. To be sure, if such cases began to dominate tort law—as a result, say, of technological changes or what have you—then we might have good reason to revise our view that tort law is a matter of corrective justice.

Instead of asking whether *tort law* is best understood on efficiency or justice grounds, some economic analysts suggest that we ask the different question of what best explains the general set of institutions and practices of *risk regulation*. Even if corrective justice provides the better explanation of tort law understood as a distinct and autonomous body of law, it fares

---

[20] By contrast, a hybrid account in which efficiency or utility maximization enters at the grand level of political theory—not as a way of determining the enforceable duties, but rather as a way of justifying a practice of enforcing duties as a matter of corrective justice—might be a more tenable alternative. From that point of view, one could argue that it is best on utilitarian or efficiency grounds to have institutions like tort law that focus on corrective justice. The problems I have noted arise only when we try to integrate an efficiency theory of wrongs and duties with a corrective justice account of why we enforce them.

[21] I believe this is true in the case of *Hymowitz* v. *Eli Lilly and Co.*, for example.

worse than economic analysis as an account of *our general practices of risk regulation*. In fact, these analysts argue, tort law is not an autonomous body of law; it is just one of many parts of the law that have to do with regulating risk. Economic analysis provides the best explanation of tort law because tort law is an integral part of the institutional strategy of efficient risk regulation. Seeing tort law this way also allows us to uncover important connections between it and other parts of the whole.[22]

To argue this way is, of course, to adopt the familiar strategy of meeting an objection by changing the subject. Even a sympathetic critic of economic analysis may be taken aback by the swiftness with which economic analysts are prepared to abandon their longtime poster child—the private law of tort. Moreover, the fact—if it is one—that regarding tort law as part of a general approach to risk regulation fits better with the methods of economic analysis is, at best, a question-begging reason for shifting the subject-matter of inquiry. This is so even if there is a sense in which the current boundaries between various bodies of law are arbitrary. It is one thing to claim that the current divisions are neither fixed nor reflective of some natural ordering; it is another to claim that they are arbitrary in some sense that would license our ignoring them from the standpoint of theory, or abandoning them in practice. Even were the categories arbitrary in the sense of being "conventional" and neither "natural" nor "essential," that would not, by itself, justify ignoring or abandoning them. Still less would it be a reason for replacing them with the preferred economic set of categories.

The justification of the basic conceptual categories of tort law does not rest on showing that they reflect an independent moral order or that they are somehow conceptually indispensable. For example, it is not necessary to show that the distinction between "causing harm" and "failing to prevent harm", which is so fundamental to the law of torts, marks a independent moral difference. By analogy, utilitarian moral theory does not regard as fundamental the differences among causing harm, not preventing harm, and failing to benefit. Still, a utilitarian can allow that some of these differences are reflected in different parts of the law for good utilitarian reasons. Though the boundaries between categories of thought in law may not mark inherent moral differences, they may nonetheless be justifiable. Only categories that are arbitrary in the sense of obscuring a deeper understanding of the phenomenon without practical worth, or in the sense of lacking adequate moral justification, should be ignored or abandoned.

---

[22] I am not exactly sure what the argument for this claim is, in part because I do not know what the content of "risk regulation" is taken to be, and what, therefore, we are to think of as our legal practices of risk regulation. I do not take up these issues here and simply bracket the question for now. My interest here is more methodological than substantive. I want to know why the fact that economic analysis might provide the better explanation (in the interpretive sense) of risk-regulatory practices should count as a reason to think that economic analysis provides, therefore, the better explanation of tort law.

The question then becomes whether or not the categories reflected in our tort practices are indeed justifiable—both morally and theoretically. From the standpoint of the moral question we have, as I noted above, yet to hear a genuine defense of the view that the existing categories are objectionable on independent moral grounds, much less that they should be replaced by the category of economic efficiency. From the theoretical standpoint, however, we may wish to revise our categories if there are simpler or more elegant alternatives or if, as currently conceived and expressed in practice, they fail to hang together in a coherent way with other important concepts. Considerations like these may yet motivate the move to regarding tort law as merely a part of a larger body of risk-regulatory institutions.

Still, the point remains that we do not revise our boundaries between bodies of law just because we can, or because doing so suits our favorite theory. We cannot decide, as it were, to drop the category of tort as uninteresting or unimportant just because it would be more convenient for economic analysis to substitute the category "practices of risk regulation" for it. From the theoretical standpoint, any such revision must be motivated by recalcitrant problems with the categories as currently conceived—for example, by phenomena the current architecture does not capture or which it illuminates for us only dimly. Revisions can't be justified on the grounds that our favorite theory isn't working.[23]

Are there, then, sufficient reasons for revising our pretheoretic conception of tort law—for effacing the boundaries between tort and other bodies of law and substituting the law of risk regulation for this set of practices? One possible reason has already been suggested: a concept of tort law that is bound by its traditional categories may obscure important connections among different bodies of the law. This would amount to a failure of the traditional conception—and of theories based on or supporting it—to reflect the theoretical norm of *consilience*. Thus, the economist could claim that if we view tort law through the lens of economic analysis, we can

---

[23] Theoretical–conceptual revision is a rational enterprise; each departure from the existing scheme of concepts requires a reason. Thus, we begin with the smallest changes. Only as a last resort do we jettison the core of the distinctions, categories, and beliefs with which we have proceeded. In the case of the law, we thus have prima-facie reason to retain the various distinctions within it—torts, contract, criminal law, and so on—as well as the categories embedded in each of these bodies of law. We needn't show nor must we assume that these distinctions are indispensable, or that they track some independent moral order. However, we do not revise or reconceptualize the law until we have reason to doubt the value or usefulness of our existing categories.

In the pragmatist tradition this is often expressed as the "belief–doubt" principle. On this view, the Cartesian foundationalists have it all wrong. We do not suspend all belief pending some foundation of indubitability on which to ground it. Rather, we treat the set of beliefs that we happen to have as in no need of justification or foundation—indubitable or otherwise. Of course, our belief set is certain to contain some falsehoods, and we should be prepared to doubt and to revise any particular belief in the light of new experience or better theory.

better understand the coherence of our general risk-regulatory practices. The better a theory of law is at unifying distinct areas of inquiry, the more attractive the theory is.

These considerations seem to provide an entirely different and better argument on behalf of the economic analysis of tort law. Even if economic analysis does not have a good account of our pretheoretic conception of the bilateral structure of tort law, considerations of consilience may compel us to look beyond tort law to other areas of the law—including parts of administrative law and regulatory law generally. The price we must pay in order to see these connections clearly is that we must revise our pretheoretic understanding of the bilateral structure of tort law. What once seemed necessary to our understanding of tort law must be abandoned or rethought. For example, the victim–injurer relationship once appeared to be of fundamental normative significance; in revising our understanding of the tort law in the interest of consilience, we abandon or reinterpret the normative significance of that relationship. We see a lot more in the law and in the way its component parts hang together when we give up the view that in torts the victim and injurer are deeply connected in the way we might otherwise have thought they were.

This is the right kind of argument, but it is not yet a successful one for replacing the category of torts with that of risk regulation. There are many perspectives from which we might look at a body of law: the point of view of private parties concerned to plan their affairs; the point of view of those who have been mistreated by others; the point of view of lawyers, judges, and perhaps of reformers. The economic analysis of risk regulation seems to take this last perspective only, and in doing so renders the other perspectives nearly unintelligible. For in asking us to revise our pretheoretic conception of tort law, it requires that we abandon the view that victims sue injurers because they have been wronged by them.[24] We see lots of connections from the reformer's point of view, but at the cost of our inability, perhaps, to comprehend law from other points of view.

Thus, we do not yet have an argument for the economic analysis of tort law, but, rather, only the outlines of what such an argument might look like. At the very least, proponents of economic analysis will need to show in more detail the ways in which economic analysis illuminates the connections between torts and risk regulation; they will also need to defend the view that making those connections more perspicuous is worth sacrificing the existing conceptions, which illuminate tort law's bilateral

---

[24] Of course, alleged victims may have all sorts of subjective reasons for suing their alleged injurers; in most cases they do so because they believe they can thereby secure some financial reward. The point here is not about the subjective beliefs of litigants, but, rather, about the norms the participants understand to be governing the practice.

structure.[25] Still, the importance of the norm of consilience to theory construction authorizes an implicit challenge to the corrective justice account, one that we ought to take up. It would be a failing of the corrective justice account if it could explain tort law only by isolating it from other areas of the law or of political morality. Indeed, if it is a good account of tort law, we should expect corrective justice also to illuminate a broader domain of our social practice. After all, the conceptual categories central both to tort law and to corrective justice—categories like responsibility, wrong, repair, and so on—are also important to our pretheoretical understanding of other parts of the law and of our political institutions more generally. The burden of the corrective justice theorist is thus not to show that corrective justice unifies tort law with regulatory practices in particular, but simply to show that the explanation of tort law in terms of corrective justice reveals the ways in which tort law hangs together with other legal and political practices.

---

[25] One implication of such an account would very likely be a rejection of the fundamental importance of the public–private law distinction. So in defending the risk-regulatory explanation, one would not only have to abandon the centrality of the bilateral structure of tort law, but also have to revise our pretheoretic understandings of the differences between private and public law.

Lecture Four—
Consilience

The value expressed in the norm of consilience is that, other things equal, it is good when a theory can bring a diversity of phenomena under a single explanatory scheme—and the greater the range of phenomena thus explained, the better. A classic exemplar of this theoretical virtue is Newton's theory of gravitation, which provides a single explanation for both the motion of falling bodies and the orbits of the planets—phenomena that had previously been subjects of distinct bodies of theory.

There are different ways in which an explanation can unify a diversity of phenomena, however, and in that sense there are different kinds of consilience. In the case of the law of gravitation, the theory unifies in a reductive way. By asserting that planetary motion and the motion of falling bodies are in fact instances of, and in that sense reducible to, a single more basic phenomenon, the theory dispenses with categories that are distinctive of one kind of motion or the other, rendering principles based on such distinctions devoid of fundamental explanatory value.[1] A similar, reductive kind of unification is exemplified in moral theory by utilitarianism, which purports to offer a single principle that exhaustively explains the rightness or wrongness of any action or institution, eliminating the fundamental explanatory value of any subordinate principle.[2]

A theory may unify diverse phenomena without eliminating the need for subordinate principles and categories, however. The consilience of such a non-reductive theory may lie in its showing how a single principle ties together and illuminates the relations among a number of distinct explanatory elements—including, perhaps, other principles.[3] The kind of consilience

---

[1] In claiming that reductive consilience renders the reduced theory or concept devoid of fundamental explanatory value, I do not mean to claim that the reduced theory can play no heuristically or otherwise valuable explanatory role. If the "folk psychology" of beliefs and desires were ultimately reduced to a neural network theory of the mental, for example, it would not follow that explanations of actions in terms of an agent's beliefs and desires would cease to have practical value—however, the folk psychology would not provide a deep or scientifically significant explanation.

[2] In terms of its reductive consilience, utilitarianism might provide the most comprehensive explanation of both law and morality. Mill and others have argued that aside from expressing the moral truth, utilitarianism can also *explain* much of the law as well as much of our common-sense morality. Whether or not it does explain these things depends, of course, on a host of other factors besides its comprehensiveness. I owe this point to Martin Stone.

[3] The sense of "ties together" will be developed more fully below. For the moment, however, it should be clear that not just any demonstration of a relationship between two explanatory

we seek in a theory, whether reductive or not, depends on the kind of phenomenon to be explained.

In the defense of the economic account outlined at the end of the previous lecture the consilience of the account is seen in its ability to unify a variety of different areas of law and other regulatory practices by reducing these apparently distinct phenomena to instances of a single more basic practice of efficient risk regulation. The principle of efficiency exhaustively explains the whole range of these institutions, and principles based on the distinctness of these institutions lose any fundamental explanatory power; more, such principles are even held to be misleading and to obscure the phenomenon being explained. When we understand the way in which tort law is an application of the same principle as, say, contract or parts of administrative law, we have (it is claimed) achieved a deeper and clearer understanding of the kind of institutional arrangement tort law is. Part of this deeper understanding involves seeing that our earlier way of conceptualizing these diverse practices as fundamentally distinct must be discarded. The practices have been exhaustively explained by the principle of efficiency, and the traditional categories add little, if anything, to our understanding.

Other things equal, the consilience of the economic analysis is an attractive aspect of the theory. It would be wrong, however, to suppose that the economic analysis has cornered the market on theory consilience, or to assume that the kind of consilience we should be striving for in a theory of tort is reductive consilience. A nonreductive explanation of a body of law can exhibit its consilience by showing how that body of law figures as an integral part of the law as a whole, and perhaps by showing further how the law figures in the broader context of our moral and political practices. Indeed, such an explanation might unify a range of legal practices precisely by showing why the principles realized or expressed in a given body of law are unique to it, and are neither generally applicable across all legal contexts nor dispensable in favor of some generally applicable principle. Thus, tort law and criminal law might be unified in this sense by a theory that showed why we need these distinct bodies of law, each with its distinct and ineliminable principles. A successful theory of this sort would explain how the modes of practical reasoning and substantive principle realized in each part of the law express

---

elements should count as unifying them or tying them together. For example, it would be perverse to say that we have unified distinct explanatory elements by showing that they are parts of mutually exclusive explanations, or by showing that they derive from contradictory initial assumptions. One of the burdens of this lecture is to show that there is meaningful sense in which we can unify explanatory elements or theories without reducing them to some more basic and more comprehensive theory.

fundamentally or unavoidably (perhaps even necessarily) unique features of that part.[4]

I have argued that the content of concepts is given by the inferential roles they play in the various practices in which they figure. Many of the concepts that figure in tort law—responsibility, wrong, duty of care, repair—figure in other practices too, including other legal practices, our public discourse on politics and policy, and our everyday moral judgments in a variety of contexts. It is reasonable to suppose that an adequate understanding of tort law should be sensitive to the role that its central concepts play in these other practices too; and it is to be hoped that a theory of tort law will shed light on other of our legal and political practices. We need not, of course, show that tort law is connected to the set of institutions available for allocating risk; that is the burden that economic analysis has taken on, but it is certainly not an adequacy condition for a theory of tort law as such. The norm of consilience tells us only that a theory that explains tort law in terms of a given set of principles is better to the extent that those principles can also explain other practices; in this way, the theory contributes to a more comprehensive understanding of the whole.

In this and the next lecture I defend a certain view about the relationship between tort law and our redistributive institutions, and between the principles of corrective and distributive justice. I argue that the institutions of tort law and our redistributive institutions together articulate the requirements of fairness with respect to allocating the costs of life's misfortunes.[5] Moreover, the idea of fairness common to these institutions is itself an aspect of a more general principle of fairness: fairness with respect to the terms of interaction among free and equal persons in a cooperative endeavor. The consilience of the corrective justice account is seen in the way it fits into a broader understanding of our legal, moral, and political practices—illuminating this range of practices without eliminating their distinctness.

---

[4] The basic point is simply that a good explanation can show how various parts of the whole differ from one another in some systematic or principled way, and how their doing so contributes to the coherence of the whole. In the limiting case, such an explanation might demonstrate that different parts of the whole are necessarily distinct, and that the principles or concepts involved in each are unique. My claim is not, however, that a non-eliminative consilient theory *must* establish the uniqueness of the principles expressed in different bodies of the law; only that consilience does not require showing that distinct bodies of the law have a common root. Nor am I claiming that the principles expressed in the criminal law and tort law are unique to each.

[5] In saying that these practices articulate certain of the requirements of fairness, I mean, in the first instance, that they operate together to express a certain *conception* of fairness. That conception may not reflect, wholly or even in part, the substantive requirements of fairness. However, in so far as these practices constitute an important subset of the overall set of practices in which fairness figures, it would bizarre in the extreme if the substantive content of fairness—which I take to be given by the overall set of practices in which it figures—were not in some significant measure reflected in the conception of it articulated by the practices of distributive and corrective justice.

There is a basic pretheoretical distinction between misfortunes owing to human agency and those that are attributable to no one's agency. The traditional philosophical distinction between corrective and distributive justice reflects, among other things, this pretheoretical distinction between kinds of misfortunes.[6] Part of the connection between redistributive institutions and tort law is that together these institutions embody the requirements of fairness with regard to how we allocate the costs of life's misfortunes. The difference between the principles articulated in these institutional practices reflects the distinction between misfortunes owing to human agency and those which are no one's responsibility.[7]

Given this distinction, it is natural to suppose that the difference in the requirements of fairness with respect to these different domains reflects the role the concept of personal responsibility plays in each. Corrective justice says, in effect, that fairness in keeping track of the costs of life's misfortunes owing to individual human agency requires the imposition of a duty of repair for the compensable harms for which one is responsible: those owed, in an appropriate way, to one's agency. That is, I have a duty to repair your loss as a matter of corrective justice just because your loss is an outcome for which I am responsible.

In contrast, the scope of one's duties to come to the aid of others is not usually thought to be limited to alleviating the misfortunes for which one is responsible. Many duties of distributive justice are thought to require coming to the aid of others (typically indirectly, through redistributive taxation) to alleviate certain misfortunes for which one is not responsible. Corrective justice is a distinct kind of justice because the duties imposed by it are grounded in the "responsibility-for-outcome" relationship. This, in any case, is the pretheoretical intuition that most of us share and which is reflected both in the philosophical distinction between corrective and

---

[6] It is important to stress that this is not a theoretically precise distinction between kinds of misfortune. That, indeed, is one of the main points I hope to make in this lecture. In order to articulate with precision the difference between the misfortunes for which human agents are responsible, and the misfortunes for which no one is responsible, we need to appeal to the whole conceptual and practical apparatus of the tort law. Once the tort law has clarified the class of misfortunes for which no individual is responsible, however, we confront the question of whether to hold those misfortunes in common as a society, or to let the losses lie where they fall. This of course is a question of distributive justice. This much might suggest that corrective justice is prior to distributive justice, in that the former delimits the scope of the latter. Actually, the dependence goes in both directions. For example, if we decide as a matter of distributive justice to hold in common some class of misfortunes—say, all of the costs of innocent or negligent accidents—we remove it from the area of misfortunes for which tort law allocates the costs. Distributive and corrective justice thus work together to sort out the costs of life's misfortunes.

[7] Even as our institutions embody principles that reflect this distinction in the sources of misfortune, our view about what this distinction comes to is revisable in the light of the institutions we settle on as reflections of it. For me, this is just another illustration of the basic pragmatist commitments to the primacy of practice, to the constitutive relationship between practice and concept, and to the rejection of semantic atomism.

distributive justice, and in the distinction between tort law and our redistributive institutions.

The question of what outcomes an individual is responsible for is intimately related to the question of who should bear the costs of particular misfortunes. But what exactly is the relationship between outcome responsibility and the justified allocation of costs? Some might hold that the burdens of life's misfortunes should always be allocated according to some notion of outcome responsibility that appeals to the causal history of the misfortunes. One could argue, for example, that if B's loss is the result of our social structure (as some claim is true of so-called "structural unemployment"), then the loss is to be redistributed among us all. On the other hand, if B's loss is A's doing, then A must bear the cost; no one else has the burden of making it good. Finally, those losses of B's that he himself has caused are his own to bear.

Notice two things about this approach. First, the causal history *may* explain why B is made to shoulder those losses he has brought on himself, and why A should bear B's loss if it is the result of A's doing. But the causal history alone does not explain what is to be done with losses that are no individual's doing.[8] Thus, liberal egalitarians can argue that *unless B is the cause of his own misfortune*, then the cost should be borne by all of us; while libertarians maintain that *unless someone else has caused B's misfortune*, then it is his own, and no one else can be made to bear any part of it. Neither argument is especially compelling on the grounds of causation alone, however. If one side or the other is to be preferred, it must be because of some more basic moral considerations.

As I see it, the relevant considerations are the requirements of political fairness as reciprocity among free and equal persons.[9] For the libertarian, on the other hand, the basic principle is one of *self-ownership*.[10] The libertarian concept of property (or rightful holdings) as well as the libertarian concept of responsibility-for-outcomes are both built up from this concept of self-ownership, in conjunction with two other concepts: causation and volitional conduct. The idea is roughly this: X owns his body; X owns all those products (desirable or undesirable) that are either the causal upshots of his voluntary doings, subject to voluntary agreements (such as employer–employee relations, by which someone else may come to own the causal upshots of one's doings) or that he has received through gift, purchase, or other voluntary transfer; X also owns whatever benefits and misfortunes

---

[8] This might be true both for misfortunes like structural unemployment (which some would hold are the effects of collective human agency) and, less controversially, for cases like earthquakes and floods, which on the face of it appear to be owed to chance alone.

[9] I develop this conception more fully in the next lecture.

[10] While there are at least as many formulations of libertarianism as there are libertarians, self-ownership animates the most influential versions of the doctrine.

might accrue to him by chance, that is, things that happen to him, or things that he finds and keeps, when they are not the causal upshots of someone else's voluntary activity, voluntary transfers, or agreements. And X owns nothing else.[11] This is a moral, and not merely a legal, sense of ownership; and moreover it is held to constrain, as a requirement of justice, the actions of the political state.

It is important to the libertarian project that we understand that this is an analysis not only of property ownership, but of outcome ownership as well—or, in other words, an analysis of outcome responsibility. It states the truth conditions for all propositions of the form: so-and-so owns or is responsible for such-and-such (where "so-and-so" ranges over persons or other responsible agents and "such-and-such" ranges over things and states of affairs).

Two features of this project are noteworthy. First, the content of responsibility-for-outcomes derives from concepts—self-ownership, causation, and volition—whose normativity is purportedly prepolitical; that is, the content of these concepts is not supposed to derive from or depend in any way on the roles they play in any legal or political institutions. Second, for that and related reasons, the libertarian believes that legal and political institutions must conform to these conditions of outcome responsibility in order to be just. Institutions of corrective justice—like tort law—and institutions affecting issues of distributive justice (for example, the property and taxation regimes) must all reflect the libertarian doctrine of outcome responsibility. The net effect is that the libertarian supports strict liability (as opposed to fault) in tort law and rejects as unjust any coercive institutions (most notably redistributive taxation) aimed at a redistribution of wealth. Under strict liability the injurer must take back what he rightfully owns, namely, the costs that have resulted from his voluntary agency. By the same token, redistributive institutions are unjust because they violate the principle of agency by forcing individuals to bear the costs of misfortunes that have befallen others, when those who are forced to bear the costs are not responsible for them in the relevant sense.

The libertarian position entails three claims that warrant our particular attention. The first is that there is a general concept of moral responsibility for outcomes that applies across *both distributive and corrective* contexts. The second is that this concept of moral responsibility for outcomes is prior to and imposes constraints on political or legal institutions—so that, in order to be just, such institutions must satisfy or conform to the requirements imposed by the principle of outcome responsibility. The third claim,

---

[11] Another familiar way of characterizing libertarianism—in terms of the principle of maximum compossible negative liberty for each—can be shown to derive in the end from the more basic commitment to self-ownership.

implicit in the other two, is that the underlying problems and principles of distributive and corrective justice are the same, and in particular that justice in allocating life's misfortunes is always a matter of ownership.

I shall not rehearse the standard objections to the libertarian theory of distributive justice (many of which I find compelling). The concerns I want to explore are less familiar and reveal problems with the libertarian approach as it applies to both distributive justice and tort law. The key idea in libertarianism is that one owns the causal upshots of one's actions. The untoward causal upshots of one's actions are their *costs*. Libertarianism claims that it is unfair to displace the costs of one's activities onto others; and it is unfair for the state to require anyone to bear costs that are not the costs of his own activity—costs that are not owed to his agency and which are not his doing. It is this picture of the costs of one's activities that leads libertarians to defend a theory of strict liability in torts and to oppose schemes for the involuntary redistribution of wealth.[12]

The consistency of these positions cannot be denied; indeed, they stand or fall together.[13] The fundamental reason both views must be rejected is that libertarianism offers what I have called a "naturalistic" interpretation of the concept of the costs of an activity, when, in fact, the concept of an activity's costs cannot be given content independently of some normative standard of care. An example will illustrate the objection.

Suppose my cows trample your corn. Is this a causal upshot of my voluntary doings (in which case I own the damage and must compensate you for it) or a causal upshot of your own voluntary doings (in which case the costs are yours to bear)? I could have built a fence between our properties; or I could have supervised my cows more carefully, or chosen to raise chickens instead of cows. Thus, but for my voluntary doings, the damage would not have occurred. The problem is that you too could have taken steps that would have avoided the costs. You could have built a fence, or planted your corn out of trampling range of my cows. But for the decisions each of us made, the harm would not have occurred.

To ask "Whose conduct imposed the costs" is like asking "Which activity —ranching or farming—is the damage to corn a cost of?" This is a question to which there simply is no naturalistic answer. The answer we need must take its bearings from a different, and plainly non-naturalistic, question, namely "What duties of care do we owe one another?" If I *ought* to have taken precautions—built a fence, supervised my cows more carefully, or the like—then the damage to your corn is a cost of ranching not farming. On the other hand, if I had no such duties, or if you had a duty to guard against errant cows, or a responsibility to farm a greater distance from the

[12] The conjunction of these two views is characteristic of the work of Richard Epstein.
[13] I have criticized these and related views in detail elsewhere. See Coleman and Ripstein, "Mischief and Misfortune".

property line, then the damage to the corn is a cost of your activity, not mine.[14]

This means that the concept of an activity's costs is a normative, not a naturalistic, notion.[15] Yet it is the mistakenly naturalistic conception of an activity's costs that underwrites the conjunction of views characteristic of the libertarian position—namely, strict liability in torts and anti-redistributivism. Once we recognize the standard of care as partially constitutive of the concept of an activity's costs, the principle of strict liability goes out the window. Even if fairness requires that I repair the costs my activities impose on others, we cannot identify which costs are the ones I have imposed without first establishing the scope of my duty of care to others.

Moreover, what I owe to others is not necessarily limited to the sphere of those costs that I have in some way brought about. The appropriate duty of care may entail that I must bear some part of the costs of the misfortunes that have befallen the disabled, the infirm, the poor, and the otherwise disadvantaged—quite apart from any role my causal agency has played with regard to those misfortunes. What costs are mine to bear is in the first instance a matter of what duties I have to come to the aid of others, and is not necessarily a matter of what I have done to them, or failed to do for them.

Stephen Perry has offered a similar but importantly different objection to the libertarian conception of outcome responsibility. Perry notes that the libertarian reliance on ownership, spelled out in terms of causation, leads to indeterminacy. If X is strictly liable for the causal upshots of his voluntary actions, then in most cases both the injurer and the victim own the victim's loss. This is because, in general, some voluntary actions of both parties are "but-for" causes of the harm. A principle of strict causal liability leads not to strict injurer liability—as some, like Richard Epstein have thought—but to indeterminate liability.[16]

Instead of analyzing outcome responsibility in terms of volition and causation, Perry analyzes it in terms of foreseeability and avoidability. Outcomes an agent can foresee and avoid—and, in that sense, outcomes the agent can control—are ones for which she is outcome-responsible. On Perry's account, the criterion of outcome responsibility determines the class of persons who can justly be held responsible for an outcome. In any

---

[14] For a much fuller development of these ideas, see ibid.

[15] That the concept of an activity's cost is normative in this sense is not an idea that is foreign to economic analysis. However, for reasons I discuss elsewhere, the particular economic analysis of the normative concept of a duty of care—which is at the core of the idea of an activity's costs—is not persuasive. (See ibid.) My target at the moment is the libertarian, however, and not the economist.

[16] See Stephen Perry, "The Impossibility of General Strict Liability" *Canadian Journal of Law and Jurisprudence* 1/2 (July 1988) 147–71.

accident the loss can justly be imposed only on those who could foresee and avoid the accident. This leaves open the question which member or members of the outcome-responsible class ought to bear the costs. On Perry's account, that is where the concept of fault comes in. The party who is at fault must bear the cost. Thus, liability in torts represents two distinct related ideas—outcome responsibility and fault.[17]

Perry conceives outcome responsibility as a *necessary condition* of just liability. Individuals who are outcome-responsible are the only suitable candidates for liability; but being a suitable candidate is not sufficient to justify the imposition of a cost. In addition, one must also be at fault in the relevant sense. One must, in other words, have had a *duty* to avoid the harm; and the harm that occurs must be a consequence of one's failure to discharge that duty.

The difference between Perry and the libertarian is thus threefold: first, Perry analyzes outcome responsibility in terms of foreseeability and avoidability rather than in terms of volition and causation. Second, he supplements the criterion of responsibility with the principle of fault; an agent's outcome responsibility for a harm is a necessary, but not a sufficient, condition for imposing on her the costs of the harm. And third, unlike the libertarian, Perry does not explicitly derive from his conception of outcome responsibility any prescriptive implications for institutions affecting the issue of distributive justice.[18]

Nonetheless, Perry's view appears to have at least two key features in common with the libertarian's. First, while the libertarian and Perry defend different conceptions of outcome responsibility, they hold in common the

---

[17] To avoid misunderstanding, it is important to note that the relevant concept of responsibility for outcomes—whether the libertarian's, Perry's, or my own—is not intended to capture or to track the appropriate practices of assigning blame and praise to agents. None of the parties to this debate believes that, in order to be *responsible for an outcome*, an agent must be in the sort of relationship to it that would make her blameworthy if it is a bad outcome, or praiseworthy if it is a good one. An agent might be excusable with respect to some or all of the outcomes for which she is responsible—perhaps because she acted on a mistaken judgment, or under duress, or in nonculpable ignorance; yet the outcome might nonetheless be the agent's responsibility. It may be hers to own up to, though the act which produced it may not reflect unfavorably on the agent's character or motivation. Finally, even when an agent is, say, blameworthy for an outcome that is her responsibility, there need be no proportionality between the blame and the outcome responsibility: an agent who is only slightly blameworthy may be liable for an enormous loss, because she is outcome-responsible for it.

[18] It is not obvious how close or how far apart Perry and the libertarians are on this last point. For the libertarian, outcome ownership is the basic principle that fully expresses the requirements of political fairness. It has strong moral implications in the following sense: If person X is outcome-responsible for harm Y, then it is prima facie just to hold X liable to repair Y. If X is not outcome-responsible for Y, then it is not just to hold X liable. This applies to all forms of liability, whether in tort, contract, regulation, or redistribution. I have already shown that Perry is committed only to the weaker claim that if X is not outcome-responsible for Y, then she cannot be held liable *in tort* for Y. There is nothing in Perry's account that requires him to claim that outcome responsibility similarly constrains the imposition of liability in other institutional contexts, or that the *same* principle of outcome responsibility applies as a constraint in those contexts.

view that the conception of outcome responsibility relevant to tort law is independent of our institutions of responsibility. That is to say, outcome responsibility does not depend on what kind of tort and redistributive institutions are in place in a given society. This forms the basis of the second common feature between Perry and the libertarian, namely the view that this independent conception of outcome responsibility provides invariant conditions on the justice of tort institutions—in other words, conditions that are unaffected by other legal and political institutions and practices, and whose content does not itself depend on the tort institutions in place.

It would be unfair to place too much emphasis on these similarities. Despite sharing with the libertarian the view that the content of outcome responsibility is independent of our social institutions, Perry does not maintain that the normative implications of outcome responsibility for tort law are thus independent. In this respect, his view is not far from mine. Where I differ with Perry is not so much in the analysis he provides of liability, but in what his analysis seems to imply in the realm of action theory. To say that an individual is responsible for some outcome is, on the face of it, to say that the outcome is that person's *doing*—a part of the world that is appropriately ascribed to her agency. Perry seems to suggest that the conditions of foreseeability and avoidability suffice as an analysis of how states of affairs in the world are to be assigned to individual human agency. Once that assignment is made, our institutions of responsibility (for example, tort law) then enter in order to determine when something *I have done* is also something *I should bear the cost of.*

In contrast to this view, I maintain that the answer to the question whether some part of the world is my doing will always depend on what is at stake in asking that question. If the question concerns what I may be punished for, or held liable for, the answer may be different than if the question concerns what I morally ought to feel remorse for, or what I should try to set right. Thus, there is no single sense of responsibility that underlies all of our practices and institutions of responsibility; on the contrary, those practices and institutions determine an array of different senses in which some part of the world can be said to be the result of my agency.

It is not obvious that Perry must deny this; after all, the only theoretical work that his notion of outcome responsibility does is to figure as a necessary condition of tort liability. If that is in fact all he means to capture with his conditions of foreseeability and avoidability, then I have no substantive quarrel with him. If one is to be justly held liable for some outcome, then one must indeed have been able to foresee it and avoid it. I submit, however, that it is extremely misleading to characterize this condition as any kind of *responsibility*. It seems, rather, simply to unpack a part of our conception of effective agency.

Only agents are the proper objects of responsibility; and only those capable of foreseeing and avoiding events or states of affairs are capable of being responsible for them. This is why, for example, infants and the (extremely) mentally incompetent cannot be responsible for anything. If we are wondering whether, in a particular instance, an agent X *could* be responsible for a state of affairs S, we might begin by asking whether or not X could have foreseen and avoided S. We would ask that not because an affirmative answer implies any kind of responsibility, but because a negative answer to either would defeat any attribution of responsibility by showing that a part of our notion of effective agency is absent.

The point is that foreseeability and avoidability do not capture any recognizable notion of responsibility at all. These conditions do not establish that X is (in any recognizable sense) outcome-responsible for S, but, rather, establish only the much weaker claim that S is an event, action, or state of affairs that X *could be* responsible for. I certainly do not deny (how could I?) that there is a notion of agency that is central to our concept of responsibility and whose content is largely, if not completely, independent of the practices in which it figures; further, foreseeability and avoidability are at least an important part of that notion of agency. What I deny is that there is any recognizable conception of *responsibility* whose content is independent of our practices of responsibility. What states, events, and actions we are responsible for depends on the practices in which our being responsible is a ground or basis for a judgment, action, or reason for acting.

In the legal context this means, first, that the appropriate conception of outcome responsibility must reflect the conditions under which the exercise of state authority is legitimate. These conditions express the constraints of fairness on the terms of interaction between persons, and reflect in turn the fundamental conception of fairness as a kind of reciprocity. It is not obvious that our extra-legal judgments of moral responsibility for outcomes, or of responsibility more generally, reflect or answer to the same set of constraints as do our judgments in a legal context. Thus, the criteria of responsibility suitable to ground enforceable duties of repair might well be different from those appropriate to non-enforceable duties (duties to apologize, to make amends, or in other ways to come to aid of others).[19]

More importantly, the way fundamental considerations of fairness are worked out in the legal–political domain may vary from one society to the next. Roughly speaking, a fair allocation scheme may rely more or less extensively on redistributive institutions versus institutions of corrective justice. The appropriate conception of outcome responsibility in a given

[19] See my article "The Practice of Corrective Justice". It is unclear whether Perry or the libertarian would deny this point in favor of a single moral conception of outcome responsibility.

society must reflect its particular division between the corrective and redis-tributive aspects of keeping track of the costs of life's misfortunes.

Finally, the appropriate conception of outcome responsibility can be articulated only in light of a given society's actual practices of corrective justice. The concept of outcome responsibility appropriate to determining enforceable duties of repair will be given its content by the structure of practical inferences embodied in the institutions of corrective justice. In sum, the coercive context, the specific division between corrective and redistributive institutions, and the actual practice of corrective justice all figure in the determination of the appropriate concept of outcome respons-ibility. Contrary to Perry and the libertarians, there can be no abstract, pre-political conception of outcome responsibility that provides a single set of constraints affecting the justice of tort institutions. Most fundamentally, I deny that the justice of our institutions of responsibility, such as tort law, depends on any prior determination of what each of us individually "owns". Rather, what each of us "owns" depends on what we owe one another; and that is a reflection of fairness as its content and requirements are expressed in our institutional, social, and moral life.

The important distinction Thomas Scanlon draws between allocative and attributive questions may be employed to clarify further the differ-ences between Perry and the libertarians on the one hand, and myself on the other.[20] The attributive question is, who is responsible? The allocative question is, who should bear the costs? Suppose we begin with the latter question. One answer might be: the person who is responsible for the loss should bear it. This would be to say that the allocative question is to be answered in the light of the principle of attribution. For example, we might say that the costs of the accident should lie where they fall unless someone is responsible for having brought it about. If someone is responsible for having brought it about, that person must bear the loss. Any other way of allocating the loss would be unfair or unjust.

That the allocative question is to be resolved in terms of the attributive principle is a commitment that Perry shares with the libertarian. Although, for Perry, attribution cannot be determined simply on the basis of outcome responsibility—fault is also a factor—outcome responsibility is a necessary condition of liability and is logically prior to the appropriate allocation of costs. By contrast, I hold that there is no conception of outcome responsibil-ity that is both necessary for and logically prior to the question of who should bear the costs of a misfortune. The relevant conception of respons-ibility can be determined only in light of what we owe one another by way of a standard of care—a determination that often reflects the allocative

---

[20] Thomas Scanlon, "The Significance of Choice" in Sterling M. McMurrin (ed.), *The Tanner Lectures on Human Values* (Salt Lake City: University of Utah Press, 1988).

issue at stake and the principles of fairness appropriate to it. In other words, the principle of allocation determines the appropriate principle of attribution—not the other way around. Once we determine what the allocative question is that a particular body of law seeks to answer, then we can determine in the light of the principle of fairness which, if any, criteria of attribution (or outcome responsibility) must be satisfied. Thus, contrary to Perry, I hold not only that responsibility is not sufficient for liability; but also that the relevant concept of responsibility itself depends on the moral–political principles of fairness that govern the allocation of misfortune's costs. This is the sense in which responsibility in torts is a matter of political morality "all the way down".

The set of relationships I have delineated between corrective and distributive issues has shown the distinctive consilience of the corrective justice account, as well as adumbrating the holism that is the topic of the next lecture. Like the libertarian doctrine, the corrective justice account is embedded in a broader explanatory scheme that points to the fundamental unity of distributive and corrective justice. But unlike the libertarian approach, the fundamental explanatory idea is not ownership, but, rather, fairness as reciprocity among free and equal persons. In the sphere of keeping track of life's misfortunes, the constraints of fairness are articulated in the roles a given society assigns to its corrective and redistributive institutions. The institutions of corrective justice in turn articulate the requirements of fairness in the domain of those misfortunes owed to human agency, and give concrete and determinate content to the key ideas of corrective justice, among them the concepts of an activity's costs and of outcome responsibility.

Lecture Five—
Holism and Explanation

Many, if not all, transparently attractive principles of morality are, at the level at which their attractiveness is transparent, incapable of regulating affairs among us. That is, they cannot give rise to particular rights, responsibilities, and duties. In order to serve as regulative principles, rather than mere abstract ideals, their content must be made more concrete. Take two principles that seem attractive enough on their face: "No one should be allowed to displace the costs of his activities onto others"; and "Each person should clean up his own mess." Arguably, both principles express requirements of fairness. It is not fair for one person to require others to clean up his mess or to displace, thereby, his costs onto them. This leaves open the question what counts as a "cost" or a "mess" of the relevant sort, and what constitutes a "displacement" or a "cleaning up" of it. Only once these terms are more fully specified can principles like the ones just mentioned regulate interactions among individuals.

The thesis I have advanced is that these key terms and concepts are made more concrete—their semantic content is more fully specified—by the social practices that articulate or embody them. Thus, we can understand certain of our social practices as ways of articulating principles of political morality. Social practices turn abstract ideals into regulative principles; they turn virtue into duty. It should be understood that the thesis is semantic, and not merely epistemic. In other words, the practices we have do not merely reveal the content of the principles to which we are committed; each practice partially constitutes that content.

Two general features of the account I have offered are its multi-level aspect and its holism. Starting at so to speak, the ground level, we have practices of corrective justice—a system of practical inferences that purports to determine when the imposition of a liability is justified. The structure of these inferences in tort law gives determinate content to its key concepts, and thereby makes explicit the requirements of the principle of corrective justice; while at the same time the principle of corrective justice organizes the concepts of tort law, explains the nature and structure of the inferences those concepts license, and in doing so, guides the practice of tort law. The principle of corrective justice, in turn, occupies a mid-level between the practices of tort law and an upper-level principle of fairness in allocating the costs of life's misfortunes. Here again the higher principle is said to be given determinate content by the practices subordinate to it, while at the same time guiding and constraining them. This is in each case the sense in which the principle explains the practice.[1]

One of the charges that is certain to be directed at any holistic account of this kind is the charge that it is circular in a way that undermines its explanatory claims. How can tort law be explained by corrective justice when the content of (for example) responsibility in corrective justice appears in part to depend on tort law?[2] How can a principle of fairness in allocating misfortune's costs explain the respective domains of distributive and corrective justice when the actual practices in those domains give determinate content to fairness? And so on.

The worry is prompted by the fact that explanation requires a kind of conceptual distance between explanandum and explanans (in the same way that justification requires normative distance between that which is to be justified and that which purports to justify). Any other approach would seem to be question-begging. It does not follow, however, that the content of the explanans and explanandum must be specified independently of one another. Indeed, from a holistic perspective the content of every concept depends to a greater or lesser degree on the content of every other.[3] On such a view the explanatory requirement of "conceptual distance" must be a matter of degree. What counts as sufficient conceptual distance will depend on the kind of explanation that is being offered.

Let us recall, then, what kind of explanation the corrective justice account is. The view I have put forward is that when we see the inferential practices of tort law in the light of the principle of corrective justice, they hang together in a way that makes the best sense of those practices. Add to this the fact that tort law is plainly a normative practice, and that the way corrective justice makes sense of it is by expressing the norm that governs it. One way of stating the nature of the explanation, then, is to say that it enables us to see how the constituent parts of the practice hang together by expressing the norm or principle that governs the practice.

One of the conditions of adequacy for this kind of explanation is, of course, that the principle that putatively governs the practice be capable of doing so. The conceptual distance required, in other words, must be great enough that the principle of corrective justice can actually govern the

---

[1] The multi-level metaphor is intended to capture (very roughly) different levels of *abstraction*. A more common metaphor for a holistic or semi-holistic model like mine is the metaphor of a web, in which the distance of a belief from the center reflects (very roughly) different levels of *importance*. I am not suggesting that fairness is more important than the concepts that figure in tort law, or the like. I introduce the multi-level picture simply to help readers grasp the way in which principles, the concepts implicated in them, and the practices in which they figure constrain and inform one another along a dimension of (roughly) concreteness–abstraction.

[2] This of course was one of the main conclusions of the previous lecture.

[3] This is a limiting case of the non-atomistic semantics to which I am committed.

practices of tort—which means at least that it must be able to pick out instances where the practice has failed to conform to the principle. A regulative principle that was satisfied by whatever practice happened to fall under it would be no regulative principle at all. The challenge of circularity may thus be phrased more pointedly as follows: if the practices of tort are what give determinate content to the principle of corrective justice, then what would count as a *wrong* inference, one that *did not* connect the concepts of the law in the way corrective justice says they are connected? Unless corrective justice can exert some kind of "normative pressure" on the practices it explains, then anything goes; nothing that happens in our tort institutions could count as failing to embody corrective justice. That would make the corrective justice account circular in a way that would render it unable to explain tort law.

The difference discussed in the last chapter between the libertarian view and the one I have proposed may, in part at least, reflect a similar worry about circularity. The libertarian seeks to analyze outcome responsibility in abstraction from tort institutions, and thus to specify the content of the concept of outcome responsibility independently of the practices that are regulated by that concept. If this seems to the libertarian (or to others) to be the obvious methodology for a normative theory of a body of law such as torts, that may reflect the assumption—conscious or not—that only such an independently determined norm could provide genuine normative guidance or constrain the practices of tort law from the standpoint of justice.

Naturally, I must deny that assumption; for with the method I adopt, no analytical priority is assigned either to abstract concepts and principles[4] (whether a lower mid-level one like outcome responsibility, a higher mid-level one like the concept of corrective justice, or an upper-level concept like fairness) or to the actual practices in which those concepts and principles figure. The abstract and relatively indeterminate sense expressed in the principle of corrective justice, for example, is made concrete and determinate in the practices of corrective justice; while at the same time the principle has a certain content that is independent of the practice, and is thus able to provide general guidance affecting the way in which it is articulated in practice.

There is really nothing mysterious about the fact that an incompletely specified concept or principle can provide guidance, while at the same time getting more determinate content from the practices it guides. The key is to understand that while *part* of the content of (for example) corrective justice gets worked out and made determinate in the embodiment relation I have described, tort law is not the *only* practice that contributes to the content of

---

[4] I mean a concept regarded in abstraction from some of the practices in which it figures; or a principle regarded in abstraction from some or all of the practices it purports to govern.

corrective justice. The central organizing concepts of both tort law and corrective justice—concepts such as wrong, responsibility, and duty of repair—are responsive not only to tort law, but also to the roles they play in the full range of legal, political, and moral practices in which these concepts figure.

It would be ludicrous to assert that "wrong", for example, gets all of its content from tort law. My claim is simply that it gets part of its content there, and the rest of its content elsewhere—from the criminal law, from our political ideals, and from the content of our everyday moral judgments (to name three domains in which the concept of wrong figures conspicuously). Holding the role of the concept in each of the other domains of practice as provisionally fixed allows us to take our bearings from the concept as we work out its application in some particular domain, such as tort law. This is a perfectly general methodological claim. The application of any concept in any domain may be reviewed and revised in light of its application in other domains. What we cannot do is to abstract away from all of our practices *at once* and somehow still derive determinate applications of a concept—from its *eidos*, say, or from "the natural light of reason". The claim that there is no such supernal template governing our understanding expresses the pragmatic character of the position I am advancing.

If the mid-level principle of corrective justice gets its determinate content and proper application from the practices of tort law, that principle serves in turn to provide determinate content to the upper-level principle of fairness in keeping track of the costs of life's misfortunes. In particular, it expresses the requirements of fairness in allocating the costs of misfortunes owing to human agency. The concept of fairness is thus partly determined by tort law; but it is also determined in part by all of our other moral practices—legal, political, and private—in which fairness figures. This claim expresses the holism of the account I am presenting. *The normative pressure fairness exerts in tort law is the pressure of every other practice in which fairness figures.* This insures that not every practice of repair qualifies as an instance of or instantiation of corrective justice or fairness.

An example will illustrate the way in which fairness, mediated by corrective justice, can exert normative pressure on the practice of tort law. Fairness requires (let us suppose) that no person be permitted to set the terms of interaction between individuals unilaterally. This assertion alone has a certain content independent of the law—a content sufficient for us to argue persuasively that a system of tort law cannot be fair if it employs a subjective standard of fault or negligence. The argument proceeds along the following lines.

If we simply let costs lie where they fall, then one individual can unfairly displace the costs of his activities onto another; the same is true, however, if we hold all our activity costs in common. But how are we to know which costs are owed to A's activities, which to B's, and which to no one's at all? Suppose we believe that the libertarian answer—that each should own the costs of his causal doings—fails because this standard is simply indeterminate. Then we might be led to the view that among the causal upshots of an agent's doings he should be liable for all and only those that he has *intended* or *foreseen*. However, limiting liability to intended or foreseen consequences—or to any subjective standard, no matter how sophisticated—violates a principle of fairness; for such a scheme would, in effect, allow each person's subjective mental state to determine the degree of security to which his victims are entitled. This would violate the principle of fairness that no one person may unilaterally set the terms governing his interaction with others; and in violating a principle of fairness, it violates corrective justice. So even though tort law helps make the demands of fairness as expressed in the principle of corrective justice explicit, fairness and corrective justice provide criteria by which the practice of tort law can be assessed.

It should be noted, however, that while the norms of fairness and corrective justice are moral norms, the kind of normative pressure I have been describing is, in the first instance, tied to their theoretical justification rather than their moral justification. Any subjective standard of cost allocation is inappropriate to the practice of tort law because it will run afoul of the principle that *best explains* tort law—namely, the principle of corrective justice.

The foregoing example illustrates how fairness, mediated by corrective justice, can constrain tort practices—and thus shows the way in which incompletely articulated concepts such as fairness and corrective justice can exert normative pressure on, and in that sense regulate and explain, tort law. I would now like to consider from the opposite direction the relationship between fairness and tort law, in order to indicate how the articulation of fairness in tort law actually gives content to the idea of fairness. As I argued in the last lecture, corrective justice is a way of making explicit the requirements of fairness with respect to the activity of keeping track of life's misfortunes owing to human agency. Specifically, corrective justice requires that the costs of misfortunes owing to human agency be imposed on the person (if any) whose wrongful conduct is responsible for those costs. The losses are made his by imposing on him an enforceable duty of repair. I believe these requirements to be part of the content of the idea of fairness, which is worked out more fully in the actual practices of tort and distributive justice. However, it seems plausible that there is more than one set of political and legal institutions that is compatible with a commitment to the abstract ideal of fairness,[5] and one of the consequences of my view is

---

[5] I mean the ideal of fairness regarded independently of any particular legal or political embodiments; it is abstract in the sense of being viewed in abstraction from those practices. Of course fairness could not be regarded in abstraction from all practices, or it would have no content at all.

that depending on how these institutions are structured, the actual content of corrective justice—and of fairness itself—may vary.

The case of New Zealand can serve to illustrate that the range of duties that fall under corrective justice is a contingent matter, and that such duties can vary across different legal systems. In New Zealand there are no tort actions for accidentally caused harms—whether negligent or innocent—and the costs of such accidents are instead allocated through the general tax coffers. This is a case, in other words, where a redistributive institution allocates the costs of misfortunes that in the United States are allocated under the corrective institution of tort law. It is not obvious that one scheme is more fair than the other overall. What seems likely instead is that the institutions of corrective and distributive justice vary across these societies in such a way that their overall practices of keeping track of life's misfortunes embody a similar conception of fairness.[6]

Of course that is a provisional claim. There may be a good argument, like the above argument against subjective criteria of negligence or liability, that would establish that one or the other system was unfair, or that one was decisively fairer than the other. Such an argument would turn on the conceptual resources available to us from all of the other practices and institutions—besides corrective and distributive ones—in which fairness figures.

The idea of fairness that has been implicit in the discussion to this point is central to a range of political doctrines whose roots lie in the liberal tradition. In particular, I have relied on a notion of fairness as reciprocity among free and equal individuals. This notion of fairness is bound up with other ideals, such as freedom and equality; and all of these ideals are contested, as regards both their content and their relative priorities. It may lie somewhat beyond the scope of this lecture to settle, once and for all, the most fundamental debates of modern political philosophy. I would like to conclude, however, by sketching what seems to me a particularly attractive view of what animates the best parts of the liberal tradition—including the ideal of fairness that is embodied (though imperfectly) in our institutions of corrective and distributive justice.

Libertarianism (to revisit the discussion of the last lecture) could be characterized as that form of liberalism organized around the idea of outcome responsibility, where outcome responsibility is itself to be analyzed in terms of morally prior notions such as self-ownership, agency, and a certain naturalist conception of causation. While I have rejected this conception of liberalism, I have not meant to dismiss the importance to liberalism of the concept of individual responsibility. I now want to suggest that a

[6] It is a further question whether and under what circumstances differences between legal systems may entail that different concepts of fairness are at play. An answer to this question will depend on an account of concept individuation.

certain conception of individual responsibility is fundamental to the liberal ideal. This conception expresses the special relationship each of us bears to her own life, and does not bear to the lives of others.[7] We might express the liberal view of the individual's relationship to his own life in the proposition that each of us is responsible for how her life goes.

This could be understood as a kind of moral claim about the accountability of persons—about the fact that we can and sometimes do judge and evaluate individuals or their lives as good or bad, virtuous or vicious, successful or failed, and so on. However, the sense of responsibility I mean is not just accountability. Rather, it strikes me as a kind of conceptual claim at the core of the liberal ideal: that if we are to have a certain concept of the individual as an agent, as a being who acts and is not merely acted upon, then it must be true that the individual can have a certain kind of ultimate responsibility for how his life goes. That is to say, whatever the circumstances of his birth, his social status, nationality, religion, and so on, his authority over the course of his life is superior to these things; they have no ultimate claim on the way he chooses to lead his life.[8]

The idea of responsibility that I am describing is what makes possible a very strong sense in which I can say that my life is *mine*: I lead it, I have made it, it is my doing rather than something that has happened (and keeps happening) to me. This is an ideal of the person, and not a description of how all people necessarily are. Nonetheless, the ideal represents the realization of capacities that all normal persons have. Liberalism, I want to suggest, is the tradition that derives principles of political life from this ideal, and seeks to realize those principles in practice. Liberal political institutions are best understood as attempts to make it possible for individuals to be responsible for their lives—and to make that equally possible for all.

Any life, we might say, reflects a combination of two kinds of factors: what one does, and what merely happens to one. Ronald Dworkin usefully expresses the distinction between these factors as the difference between *choice* and *circumstance*. In order to realize the idea of responsibility implicated in the concept of a life lived rather than a life had, political institutions must be arranged so that individuals' lives reflect to a greater degree, or to the greatest possible degree, their choices rather than their circumstances

[7] This fact about the special relationship we bear to our lives is part of the reason why many liberals object to utilitarianism, claiming that the utilitarian is unable to take seriously—seriously enough, or seriously in the right way—the differences between persons.

[8] Again, the relationship between this kind of responsibility and moral accountability is not my focus. I certainly do not mean to suggest that an individual is equally morally accountable for her actions, irrespective of hardship or privilege, or of the cultural and intellectual resources available to her. The basic elements of responsibility in the sense I am now using it may *be preconditions of moral judgment*, as Kant maintained (certainly if people did not have ultimate authority over how their lives go, then it would be hard to justify the desire to hold people to moral praise or blame for their lives or actions), but this kind of responsibility cannot be the whole story about moral accountability.

of birth and the subsequent influences of fortune. The goal of making it equally possible for each to be responsible for the way her life goes is what grounds the centrality of freedom and equality in liberal doctrine: freedom inasmuch as it is necessary to enable a life to reflect individual choice; and equality inasmuch as no individual is entitled to a greater benefit of circumstance than any other.

This is, as I have said, my own view of what is most central as well as what is best in the liberal tradition. I cannot undertake here to defend it against rival views. But if one were to grant the attractiveness of the picture I am describing, the errors both of libertarianism and of a certain extreme egalitarianism would be apparent. By focusing on the idea of self-ownership as primary, the libertarian singles out one of the preconditions of responsibility, namely choice—but fails to equalize those circumstances that do not reflect choice; on the other hand, a crudely egalitarian liberalism that demands absolute equality of material standards tends to eliminate the element of choice in pursuit of equal circumstances.

If the aim is to give choice the preeminent role in human life, and to do so equally for all, then institutions should be arranged so that circumstances are equalized only in so far as they are not the effects of choice. This, I would maintain, is the concept of fairness that explains the distinction between redistributive and corrective institutions, and that is imperfectly embodied in them. It is the distinction between, on the one hand, those of life's misfortunes which are the result of someone's choices—and which are owed therefore to human agency—and, on the other hand, those misfortunes which reflect the material conditions of choice. The principles of distributive justice govern the material conditions of choice, whereas the principle of corrective justice articulates the requirements of fairness with respect to the costs of misfortunes owing to human agency.[9] It does so by expressing the fact that fairness in keeping track of those misfortunes requires that the losses be imposed on the person (if any) whose wrongful conduct is responsible for them. Tort law further articulates the relevant conceptions of wrong, responsibility, and the duty of repair. Tort law tells us that the concept of wrong relevant to fairness is objective: a person can act wrongly without having a wrong intention—and thus, plausibly, without being morally culpable for what he has done (this is the lesson of *Vaughan* v. *Menlove* 132 Eng. Rep. 490 (C.P. 1837)). It also tells us that the duty of repair is to make good pecuniary but not necessarily nonpecuniary costs, that the default conception of repair is full compensation, and so on. Most importantly, tort law specifies the conditions of responsibility implicated by corrective justice. These requirements of fairness become clear to us in the

[9] At the same time both the boundaries between corrective and distributive justice, and the concept of what counts as a loss owing to human agency, are revisable notions: revisable in the light of the institutional and other practices that evolve as ways of expressing both.

circumstances that are delineated by our actual tort institutions; they could never be deduced from an abstract notion of fairness.

It would be in some ways neater, and might give the appearance of greater analytical power, to have a single principle of justice or efficiency from which one could derive a series of institutional forms and practices that would be defensible, perhaps even required by, the principle in question. But that would be to falsify the relationship between principles and the practices that articulate or realize them. The pragmatic method I have developed in this part recognizes (for good reasons, but ones I have only been able to touch on here) that practices make the content of the principles determinate, while at the same time the principles themselves hang together as an articulation of a particular liberal ideal of the person and of the relationships among persons. The content of the most abstract and fundamental principles that form a coherent conception of liberalism is only fully determined by the relationship the principles bear to one another and to their practical embodiments. The pragmatic method implies that we can hope for no more than a revisable structure of independently intelligible and mutually coherent principles and practices. Justice requires that we accept no less.

We are now in a position to redeem, in part at least, some of the promissory notes issued in Lecture 1. There I identified five tenets that characterize a certain pragmatic approach to philosophical explanations of law and legal practice. Each of these commitments has guided the argument throughout this first part of the book. A few exemplary references to the role they have played may now help to clarify these ideas further.

The first two tenets—non-atomistic semantics and practical inferential role semantics—are perhaps most conspicuous in the argument of Lecture 2. The discussion there of the inferential roles that certain key concepts play in tort practice serves to illustrate the way in which systems of practical inference operate holistically to determine a concept's content. The law-and-economics account fails as conceptual analysis because it cannot explain the inferences that the central concepts of tort law license in tort practice—indeed, the economics account would seem to suggest an entirely different structure of inference.

The third tenet—which I have called explanation by embodiment—is illustrated by the corrective justice account of tort law. The patterns of inference that give the key concepts of tort law their content are not haphazard, but can be seen to hang together in a coherent and mutually supportive structure. Corrective justice describes that structure; or, to put it differently, it expresses the principle that holds together and makes sense of the central concepts of tort law. At the same time the practices of tort law serve to realize or articulate corrective justice in concrete institutional forms. This is the sense in which tort law embodies corrective justice, and corrective justice explains tort law.

The fourth tenet, which asserts that explanations of practices must be viewed and assessed holistically—in light of one another—was illustrated by the way central concepts of corrective justice and tort law are sensitive to their meanings in the context of other practices. The notions of wrong, harm, fairness, and so on figure in criminal law, in our conceptions of redistributive justice, and in our everyday moral judgments. All of these practices help to determine the full content of the relevant concepts. This is how the principle of corrective justice, while depending on the actual practices of tort law for its full articulation, can also constrain and guide those practices.

Finally, the tenet of revisability was illustrated by the fact that while my arguments throughout have taken their bearings from conceptual analysis, nowhere in my defense of the corrective justice account have I appealed to any supposed analytic, necessary, or essential truth about corrective justice or its central organizing concepts. A positive instance of this commitment can be seen in the fact that the defense was open to the proposal, made by some economic analysts, that the concept of tort law itself should be abandoned in favor of a more general category of risk management. That proposal was rejected not on the grounds that our beliefs about the category of torts reflect analytic, necessary, or essential truths about the social phenomena, functions, or interests that tort practices concern; rather, the proposal was rejected because it could not be supported by plausible and defensible criteria of revision.

Part Two

The Possibility and Normativity of Law

Lecture Six—
Guidance and Compliance

No one denies that morality can figure in legal argument and legal practice. However, the kind of role it can or must play in law has been a topic of debate not only between positivists and their critics, but also within the positivist camp. The topic was brought into contemporary prominence by Ronald Dworkin, who in "The Model of Rules I" made the provocative observation that the legality of norms appears sometimes to depend on their substantive (moral) merits, and not just on their pedigree or social source.[1] The observation was intended by Dworkin as a challenge to the positivism of H. L. A. Hart; and while the challenge was, in many ways, misguided, it spurred positivists to address fundamental issues concerning the role of morality in law and the nature of legal authority. Largely in response to Dworkin, two different and incompatible strategies of response have been articulated. One is represented by inclusive legal positivism, which Hart himself eventually came to endorse.[2] Inclusive legal positivists maintain that there is no inconsistency between the core commitments of positivism and the existence of moral criteria of legality.[3] On the other hand, exclusive legal positivists—Joseph Raz notable among them—have maintained that

---

[1] Ronald Dworkin, "The Model of Rules I" in his *Taking Rights Seriously* (Cambridge, Mass.: Harvard University Press, 1977).

[2] In the posthumously published "Postscript" to *The Concept of Law* Hart explicitly embraces "soft positivism" (his label for inclusive legal positivism) (*The Concept of Law*, 2nd edn. (Oxford: Clarendon Press, 1994)).

[3] Among the leading sources of the inclusive legal positivist position are: Jules Coleman, "Negative and Positive Positivism" *Journal of Legal Studies*, 11/1 (1982) 139–64, repr. in M. Cohen (ed.), *Ronald Dworkin and Contemporary Jurisprudence* (Totowa, NJ: Rowman & Allanheld, 1984), and in Jules Coleman, *Markets, Morals and the Law* (Cambridge: Cambridge University Press, 1988); Jules Coleman, "Incorporationism, Conventionality and the Practical Difference Thesis" *Legal Theory* 4/4 (Dec. 1998) 381–425; Wilfrid Waluchow, *Inclusive Legal Positivism* (Oxford: Clarendon Press, 1994); Hart, "Postscript" 250–4. Ronald Dworkin, *Law's Empire* (Cambridge, Mass.: Harvard University Press, 1986). The leading work of the exclusive positivist position is Raz's *The Authority of Law: Essays on Law and Morality* (Oxford: Clarendon Press, 1979).

In this book I submit to the convention of referring to the position I defend as "inclusive legal positivism", having previously insisted on the term "incorporationism". I prefer the latter largely because it makes more perspicuous the central claim that this is a distinctive form of legal positivism according to which moral contents can be *incorporated* into law. The advantage of the label "inclusive legal positivism" is that it nicely contrasts with the alternative view—exclusive legal positivism—and many who defend a thesis similar to mine use this term. Ironically, of course, the leading exclusive legal positivist, Joseph Raz, does not use the label to describe his view. I use the label to describe his position, nevertheless, because just about everyone else thinks of his position in this way; and its central claims appear to entail the rejection of inclusive legal positivism (though, as I argue, they may not).

the legality of a norm must depend on its social source, and any appearances to the contrary must therefore be explained in some other way.

If inclusive legal positivism seems to offer the most direct way of accommodating Dworkin's observation, it is not a way that either Dworkin or Raz believes is consistent with the core commitments of positivism. Dworkin has argued that inclusive legal positivism is inconsistent with the positivist view that law is a *conventional* social practice. On his view, contentful or moral criteria of legal validity create a problem for positivism because morality is inherently controversial.[4] Controversy undermines law's conventionality. A controversial rule of recognition cannot be a "social rule", and thus cannot be a rule of recognition in the positivist's sense.[5]

By contrast, the debate between exclusive and inclusive legal positivism turns not on the controversiality of moral criteria of legality, but instead on the question of whether or not such criteria are compatible with legal authority. On Raz's view, the concept of legal authority precludes inquiring into a law's justifying (or dependent) reasons in order to determine its identity or content. Since inclusive legal positivism is committed to the possibility of criteria of legality that would require such inquiry, Raz concludes that inclusive legal positivism must be rejected.[6]

It is important to see that Raz's concern is with the very *possibility* of guidance through law—not with the *effectiveness* of such guidance. If morality is controversial, then a rule of recognition that incorporates morality into law will be a relatively ineffective instrument of social coordination—at least in so far as it will be difficult for individuals to determine the law or its content. This does not, however, raise any theoretical or conceptual problems for inclusive legal positivism, as far as Raz is concerned. He is not objecting that moral criteria of legality are *inefficient*; he is objecting they are *impossible*—because they cannot guide conduct, whereas law must, as a conceptual matter, be able to do so. Raz is concerned with the logical conditions imposed by the concept of legal guidance, not with the practical conditions under which such guidance can be effective.

All contemporary positivists accept that the criteria of legality are conventional;[7] most also accept what I call the practical difference

---

[4] In "The Model of Rules I" Dworkin took the view that the morality of a norm as a condition of legality violated the separability thesis. By "The Model of Rules II" (in *Taking Rights Seriously*) he focused on the more interesting objection that such criteria undermined law's conventionality. See Lecture 8 for a further discussion of this objection.

[5] I present this objection more fully and respond to it in Lecture 7. The idea of a "social rule" and its importance to positivism is also developed there.

[6] These are very rough characterizations of the differences between Raz and me. Our main differences are detailed throughout Lectures 7–10.

[7] This is not yet the claim that I refer to, below and elsewhere, as the "conventionality thesis". The conventionality thesis holds not only that the criteria of legality are conventional, but that they are expressed in a rule of recognition that makes law possible by imposing on officials the duty to apply all and only the norms validated under it. While all contemporary

thesis.[8] Roughly, the practical difference thesis is the claim that law must be able to make a practical difference as law: that is, a difference in the reasons for action that apply to those to whom the law is directed. Taken together, the claim that the criteria of legality are conventional and the practical difference thesis provide an interpretation of the banal and unobjectionable truth that law is a normative social practice: Under-standing the criteria of law as conventional is a way of interpreting the sense in which law is a normative *social* practice; while the practical difference thesis can similarly be thought of as an interpretation of the sense in which law is a *normative* social practice.

Characterizing positivism in this way has many advantages, not the least of which is that it enables us to locate precisely Dworkin's and Raz's objections to inclusive legal positivism. In effect, Dworkin argues that inclusive legal positivism is incompatible with law's conventionality, whereas Raz argues that it is incompatible with the practical difference thesis.[9] Thus, while both reject the possibility of positivism allowing moral criteria of legal validity, they have importantly different reasons for doing so.[10]

The burden of this part of the book is to develop and defend a particular version of inclusive legal positivism, including a conception of law's conventionality and a conception of law's authority—that is, of the sense in which law must make a practical difference in our lives. In defending my version of inclusive legal positivism from these and other powerful objections, I do not take myself to be presenting a conclusive case for the jurisprudential position I defend, nor offering a refutation of other views. My aim is primarily to show that my version of inclusive legal positivism is a coherent and plausible rival to Raz's exclusive legal positivism and to Dworkin's law-as-integrity. As I have occasion to emphasize in a number of specific contexts below, I believe that competing theories are to be evaluated not by their capacity to field this or that particular objection, but by the depth and comprehensiveness of the understanding they provide. This kind of evaluation is an ongoing enterprise.

legal positivists accept the more general claim that the criteria of legality are conventional, there is an important difference taken up in Lecture 7 between those like Hart and me, who embrace the conventionality thesis and others, like Joseph Raz, who treat the rule as a mere formulation of the criteria judges apply, and not as a rule that purports to regulate their behavior. This is one of the central debates in contemporary positivism.

[8] There are overwhelming textual and philosophical reasons to believe that Hart also endorsed the practical difference thesis.

[9] I take Raz's theory of authority to entail a version of the practical difference thesis, though the expression is not his. Scott Shapiro develops a more general objection to inclusive legal positivism that appeals to the practical difference thesis without invoking any robust theory of authority. I take up Shapiro's objection in Lecture 10.

[10] Dworkin and Raz are both committed to exclusive positivism, but in different senses. Dworkin takes exclusive positivism to be the best, indeed the only coherent, version of legal positivism: a coherent, but mistaken, jurisprudence. For Raz, exclusive positivism is not only the correct interpretation of positivism; it is the correct jurisprudential view as well.

Jurisprudence matters because law matters, and law matters because it figures in our practical lives—in our determinations of what we ought to do and why. Above all else, law is a regulative institution that governs or purports to govern our behavior by telling us what we are prohibited from doing and what we are permitted to do; what we can require of others and what others can demand of us. Law purports not only to govern aspects of our conduct, but to do so in a distinctive fashion.

For me, the central problems of jurisprudence are to explain the very possibility of legal authority—to identify its possibility conditions—and to explain its distinctive normativity.[11] If we are to make any progress in understanding the nature of legal authority, however, we must first distinguish among three distinct but related sets of questions. Each poses difficulties in its own right, and these difficulties multiply if the answer to one question is mistaken for an answer to another.

The law purports to govern our conduct, and to do so in virtue of its status as law. The first question of jurisprudence is: how is that possible? How can any particular law secure its claim to govern conduct as law? For some rules, their claim to govern conduct as law can be explained by appeal to a more basic authorizing rule. For example, the laws a legislature promulgates may be authorized by the law that authorizes the legislature as a source of law. It should be apparent, however, that we cannot keep up this form of explanation indefinitely, invoking an infinite regress of "legal" authorizations. Nor can we accept a vicious circle in which some finite set of rules putatively authorize one another. The first question, then, is how to explain the *possibility* of legal authority without appealing to legal authority itself. Following H. L. A. Hart, the view among many contemporary positivists is that legal authority is made possible by an interdependent convergence of behavior and attitude: what we might think of as an "agreement" among individuals, expressed in a duty-imposing social or

---

[11] This means that I do not take providing a theory of adjudication to be a central concern of jurisprudence. Most commentators interpret Ronald Dworkin as taking the opposite view, that is, as treating the primary responsibility of jurisprudence to be providing a theory of adjudication. I do not read Dworkin in quite that way. Rather, the theory of adjudication is important for Dworkin because, properly understood, it reveals the nature of law and of its distinctive authority. For him, law is best viewed through the lens of its coercive nature. In claiming authority, law claims that its use of coercive power is legitimate. If we understand adjudication from the perspective of an effort to exercise the state's coercive authority legitimately, then we will uncover what our underlying concept of law is. In doing that we will identify the concepts central to that understanding—including principles, right answers, theoretical disagreement (disagreement about the criteria of law), and the like; as well as the way in which these concepts hang together in a theory of adjudication.

On this reading, Dworkin's theory of our concept of law derives from the theory of adjudication. The burden of jurisprudence is not, however, to provide a theory of adjudication. Rather, the burden of jurisprudence is to explain what law is—in particular its existence conditions and its distinctive normativity—and the way to do *that*, for Dworkin, is through the theory of adjudication.

conventional rule (for Hart this is the rule of recognition). I call this claim the *conventionality thesis*.

Once we understand the possibility conditions of legal authority, we can move on to a second—related but different—set of issues: namely, *in what way* does law purport to govern conduct? Is there something distinctive about the kind of authority law claims, and if so, what is it? It is sometimes thought, for example, that the legal sanction can provide a simple and ready explanation of legal authority: we always have some reason for conforming our conduct to law's directives because there is always some threat of sanction for our failing to do so. Law governs by the threat of sanction. The problem with this sort of account is that the very possibility of a sanction attaching to some rules presupposes the existence of other rules that create the capacity or authority to sanction, and that identify to which rules the sanction applies. It would be viciously circular to explain the authority claimed by these "secondary" rules in terms of the sanction. For any legal system, therefore, there must exist an important class of rules that officials regard as authorizing the subordinate rules promulgated under them, and whose capacity to guide conduct cannot be explained in terms of sanctions.

What then is the nature and source of this distinctively legal authority? If law cannot—as a conceptual matter—purport to govern by sanction, how are we to understand its claim to govern? The prevalent view among legal positivists today is that law purports to govern conduct as a *practical authority*. The distinctive feature of law's governance on this view is that it purports to govern by *creating reasons for action*.

The claim that law governs by reasons is impossible to understand without first understanding one of the most important distinctions I will have occasion to emphasize in this book. This is the distinction (for each agent A) between (1) something's being *a reason for A to act*; and (2) something's being *a reason on which A acts*. Suppose, for example, I promise to meet you in your office at noon. My promise creates a reason for action for me—specifically, a reason for me to go to your office at noon. Suppose now that I forget my promise, but that I go to your office at noon anyway, acting on some different reason—say, to drop off a paper I have been working on. My having promised to meet you at noon was not *the reason on which I acted*, despite the fact the promise was, and remained, *a reason for action for me*.

In saying that a promise creates a reason for action, we are not saying anything about the motivational, explanatory, or causal role that a particular reason plays in one's actions. In our example, my promise cannot figure at all in the explanation of what I did. And that is why it is important to be very clear about the distinction between *a reason for action* and *the reasons on which one acts*. The latter are motivational or causal and figure in familiar kinds of explanations of actions. Reasons for action can, of course, figure in such explanations—I might have come to your office because I promised to do so—but their status as reasons for action does not depend on their figuring in causal explanations in this way. Rather than *motivating or causing* actions, reasons for action in this sense *warrant or justify* actions, impose duties and obligations, and confer rights and privileges. They are reasons in the sense of being normative *grounds* for action.

It is crucial to understand that in claiming that the distinctive way in which law governs conduct is by creating reasons for action, we are saying that law purports to govern by creating duties, obligations, rights, and privileges; it governs by creating *grounds* that *warrant* actions. Thus, in saying that law governs by creating reasons for action in this sense, one is *not* claiming that compliance with law's directives—and thus with the reasons law creates—must be motivated by those reasons or by the law's directives. Law governs by reasons that ground or warrant duties, but compliance need not be for the reason that the law demands it. (Though of course it may be for that reason: that is the special case in which the law is the reasons for compliance.)[12]

To this point I have distinguished between two different but related issues pertaining to the nature of legal authority. The first concerns the existence conditions of law and thus the possibility conditions of legal authority: how is legal governance possible? The second concerns the nature or kind of governance law purports to provide. As most contemporary positivists understand it, law purports to govern by creating reasons for action that, for example, ground rights and impose duties.

Finally, we come to a third set of questions, one that concerns the conditions, if any, under which the reasons the law purports to create are moral reasons. Or to put it slightly differently: the third set of questions concerns the conditions of *legitimate* authority. It is one thing to say that law purports to govern conduct, and to do so by creating reasons that are duties and obligations; it is quite another thing to say that the reasons the law creates—the duties it imposes—are moral ones. This is the problem of specifying the conditions of legitimate authority. Though a jurisprudential theory might conclude with the third set of questions, by identifying the conditions of legitimate authority, it begins with the first set of questions, by asking how governance by law is possible.

---

[12] Jurisprudence is the study, in part, of how law purports to govern conduct. It is not the study of how law secures individual compliance with the rights and duties it creates by its directives. In claiming that the law's distinctive normativity consists in its being a practical authority that gives rise to reasons for action, one is not claiming that the law must be the reason for one's compliance with it. There is no reason why someone committed to the argument that I have just outlined would have to deny that the law secures compliance with the bulk of its directives through sanctions. The fact that the sanction cannot be an account of law's distinctive normativity does not preclude it from being the best explanation of why most individuals comply with the law's reasons most of the time.

The conventionality thesis is an answer to this question. Whereas all positivists agree that wherever there is law, there are conventionally accepted criteria of legality, the conventionality thesis claims that these criteria are expressed in a rule that purports to impose an obligation on officials to evaluate conduct according to all and only those norms that satisfy the criteria set out in it. The difference is important. Joseph Raz, for example, accepts that the criteria of legality are conventional, but denies that the rule articulating those criteria must be a regulative rule. Hart and I, on the other hand, claim that it must be a regulative rule if the conventionality thesis is to be an answer to the question of how legal governance is possible.

Lecture Seven—
The Conventionality Thesis

The law purports to govern our conduct, and to do so in virtue of its status as law. The first, and perhaps the most philosophically difficult, question of jurisprudence is: how is that possible? What accounts for the fact that a particular rule can make demands on our conduct in virtue of its bearing the mark of law? In some cases, a rule's claim to govern conduct as law can be explained by appeal to a more basic authorizing rule. For example, the laws a legislature promulgates may be authorized by the law that authorizes the legislature as a source of law. It should be apparent, however, that we cannot keep up this form of explanation indefinitely; for instead of explaining the possibility of law's claim to govern our behavior, we would simply be assuming that possibility by an infinite regress of "legal" authorizations. Nor can we accept a vicious circle in which some finite set of rules putatively authorize one another. The problem, in a nutshell, is how to explain the possibility of legal authority without appealing to legal authority itself. The recognition of this problem marks the beginning of jurisprudence.

Historically, jurisprudential theorists have adopted one of two alternative solutions: each explains the possibility of legal authority in terms of something other than legal authority. In the case of the natural law tradition, the possibility of legal authority is explained in terms of *moral* authority. There are numerous variations on this theme, and I mention only a few to provide a feel for the strategy of argument. On one view, legal authority is the institutional embodiment of the natural law, and thus is to be explained as being made possible by natural law; a related view is that legal authority is made possible in so far as it is an expression of God's will; alternatively, legal authority is sometimes said to be derived from (and in that sense made possible by) the correct political morality, and in that case legal authority is an institutional expression or realization of political morality. The key to all such arguments is that the concept of legal authority is explicated in terms of, broadly speaking, moral authority. This is one sense in which the concepts of law and morality are thought to be conceptually connected.[1]

The prevailing view is that what distinguishes legal positivism from natural law theory is that the former denies what the latter asserts—namely, that there is a conceptual connection between the concepts of law and morality. In the context of current discussions of the possibility conditions of legal authority, this denial amounts to the claim that the

---

[1] Being conceptually connected in this way does not immunize law from moral criticism, nor does it preclude the natural lawyer from explicating in some other way the distinctive way in which law purports to govern human action.

possibility of legal authority is not to be explained as being an instance of moral authority.

Positivism claims that the possibility of legal authority is to be explained not in terms of substantive morality, but, rather, in terms of certain *social facts*. Call this the "social fact thesis"; no claim is more central to legal positivism.[2] John Austin's legal philosophy provides an important nineteenth-century example of the approach. For Austin, law is "the command of a sovereign-properly-so-called". The sovereign is conceived as an actual person: that individual who has secured the habit of obedience to his commands and who, himself, is not in the habit of obeying anyone.

There is no infinite regress or vicious circle in this account—the chain of authority is firmly anchored in the person of the sovereign, who is in turn defined without a circular appeal to law (the sovereign is not, for example, defined as the legally authorized source of law). Yet Austin's solution does not rely on introducing a new set of normative terms. Legal authority is a matter of "hard facts" about habits of obedience and patterns of sanctioning.

Austin's explanation of law's existence conditions in terms of habits of obedience came under devastating attack by positivism's greatest contemporary proponent, H. L. A. Hart. In the first place, the sovereign in many cases is no single individual but a collective body, such as a legislative assembly. Even if everyone else is in the habit of obeying the assembly, there is no explanation on Austin's account for the procedural rules (among others) that bind the assembly's members. Moreover, even when a single individual is the sovereign, as in the case of an absolute monarch, Austin can provide no explanation of the rules of succession, which authorize the transfer of sovereignty from a monarch to his heir. A deeper and on Hart's view more important objection is that in effectively reducing authority to habits, Austin throws out the baby with the bath water: for the idea of legal authority is the idea that the law claims to provide *reasons* for acting, and not simply that it exploits a habit of obedience.

Hart's own formulation of positivism retains the social fact thesis, while avoiding the difficulties of Austin's account. Hart's position—widely misunderstood and mistakenly criticized—is that law is made possible by an interdependent convergence of behavior and attitude: a kind of *convention* or social practice that we might characterize as an "agreement" among officials on the criteria for membership in the category "law".[3] The relevant social practice is comprised of two elements: convergent behavior and a critical reflective attitude toward that behavior—an acceptance of it. In other words, officials behave in a manner that is consistent with their

---

[2] For a fuller discussion of the social fact thesis and an explanation of why it is more central to legal positivism than is the separability thesis, see Lecture 11.

[3] The idea of agreement is slightly misleading in this context since a formal act of agreement is not necessary to Hart's or to my account. Below I reformulate this idea in terms of participation in a social practice having a certain normative structure.

following the same rule for validating laws; and this reflects a set of normative commitments which endorse the convergent behavior as justified, and which would condemn deviations from it. This reflective, critical attitude is the so-called "internal point of view". It is expressed in and manifested by, but is not reducible to, the behavior of offering justification and condemning non-compliance.

For Hart, this practice of officials creates and sustains criteria for membership in the category "law". Law is made possible by the existence among officials of a practice of adhering to criteria of legality or validity. The rule that captures this practice is what Hart calls the "rule of recognition": it is the signature of a legal system. The rule of recognition is a necessary, but not a sufficient, condition for law. In addition, Hart identifies various efficacy conditions: e.g. that the bulk of the populace comply with the rules recognized under the rule of recognition.

Law exists (is actual) when there is a rule of recognition and rules valid under it that are generally followed by the majority of the population. Acceptance of the rule of recognition from the internal point of view by officials is a conceptual requirement of the possibility of law; acceptance from the internal point of view by the bulk of the populace is neither a conceptual nor an efficacy requirement. Even if they characteristically do, the majority of persons need not *as a conceptual matter* adopt the internal point of view toward the behavior by which officials validate law, nor toward the subordinate rules that are validated under the legal system. Of course, it may be desirable on efficiency grounds that a population treat law as legitimate or obligation-imposing, since fewer public resources might then be required to insure compliance.[4]

An additional feature of Hart's account that differentiates it in a fundamental way both from Austin and from some more recent positivists, such as the Scandinavian realists, is that Hart explicitly rejects a certain reductive approach to the analysis of law. As we saw above, Austin reduces legal authority to power and habits of obedience; the Scandinavian realists reduce law to predictions of untoward consequences in the event of non-compliance and thus—by Hart's lights as well as my own—define the internal point of view out of existence.[5] The failure here is not, as some have mistakenly thought, limited to the reductionist's inability to account for the obvious *empirical* fact that individuals sometimes comply with law because the law requires it. Rather, the failing is also, and more significantly,

---

[4] To say that it is desirable that individuals find the law legitimate and obligation-imposing is not to say it is invariably desirable that when individuals comply with the law, they act on the reason the law provides. That they should act on law's reason may normally be preferable to their acting because of sanction; but in many cases, for example the case of a law prohibiting murder, it is of course preferable that individuals act not on law's reason but on the independent moral conviction that innocent human life is valuable and not to be destroyed.

[5] The work of Alf Ross exemplifies this approach. See *On Law and Justice*, trans. Margaret Dutton (Berkeley: University of California Press, 1959).

conceptual. Law is not *possible* unless officials accept the rule of recognition from the internal point of view; that is, law is possible only if the relevant officials treat the rule as their reason for compliance with it. By defining the internal point of view out of existence, the reductionist is left with no way of explaining the very possibility of law.

Like every legal positivist, I maintain that the possibility of law is to be explained in terms of social facts. Like Hart, I further maintain that the possibility of legal authority is to be explained in terms of a *conventional* social practice, namely the adherence by officials to a rule of recognition that imposes a duty on them to apply all and only those rules valid under it. This is the conventionality thesis. In explaining the possibility of legal authority in terms of a rule of recognition, the conventionality thesis gives content to the idea that law is a normative *social* practice which, while satisfying the social fact thesis, nevertheless avoids *reducing* legal authority to social facts. The conventionality thesis provides an answer to the first of the three sets of questions pertaining to legal authority identified in the previous lecture: what are the possibility conditions of legal authority?

The conventionality thesis figures prominently in the remainder of the argument of this book. In this lecture I wish to clarify a number of important philosophical issues surrounding that thesis (some of which I have briefly alluded to already) and in doing so, to articulate my particular version of it. (1) I begin by considering the widely misunderstood relationship between the rule of recognition and the social practice of officials. (2) I go on to argue that, contrary to the views of many positivists, the rule of recognition purports to be, and can be, a duty-imposing rule. This leads to the general question of how the rule of recognition can impose duties on those whose conduct it purports to govern, and to the particular question of what role, if any, the internal point of view plays in the explanation of the normativity of social rules. (3) I close by considering the objection that to explain the existence conditions of legal authority in terms of a rule of recognition whose existence depends on the behavior of "officials" is, in the end, to explain law in terms of law. According to this objection, rather than counting as a solution to the problem it addresses, the rule of recognition merely reformulates or restates the problem. I begin with the relationship between the rule of recognition and the relevant social practice.

1. Though many writers—Hart himself occasionally—identify the rule of recognition with a social practice, the two cannot possibly be the same thing. The rule of recognition is a rule, and thus an abstract, propositional entity.[6] The practice is constituted in part by behavior, and is thus not a propositional entity. The rule has conditions of satisfaction; the practice

[6] I am extremely grateful to Scott Shapiro for discussions that have shaped my thinking about the issues that I take up in the section on the relationship between the rule of recognition and the behavior of officials.

does not. If the rule is not identical with the practice, what is the relationship between them?

The most important point about the relationship between rule and practice is that the rule of recognition comes into existence as a rule that regulates behavior only if it is *practiced*. The practice, we can say, is an existence condition of the rule of recognition. This feature falls out of the fact that the rule of recognition is a social or conventional rule: like the convention of driving on the right-hand side of the road, its claim to govern conduct depends on its being generally observed.[7] By contrast, the legal rules that are validated by a rule of recognition purport to regulate behavior regardless of whether or not those rules reflect actual practice. For example, a valid law setting the legal drinking age at twenty-one years purports to regulate conduct despite its being flouted.[8] Thus, while the rule of recognition can impose an obligation on officials (to evaluate conduct by applying all those rules that satisfy the criteria of legality set forth in it) only in so far as it is actually practiced, this conventional rule in turn grounds the claims of the rules validated under it to regulate conduct regardless of whether or not those subordinate rules are adhered to. Put precisely, while the claim to legal authority requires that all laws be capable of regulating conduct, the claim of legal norms generally to regulate conduct depends on the existence of a rule whose own claim to do so depends on its being practiced.[9]

Scott Shapiro has expressed very much the same point in a slightly different, and helpful, way. Shapiro claims that the distinctive innovation of Hart's positivism is the claim that (legal) *norm-governed* behavior is made possible by (legal) *norm-guided* behavior. Norm-guided behavior is behavior in which the norm is the reason on which the agent acts; norm-governed behavior is behavior that is subject to a norm. The vast majority of legal rules purport to *govern* behavior whether or not they are practiced, that is, whether or not they actually *guide* behavior. But the possibility of a legal rule's governing depends on the analytically or conceptually prior existence of a convention among officials, a convention whose ability to govern their behavior depends on their being guided by it.

---

[7] For the purpose of this example, I treat the practice of driving on the right as merely a convention, not as a practice required by law.

[8] In this sense, a *law* requiring driving on the right-hand side of the road could regulate conduct independently of its being practiced. Its claim to provide a reason for driving on the right would stem not from its being a conventional practice, but from its being a legally prescribed practice.

[9] Another example: If I "adopt the rule" of running for one hour three times a week, I have not yet brought that rule into existence *as a regulative rule*, that is, as something that can give me reasons for acting (I may, of course, have reasons for running that are not created by any rule—for example, running may be good for my health). Even if, having decided to run three times a week, I am henceforth disposed to criticize myself for failing to adhere to that decision, I have still not given myself a regulative rule until I have practiced it to some degree (think how odd it would be to say, "I make it a rule to run one mile three times a week, but never actually do so"). This is one feature that social rules have in common with self-imposed rules.

This brings us to a related point about the relationship between rule and practice. It is often said, mistakenly, that because the rule of recognition is a social or conventional rule, its *content* is constituted by the behavior of officials; and that because its capacity to impose duties depends on its being practiced, the scope of the obligations it imposes on officials is coextensive with their actual behavior. The issues of semantic content and scope of obligation are of course closely related, but let us set that aside for the moment and focus on the claim about content. The standard view, implicit in almost all writing on the subject, is that because the rule depends on convergent behavior for its existence as a regulative rule, its content is determined fully by that behavior. Those who object to characterizing the rule of recognition as a conventional rule have exploited this standard view in order to undermine the conventionality thesis.

Here is the worry. If the content of the rule is determined by the convergent behavior, it seems to follow that whatever description captures the range of that convergence just is the rule of recognition. This would be at best a cramped and unilluminating form of explanation—in effect, we would be saying, "Whatever it is that officials do, they are following a rule whose content tells them to do that." Moreover, some have thought that if the behavior determines the content of the rule, then the scope of obligation imposed by the rule of recognition must be coextensive with the actual convergence of behavior of officials. But in that case, the rule could impose no duties beyond the scope of convergent behavior, and thus no behavior could fail to satisfy the rule of recognition. All and only convergent behavior would be subject to the rule, and there would be no sense in which it could govern behavior that failed to converge. Here it is difficult to see in what sense we would be talking about a rule at all.[10]

---

[10] It is this unhappy formulation of the relationship between behavior and rule that Dworkin's arguments implicitly target (I address his arguments in depth in Part III). The mistake here lies at the other extreme from the mistake noted earlier—namely, the failure to recognize that being practiced is an existence condition of a social rule (as it is for self-imposed rules). Those who fail to recognize that practice is an existence condition of social rules will not be tempted to question the possibility of disagreement about the content of the obligations imposed by social rules, or to wonder how a social rule can give rise to a particular obligation in a case in which there is no established convergent practice. By contrast, while Dworkin rightly notes that being practiced is an existence condition of a social rule, he takes this to mean that the convergence of behavior *fully determines the content* of the rule and, thus, delimits the scope of the obligations it imposes. It is this mistaken interpretation of the relationship between rule and practice that Dworkin's objection seeks to exploit.

A view about social rules may fail either by holding that the mere adoption of a rule is sufficient for its existence as a social rule; or by holding that the practice of a social rule determines its content. In what follows, I offer a view that steers a middle course between both of these mistaken extremes. The appropriate account is one that explains what is distinctive about social rules—namely, that their existence as regulative rules depends on their being practiced—while also explaining how they are similar to other (non-social) regulative rules, in so far as their capacity to regulate is compatible with disagreement about the nature and scope of the duties they purport to impose.

While the objection seems quite powerful, it is able to get off the ground only by presupposing a mistaken picture of the relationship between the content of the rule of recognition and the convergent behavior (a picture that, regrettably, is owed in part to positivist supporters of the conventionality thesis). The mistake is to suppose that the semantic content of the rule of recognition is determined by the range of the convergent behavior. To make this mistake is not to take seriously the claim that the practice of officials is a practice of *following a rule*. For there must always be a gap between the mere description of rule-guided behavior and the content of the rule that guides it.

The point is familiar from a variety of sources, most famously perhaps from Wittgenstein's *Philosophical Investigations*. A pattern of behavior can never fully determine the content of a rule, because any pattern of behavior is consistent with an indefinite number of different rules, each of which "covers" past behavior, yet each of which would result in different future behavior.[11] If the behavior alone determined the rule, then the rule would be so indeterminate that any future course of behavior would be consistent with it—which is to say that there would be no rule at all.

The crucial point is that in saying that there is a *practice* of officials of adhering and conforming to certain criteria as constitutive of the class "law", we mean to be asserting more than that their behavior converges on applying these criteria. In order for their behavior to constitute a *practice* in the relevant sense, it must reflect a shared grasp of the rule they are applying. The practice requires not only that officials' past behavior has accorded with the rule, but also that they share a grasp of how to "go on" or to "project" the rule to cover future behaviors. They must tend to agree, in other words, on which future behavior will accord with the rule and which will not. This commitment to going on in a particular way is part of what distinguishes merely convergent behavior from rule-following behavior.[12] Here we are merely emphasizing that officials really do *follow* the rule of recognition, in the everyday sense of "following" that we always mean when we say someone follows a rule. It is only in this sense that the rule of recognition is capable of having explanatory power with regard to officials' behavior.

[11] Nelson Goodman has shown that an analogous problem arises in the area of confirmation theory. Suppose "grue" is a predicate that applies to any object that is seen to be green when first observed before a given time t, or that is seen to be blue when first observed after t. The same evidentiary base at t seems to provide equally good confirmation for "all emeralds are green" and "all emeralds are grue". See Nelson Goodman, *Fact, Fiction and Forecast*, 4th edn. (Cambridge, Mass.: Harvard University Press, 1983), 74 ff.

[12] This idea is further developed below and in Lecture 11. I argue that social practices are constituted by social rules that are best characterized as "frameworks of interaction". Their existence depends on "shared intentions", the full content of which is filled out as the participants go along. In that sense, social rules are parameters within which the terms of ongoing interaction are negotiated or evolve.

A related point, articulated first by Wittgenstein in his discussion of rule-following, is that the grasp of a rule—the ability to "go on"—cannot be exhaustively articulated in propositional form. Saul Kripke has explicated this point forcefully, showing that even the apparently hard-and-fast rule for our practice of addition cannot be stated in such a way that it uniquely determines what we all know to be the criteria of correctness for that practice.[13] There is always the possibility of interpreting a propositional expression of the rule of addition in an indefinite number of non-standard ways. Since in fact we all converge in interpreting it in the same way, our understanding of the practice must go beyond propositional knowledge.

It should be unsurprising, therefore, if participants in a convergent or conventional practice—such as that explained by the rule of recognition— were to provide somewhat different formulations of the rule they were following; especially if they were asked to specify it in all its details, or to project it to cover a range of difficult hypothetical cases (here the analogy with addition breaks down: not all rules have a standard interpretation which admits of no variations). We should not want to overstate the degree of allowable disagreement or difference in formulations, however; if the same rule is being followed, then participants must share a grasp or understanding of the rule that is reflected both in convergent behavior and in broadly shared understandings of the rule's application to a range of paradigms and hypotheticals.[14] At a minimum, they must share a framework of interaction.

Instead of saying that the content of the rule is determined by the convergent behavior, we might say that the behavior *fixes* the rule.[15] By this I mean, first, that the behavior can help us to identify which rule is being practiced; certainly it can eliminate the vast majority of potential candidates. Moreover, given the background of a common culture and language (in which the capacities needed to grasp the standard interpretation of a rule are embodied) the convergence of behavior can suffice to enable succeeding generations of officials to gain the requisite grasp of how to "go on", thus enabling legal systems to persist over time.

We come finally to the relationship of the rule of recognition to the internal point of view. Hart's introduction of the internal point of view into jurisprudence is one of his great contributions. Unfortunately, his occasionally equivocal use of this term has led to at least as much confusion as insight. As I characterized it above, the internal point of view is an attitude of the participants toward a pattern of convergent behavior. Hart suggests

[13] See Saul Kripke, *Wittgenstein on Rules and Private Language: An Elementary Exposition* (Cambridge, Mass.: Harvard University Press, 1982).

[14] Each case is revisable at any given time, but they are not all revisable at once. See Lecture 11 for a discussion of the impact of this claim on Dworkin's "semantic sting" argument.

[15] I am grateful to Scott Shapiro for suggesting this way of putting the point.

in some contexts, however, that the internal point of view is an attitude not toward patterns of behavior, but toward *rules*. This has led to a variety of misunderstandings about the role of the internal point of view.

Hart often refers to social rules as having an "internal aspect". Many writers in the field take this to mean that the rule of recognition is a social rule that is itself accepted from the internal point of view, or in other words that the internal point of view is simply an attitude (acceptance) taken toward the rule. While not strictly incorrect, this characterization obscures the key element of the relationship between the internal point of view and the rule of recognition, namely the fact that the internal point of view is an *existence condition* of the rule. There is no rule of recognition independent of convergent behavior toward which participants take the internal point of view. It is the shared attitude toward the pattern of behavior that constitutes the fact that the behavior is governed by a rule.[16]

A social rule exists when convergent behavior is conjoined with a critical reflective attitude toward that behavior. The critical reflective attitude is the internal point of view. Its object, in the first instance, is the pattern of behavior, not the rule. The existence of the internal point of view is what marks the difference between regularized behavior—or behavior that people engage in "as a rule"—and rule-governed behavior—behavior that is *regulated by a rule*. If the majority of those whose behavior has converged in some way (for example, habitually) do not share the view that their behavior in the convergent area is governed by a rule, then it is not governed by a social rule. A social rule's ability to govern behavior depends on the fact that individuals take the convergent behavior of themselves and others to be guided by the rule.

In contrast, compliance with most ordinary rules does not imply taking the internal point of view toward them. One might comply with a moral rule for fear of an afterlife in hell, for example; or one might comply with the tax law for fear of imprisonment. This would not be to take the internal point of view toward the rule. To take the internal point of view toward rule-governed behavior is to take the rule—and not an external sanction—as the reason for one's compliance. This is the difference between merely *complying* with a rule that governs one's behavior, and being *guided* by that rule. In the latter case, but not the former, the rule is the reason for compliance.

Of course one could take the internal point of view toward moral rules or tax laws; some people do. But the relationship of the internal point of view to such non-social rules would still be different from its relationship to the rule of recognition, and to social rules more generally. For one could in

---

[16] This is a conceptual point about what it is for something to be a social rule—not an explanation of how social rules create or give rise to reasons for acting. See below for a discussion of the way in which this shared reflective attitude contributes to an explanation of the normativity of the rule of recognition.

principle take a non-social rule as the reason for one's compliance even if no one else did. By contrast, if there is no general practice of compliance with the rule of recognition, there is no rule of recognition, and a fortiori one cannot take it as a reason for action. This is the key to the special relationship of the internal point of view to the rule of recognition. The widespread adoption of the internal point of view by officials toward their convergent behavior—as evidenced in consistent appeals to the rule as a basis of justification or condemnation—is *an existence condition of the rule, and thus a possibility condition for the rule's providing reason for action.*

As we saw earlier in this lecture, the claim of rules subordinate to the rule of recognition to regulate conduct does not depend on their being practiced, but depends instead on another rule—the rule of recognition—whose claim to regulate conduct does depend on *its* being practiced. The point currently under discussion is analogous. The claim of subordinate rules to regulate behavior does not depend on anyone's adopting the internal point of view toward them, though it does depend on the existence of a rule whose own existence depends on the bulk of those whose conduct it purports to regulate (i.e. officials) adopting the internal point of view toward *it*.

Let me summarize this discussion of the relationship between the rule of recognition and the practice of officials. Being practiced is an *existence condition* of the rule of recognition. The practice consists in a convergence of behavior and an internal point of view. The convergent behavior fixes the rule, but does not determine its content; nor does the range of convergent behavior determine the scope of obligations the rule purports to impose. As with any rule, the content of the rule of recognition extends beyond any finite pattern of behavior; and as with any obligation-imposing rule, the obligations the rule imposes are determined by its *content*, and are not limited to the convergence of behavior of those subject to the rule. Finally, the internal point of view is a necessary element of the practice of a rule of recognition, and is therefore itself an existence condition of the rule. However, the claim of subordinate rules to regulate behavior does not depend on anyone's adopting the internal point of view toward them.[17]

---

[17] This is why "sanction" or "command" theories—views that, as Hart puts it, "leave no room" for the internal point of view—fail as a *conceptual* matter. It is not just that they ignore the obvious fact that some people comply with the law for the reason that the law requires it; rather, as I emphasize below, failure to countenance the internal point of view makes it impossible to explain the very possibility of legal authority. Similarly, Hart's argument is *not* that it is preferable for the law to secure compliance through individuals' adopting the internal point of view. Rather, Hart claims that the internal point of view is a conceptual necessity of legality. I take this issue up in Lecture 12, in a discussion of Stephen Perry's interpretation of Hart as a normative jurisprudent. That claim comes under severe attack in Scott Shapiro, "The Bad Man and the Internal Point of View" in Stephen J. Burton (ed.), *The Path of the Law and its Influence* (Cambridge: Cambridge University Press, 2000).

2. I turn now to the second main topic of this lecture, the question of whether the rule of recognition can be a duty-imposing rule. Hart famously distinguishes primary from secondary rules: primary rules are those that purport to impose obligations, whereas secondary rules confer powers. The rule of recognition is on Hart's view the most important of the secondary rules, and thus is typically conceived as a power-conferring rather than a duty-imposing rule.[18] Some commentators have noted that because the rule of recognition simply states what the criteria of legality are, it should be thought of as neither power-conferring nor duty-imposing. This has prompted some theorists sympathetic to Hart's overall project to redraw the distinction between primary and secondary rules. They prefer to say that primary rules claim to impose obligations, while secondary rules are rules about primary rules; secondary rules are in this sense second-order or meta-rules. They include rules of legislation, which enable individuals to make, amend, and alter primary rules; rules of adjudication, which establish the power to adjudicate disputes and the conditions under which that power can be legitimately exercised; and finally, the rule of recognition, which sets out the criteria of legality.[19] The rule of recognition is a rule about other rules, but on this view it is neither power-conferring nor duty-imposing. Rather, it merely states when norms that purport to be power-conferring or duty-imposing are valid law; or, to put it slightly differently, it states the test which norms must satisfy in order to be law.

Joseph Raz, for example, adopts what we might call a "semantic" conception of the rule of recognition. He acknowledges that the criteria of legality are conventional in the sense that their existence depends on the practice of officials, and not on the quality of argument that can be mustered on their behalf. He is committed, as well, to the view that these criteria constitute a "test" of legality—criteria of membership in the category "law". He does not, however, treat the statement of these criteria as a *regulative rule* that purports to govern anyone's behavior. In that sense, he treats the rule of recognition as having a *semantic* character only. Put another way: the Razian view is that wherever there is law there must be, as an analytic matter, criteria that constitute a test of the legality of any norm.

---

[18] In fact, despite classing it among the secondary, power-conferring rules, Hart treats the rule of recognition primarily as a duty-imposing rule: that is, a rule that purports to impose a duty on officials to evaluate conduct in the light of norms that satisfy the criteria of legality set out in it.

[19] To say that the rule sets out the criteria of legality is ambiguous. It could mean that the rule simply marks some norms as valid law, and thus renders the law *determinate*. But it could mean that in addition to that, the rule plays the role of enabling individuals to identify which of a community's norms are its laws, and thus makes the law *determinable*. Making the law determinate in this sense would be an *ontological* function of the rule of recognition, while making the law determinable would be an *epistemic* function. The key point here is that on either interpretation, the rule of recognition may appear to be neither power-conferring nor duty-imposing.

These criteria can in principle be articulated in propositional form, and that proposition may be called the "rule of recognition". Understood thus, however, the "rule" is not part of the community's law; it simply states what the criteria of legality in a given community are. In doing so, it guides no one's conduct and imposes no duties. It is just a conceptual tool that helps those of us who think about law to organize our thinking about it.

Thus, in claiming that the criteria of legality are conventional, one is not thereby committed to the existence of a rule of recognition as a potentially duty-imposing or regulative rule; it remains a matter of dispute among legal positivists whether or not it is necessary or helpful to invoke the concept of a rule of recognition in any sense that goes beyond the semantic conception. Raz thinks not, while a number of positivists—Hart and I among them—have characterized the rule of recognition in a stronger sense, as a rule that purports to impose a duty on officials: specifically, the duty to evaluate conduct by appealing to all and only those norms that are valid under the rule.[20] Typically, the reluctance of those positivists who have shied away from characterizing the rule of recognition as a duty-imposing rule stems from doubts they have about the possibility of conventional rules to create or impose duties. Thus, one burden that falls to those who view the rule of recognition as purporting to impose a duty on officials is to explain how conventional rules can be duty-imposing. This is a serious challenge to the conventionality thesis, and I respond to this challenge below.

To be perfectly fair, there may be no theoretically compelling reason to say that the duty judges have to evaluate conduct by appealing to all and only those norms that are valid under the rule is a duty that originates in, or is explained by, the rule. One might wish to reserve the expression "rule of recognition" to mean a merely semantic entity that captures the content of the criteria of legality without imposing any duty. Nonetheless, if one does not treat the rule of recognition as a duty-imposing rule, one still needs to explain why, and under what conditions, judges are obligated (or have reason) to apply the criteria of legality, as well as how the fact that other judges apply the criteria can be a reason for each judge to do so. Even if it is not strictly speaking necessary to explain these things in terms of a rule of recognition, it is both natural and perhaps helpful to do so. It reflects the ordinary way in which we characterize or talk about conventional practices and authority—that is, as rule-governed concepts. At the same time, speaking in terms of free-standing criteria of legality does not eliminate any of the

---

[20] In saying that the rule of recognition purports to impose a duty on officials to evaluate conduct in the light of all and only those norms that satisfy the conditions set forth in a rule of recognition, I mean to include norms immediately valid under the rule as well as norms that are not immediately valid under the rule, but to which officials are directed by the immediately valid norms.

philosophical puzzles that a positivist must confront. On balance, it seems preferable to follow Hart by understanding the criteria of legality as being expressed in a rule of recognition that purports to be a regulative or duty-imposing rule.[21] In the end, however, it may be of little importance whether or not the term "rule of recognition" is attached to the explanation of the purported duty; what is important is to explain—in a way consistent with the positivist commitment to the conventionality of law—the nature and possibility conditions of the duty of officials to apply the criteria of legality.

One of Hart's most familiar and important objections to Austin is that his analysis of law in terms of commands and habits of obedience is incapable of explaining law's normativity—that is, law's claim to provide reasons for action. Because habits are not reasons, an analysis that reduces law to habits lacks the resources necessary to explain the role law plays in our deliberative and normative lives. This is why Hart places at the center of his analysis of law the concept of a rule. Rules can be reasons for action in a way in which mere habits cannot be.

It is a further and important philosophical question how, or in virtue of what feature, a rule purports to be reason-giving. In the case of the rules of critical morality, the claim to provide reasons for action derives from the claim to truth; or, put slightly differently, from the fact that such rules can express bona fide moral reasons independently of whether or not anyone heeds them. The existence of such rules as normative entities does not require that they be practiced or accepted. The opposite is true of social rules, however, whose existence as regulative rules always depends on their being accepted and practiced. This is important in the present context because the rule of recognition is, according to positivists, a social rule and not a rule of critical morality.

The rule of recognition can be a reason for action only if social rules can be reasons for action. What we need is an account of how social rules, which purport to be reasons for action independently of their content, can nevertheless be bona fide reasons. Providing such an account is especially important to the theory being developed here, because the existence of a rule of recognition is being put forward as part of the explanation of the very possibility of legal authority. Since the claim of rules subordinate to the rule of recognition to provide reasons for action depends on their being authorized by the rule, it is crucial that we be able to explain *its* normativity.

It is reasonable to suppose that such an explanation will follow from a more general account of the normativity of social rules. Like any social rule, the rule of recognition exists only if there is a convergence of behavior

---

[21] The idea of legal authority is, for a positivist, tied up with the concept of a rule. Understanding the possibility of legal authority in terms of an authorizing rule and not just free-standing criteria of legality enables us to explain the concept of legal authority in terms of rules; and to do so in a way that creates no additional conceptual problems.

conjoined with the reflective, critical attitude that Hart calls the internal point of view. The internal point of view thus marks the difference—on Hart's account—between mere convergent or regular behavior (habits of obedience, for example) and social-rule-guided behavior. It is natural to read this account as entailing the claim that the internal point of view *explains the rule of recognition's normativity*. The rule of recognition is capable of regulating the behavior of officials—capable, in other words, of imposing a duty on them to evaluate conduct by applying the standards that satisfy the criteria set out in it—*just because* the rule is accepted from the internal point of view.

Having read Hart this way, many commentators have gone on to assail the claim that the internal point of view could transform a behavioral fact (a regularity of behavior) into a normative fact (the existence of a regulative rule). How, these critics ask, can a rule give reasons or impose an obligation just because people treat it as doing so? A rule cannot be said to impose an obligation simply because those individuals who are its intended subjects *believe* they are obligated by it. To hold otherwise is to engage in a form of objectionable "bootstrapping", in which that which purports to explain the normativity of the rule of recognition—the internal point of view—is partly constitutive of what is to be explained.[22] On the other hand, if Hart does not claim that the internal point of view explains the rule of recognition's normativity, he appears to have no explanation of it.

Though nearly universally accepted as devastating to Hart's project, the objection is not, in the end, persuasive. Social rules can be reasons for action, and properly understood, the internal point of view is pivotal to the explanation of how they can be. Moreover, though a conventional rule, the rule of recognition can nevertheless be a duty-imposing rule. The internal point of view, however, plays no role in the explanation of how conventional rules can be duty-imposing. The arguments for each of these claims—that social rules can be reasons, and that they can impose duties—draw on important, but largely overlooked, distinctions, and require a more philosophically sophisticated understanding of the internal point of view.

Let us begin with the important distinction between the claim that the rule of recognition can be a *reason* for acting, and the very different claim that the kind of reason it provides is a *duty*—specifically a duty to evaluate conduct in the light of all and only those norms that satisfy certain criteria of legality. The conventionality thesis entails both of these claims, but they

---

[22] Though the objection is sometimes formulated this way, it is not clear that, as a formal matter, A's being partly constitutive of B makes it objectionable to explain some feature of B by appealing to A. There need be nothing objectionable about an explanation of that form—though of course not every explanation like that will be a good one. The present objection is most charitably understood as asserting that Hart offers a bad explanation of this form—not that this is a bad form of explanation.

are importantly different. First, if legal governance or legal authority is made possible by rule guidance in the form of adherence to a social practice that guides the behavior of officials, then we need an account of how certain social practices can be *reasons*—how social facts can be norms. Not every reason is a duty; however, both Hart and I treat the rule of recognition as purporting to be the source of judicial duty or obligation, that is, as the explanation of the duty judges have to apply certain criteria of legality. Thus, we need an account of the possibility of social rules being reasons, as well as an account of the distinctive kind of reason the rule of recognition purports to be—namely, a duty to apply certain criteria of legality.

The criticism of Hart just outlined treats him as attempting to show that the internal point of view can explain how a social rule of recognition could be a *duty-imposing* rule. I do not believe, however, that Hart meant the internal point of view to explain how the rule of recognition could be a source or explanation of judicial *duties*. In any case, I certainly hold no such view. The internal point of view figures in the explanation of how social rules can be reasons for action: how certain practices can be norms. It is not an explanation of the character of the reason that a social rule can provide. Thus, while Hart's critics may be right to insist that the internal point of view cannot explain the rule's capacity to impose a duty, their criticism is probably misplaced.

In order to understand how social rules can be reasons, and to demonstrate the role of the internal point of view in that explanation, it is important that we begin with a proper understanding of the internal point of view.[23] Hart's critics mischaracterize the internal point of view in a way that makes it seem impossible that it could even *enter into* an explanation of the rule's normativity. If we regard the internal point of view as simply the *belief* among officials that their behavior is governed by a rule, then it is indeed difficult to see how this belief could give rise to a regulative rule or a reason for acting. If convergent behavior alone cannot create reasons for action, then how can convergent behavior conjoined with the belief that the behavior is rule-governed create such reasons?

Put this way, the objection is compelling; but, as I said, this mischaracterizes the internal point of view. The internal point of view should not be understood as a belief of any sort, but, rather, as the exercise of a basic and important psychological capacity of human beings to adopt a practice or pattern of behavior as a norm. This capacity can be given a philosophical analysis in terms of behavioral and psychological dispositions—among them, the disposition to conform to the norm or rule, to evaluate oneself

---

[23] Hart's introduction of the internal point of view is one of the great contributions *The Concept of Law* makes to legal philosophy. But this notion has also been a tremendous source of confusion. I try to sort through some of this confusion in "The Internal Point of View" (essay on file with the author).

and others on its basis, and to form certain beliefs and other intentional states associated with such a commitment. However, there may be no further *philosophical* explanation of the grounds or source of this capacity. Its existence is to be explained in some other way—causally, sociologically, biologically, or, more broadly, by invoking an evolutionary argument that identifies the adaptive value of such a capacity (for example, its useful- ness to individuals in enabling them to undertake projects and to secure the gains of coordinative activity). Understood in this more sophisticated sense—not as a belief, but as the exercise of a basic capacity to adopt a pattern of behavior as a norm—the internal point of view is essential to the explanation of the rule of recognition's normativity.

We can illustrate the role the internal point of view plays in this story by considering the case of a self-imposed or "personal" rule—say the rule I might adopt to do 100 sit-ups every day. If I should happen to be in the habit of doing that many sit-ups every day, my habit of doing so gives me no reason to do sit-ups. Of course I already have plenty of good reasons— having to do with health and fitness—for doing such exercises; but my *habit* of doing them does not add any further reason. Now suppose that I take a certain stance toward my doing sit-ups each day, a stance we can characterize as "adopting the behavior as a norm". This stance can be explic- ated in terms of a set of normative dispositions: the disposition to conform to a certain standard of behavior, and to engage in reflective evaluation of my conduct on the basis of that standard. By thus adopting my behavior as a norm (and provided I regularly conform to it) I have made the behavior a rule or norm for me. In doing so, I have created a reason that is additional to and different from the reasons of fitness and health that I already had.[24] The internal point of view creates an analogous reason for those who adopt it. In this sense, the internal point of view actually *does* "turn behavior into a rule"; it turns a social fact into a normative one. Hart's emphasis on the explanatory value of the internal point of view is thus vindicated.[25] Social rules can be reasons for action, and the internal point of view figures pro- minently in the explanation of that fact.[26]

---

[24] The existence of the additional reason is apparent if we consider how it can affect my motivations (that is, adopting the rule might strengthen my will to do what I already have good reasons to do).

[25] I am extremely grateful to Christopher Kutz for suggesting this interpretation of the internal point of view along Gibbardian lines.

[26] In saying that law is normative, one is saying that the language of the law is the language of obligation, right, duty, privilege, and so on. An account of the law's normativity must at a minimum make this fact about law intelligible. In claiming that the language of law is the language of "ought", one is not thereby committed to a certain view of the *nature* of the legal "ought"; nothing about whether it is a moral "ought", a prudential "ought", or some other kind altogether. One illuminating way to read Hart's objection to Austin is to see him as claim- ing that Austin's theory—which reduces law to power, habit, and command—lacks the resources to make intelligible the appropriateness of the normative vocabulary of the law; that

However, while the internal point of view explains how the rule of recognition can create reasons for acting, this does not yet explain how those reasons can be *duties*. If I can create a reason by adopting a pattern of behavior as a norm, then it would seem that I can subsequently *extinguish* the reason that norm provides simply by withdrawing my commitment to it. Yet it is the nature of duties that those bound by them cannot voluntarily extinguish them as reasons. It would be odd if not incomprehensible to say that the reason my self-imposed rule creates for me to do sit-ups is a *duty*; for if I withdraw my commitment to follow that rule, then I extinguish the reason it creates. The many other reasons I have for doing daily sit-ups remain, but the reason I create by adopting the rule disappears.[27]

it lacks the resources to make out distinctions that are central to legal practice, for example, between being obligated and being obliged. In contrast, Hart claims, an analysis in terms of rules and an internal point of view has the resources adequate to make the deployment of the normative language of law intelligible. The concepts of obligation, authority, right, and duty make sense in the language of rules; and the internal point of view signals acceptance or commitment to rules as legitimate. That is why I am inclined to view the primary function of the internal point of view in Hart's theory as *epistemic*. It is a reliable indicator that individuals treat the law as reason-giving. For Hart, it indicates the existence of norm-governed behavior, and thus renders the use of the normative language of law intelligible.

Hart's commentators have demanded more, however, of the internal point of view. They have read Hart as claiming not just that the internal point of view is a mark of law's normativity that helps us explain the appropriateness of the distinctions drawn in law between, for example, being obliged and being obligated; but that the internal point of view is the *source* of that distinction. Social rules obligate because they are accepted from the internal point of view. If this is Hart's argument, they claim, it is a bad one. Believing one is obligated does not make one obligated. It should be clear that I, for one, doubt that Hart ever claimed or meant to claim that the internal point of view turns a habit into an obligation.

Those who wish to saddle Hart with this obviously bad argument make either of two moves in response. Either they just reject his account outright, or, if they are more sympathetic, they reinterpret him. Instead of explaining how social rules of recognition can obligate, they take Hart to be providing a social-scientific account of the existence conditions for a legal system. On this reading, Hart is claiming that a legal system exists when a group of individuals—officials—believe that they are under an obligation to apply certain criteria of legality. Hart's answer to this question, his friends suggest, may be wrong, incomplete, or less than fully satisfying—but at least it is not fatuous.

It may well be that among Hart's projects is to provide a social-scientific account of the existence conditions of a legal system; but I doubt that Hart should be read as claiming that among those conditions is that officials must believe they are obligated to apply certain criteria for assessing conduct. Even if Hart did not think the internal point of view explained how social rules can obligate, he did believe, I have argued, that the internal point of view could figure in an explanation of how social rules could be reasons for acting. Whether the account I defend is also Hart's view is neither here nor there. It is consistent, and of a piece, with Hart's jurisprudence.

In my view, the internal point of view plays several roles. It helps make intelligible the normative discourse of law and is thus a reliable indicator of an "ought", and thereby help make intelligible the aptness of the normative language of law. It is an existence condition of social rules and, a fortiori, of the rule of recognition. Finally, and most importantly, as I argue above, it is part of the explanation of how social rules can be reasons.

[27] I am extremely grateful to Ken Himma for impressing this point on me. Much of the discussion that follows has benefited greatly from his insightful thoughts on the relationship between duties and the internal point of view.

The situation is no different if the same behavior is adopted as a personal rule by others besides me. If each of 1,000 people decides to do daily sit-ups, then there are 1,000 new personal rules, each providing a new reason for acting for the individual who adopts the rule, and each extinguishable as a reason by that individual. Such reasons cannot be characterized as duties, for it is in the nature of duties that one cannot—at least not in the usual case—autonomously extinguish a duty.

By analogy, if each of 1,000 individuals separately, and as it were, "personally" commits to evaluating conduct by all and only those norms that satisfy certain criteria of legality, those separate acts of commitment do not impose any duties. There may be independent reasons—even duties—for each to evaluate conduct according to the norms that the criteria specify (for example, the content of those norms might express requirements of morality). However, the additional reason created for each by her separate, personal commitment to the criteria is a reason that can be extinguished at will by her withdrawal of that commitment. In short, not every reason is a duty, and the explanation we have offered of the capacity of the rule of recognition to be a reason falls short of explaining how the rule can impose a duty.

The solution to this problem requires that we turn our attention from the psychological capacity to adopt a practice or a pattern of behavior as a norm, and focus instead on the normative structure of the pattern of behavior to which we commit. In other words, if we wish to explain the character of the reason that the rule of recognition creates, we must look beyond the internal point of view that officials adopt toward their practice, and consider instead the structure of the practice that the rule governs.

Margaret Gilbert provides the helpful example of two people going for a walk together. Part of what distinguishes this activity from the activity of two people who are simply walking alongside one another is that the former activity has a normative structure that the latter lacks. If you and I are taking a walk together, your actions and intentions create reasons for me, and mine create reasons for you. For example, the fact that you turn to the left—or even that you intend or prefer to do so—can give me a reason to turn left. Similarly, when judges adopt the practice of applying the rule of recognition, the actions and intentions of the other judges are reasons for each; it is as though they are going for a walk together, rather than simply walking alongside one another. It is this feature of the normativity of the rule of recognition that is left unexplained by the internal point of view. For it is not just that different judges decide individually and separately to evaluate conduct in the light of standards that satisfy certain criteria, thereby creating reasons for themselves that they can unilaterally extinguish; rather, they are engaged in a practice that has a certain normative structure—where, among other things, the fact that some judges apply criteria of legality is a reason for others to do so. It is this fact about legal practice, and not the internal point of view that judges take toward it, that is the key to understanding how the conventional practice of applying criteria of legality can be a source of a duty to do so.

I cannot say whether Hart fully appreciated the difference between these two aspects of the rule's normativity—that is, its ability to be a reason for action, and the fact that the kind of practice the rule governs is one in which the behavior, intentions, and preferences of some participants are (or can be) reasons for action for others. I am inclined to believe that Hart was, at least implicitly, aware of both aspects—since he did in fact offer two different kinds of arguments regarding these different normative dimensions of the rule of recognition: one emphasizing the internal point of view, the other emphasizing the coordinative features of the rule of recognition. While his critics certainly conflated these two elements, I do not believe that Hart himself did.

Arguably, Hart conceived the rule of recognition as what we would nowadays refer to as a "coordination convention", in the formal or game-theoretic sense. Coordination conventions solve recurrent problems that arise as a result of structural features of human action. For example, when a telephone conversation is cut off, it is useful for each party to know who will call back; a convention establishing that it is the original caller who resumes the call solves the problem by coordinating the parties' actions.

Suppose it has been agreed that for some reason a legal system is a desirable thing. If there is to be law, then some group of individuals must commit themselves to applying a rule that specifies the membership conditions for the category "law". Surely there will be a broad range of possible sets of membership conditions, and each person may, *ex ante*, prefer a different set. Although each person's first preference is that all apply his favored set, each prefers (second) that all apply the *same* set—regardless of which one it is—over the (third-ranked) alternative of applying his own first-choice set while others apply their own (which is to say, the alternative of having no legal system at all). This situation reflects what in game theory is called a "battle of the sexes", or a game of partial conflict. Typically, solutions to these games are coordinating conventions, and this is how Hart seems to believe the rule of recognition is best understood. It solves a partial conflict game whose resolution is necessary if law is to be possible.

In the present context the importance of coordinative conventions is that the actions of some whose behavior is governed by them can be reasons for others. Thus, the fact that the other motorists drive on the right side of the road typically gives me a reason for doing so as well; the fact that everyone else in our group is going to the opera gives me a reason for doing so as well; and so on. Coordinative conventions create normative relationships of just the sort officials—especially judges—appear to have toward one another.

In imputing to Hart the view that the rule of recognition solves a coordination problem, I certainly do not mean to impute to him the view that *law* solves a coordination problem; rather, the rule of recognition solves a coordination problem that must be solved if law is to be *possible*.[28] To illustrate: If Hobbes is right, then the state of nature is a situation that may best be modeled game theoretically as a prisoners' dilemma. Law provides a potential solution to the prisoners' dilemma. But law can solve this problem only if legal authority is possible; and legal authority is possible, on Hart's view, only if there is a rule of recognition that sets out criteria of legality and imposes a duty on officials to apply the norms that satisfy those criteria. *The rule of recognition does not solve the prisoners' dilemma. Law solves that problem.* Instead, the rule of recognition solves a coordination problem that must be solved if law is to be possible.

Though I use the Hobbesian example of the prisoners' dilemma to distinguish the problem law solves from the one the rule of recognition solves, we need not regard law as a solution to any sort of problem at all—let alone one that can be modeled game-theoretically. Law may exist in order to make more determinate the requirements of a shared political morality, or to organize society in a way that enables individuals to be responsible for the lives they lead. Or law can create an efficient scheme of production and distribution. Law can have any number of legitimate purposes, not all of which can be usefully modeled game-theoretically. The point is just this: in order for there to be a legal system that can serve any end through rules that govern behavior, there must be a rule of recognition. That rule is not the solution to the structural problem (if any) that makes law *desirable*. It is the solution to the problem of coordinating officials on a set of criteria of legality necessary to make law *possible*.

Understanding the rule of recognition as a coordination convention has the advantage of capturing the fact that the behavior of some participants can create reasons for others. The internal point of view, moreover, has a subsidiary role to play in this explanation. To see this, recall that since each individual prefers (on the explanation we are considering) that all adopt the *same* criteria for membership in the category "law", no member has any reason to defect unilaterally—which is to say that no official has reason to apply his own first-choice set of criteria of legality. This is just another way of expressing the well-known fact that coordinating conventions are "Nash equilibria". As long as others comply, no individual has sufficient reason to defect unilaterally.

Though it is irrational for any official to apply her own criteria of legality unilaterally, it need not be irrational to defect if others do so. Thus, parties

---

[28] Thus, the familiar objection that by conceiving of the rule of recognition as a coordination convention one is committed thereby to viewing law as a solution to a coordination problem is shown to rest on a confusion.

to the coordinating convention need periodic assurance that the observable behavior of others is correctly interpreted as compliance with the "agreed upon" or conventionally accepted criteria. The requisite assurance can be provided by the causal role the internal point of view plays in affecting the expectations of officials. The internal point of view—understood as an exercise of the capacity to enter into normative commitments, and expressed in officials' public appeals to the rule of recognition as justification for their behavior, or as grounds of condemnation—gives each a reason to believe that a convention is well established and that others will continue to uphold it. It also communicates when the criteria of legality are being revised. The point here is that the *reason* an official has for believing that others will continue to comply with the rule of recognition—and thus, the reason for complying herself—rests on a *causal* story about the psychological capacity of humans to form reliable expectations about future human behavior on the basis of stable and consistent behavior and declarations about that behavior's significance.

Both the internal point of view and the fact that the rule of recognition is a coordination convention contribute to an explanation of the fact that the rule of recognition is a social rule in which the behavior of participants is authoritative with respect to the action of others. Like coordination conventions generally, the rule of recognition creates a system of interdependent and reciprocal expectations.

While I believe that the coordination convention account represents a genuine advance in interpreting Hart's position, and in our understanding of the rule of recognition, I fear that it is ultimately not an adequate solution to the problem under discussion, which is to provide an account of the rule of recognition that explains why the behavior of some judges is or can be a reason for other judges.[29] The difficulty with the coordination convention account is that coordination conventions are solutions to games in which the participants' *ex ante* preferences have a specific structure, or are ordered in certain specific ways—ways that constitute what we call "partial conflict" or "battle of the sexes" games. These are only a small subset of our social or conventional practices, however; the large majority cannot be modeled as solutions to partial conflict games. It would place an arbitrary and baseless constraint on our concept of law to stipulate that the social practice among officials necessary for the existence of a rule of recognition must always be representable as a game of partial conflict: to claim, in effect, that it is a conceptual truth about law that it can exist only if officials have *ex ante* preferences over possible criteria of law that are structured in a

---

[29] As many readers will know, I have previously defended the view that the rule of recognition is plausibly analyzed as a coordination convention. I was convinced of the inadequacy of such an account by Scott Shapiro, who also suggested the alternative account of the rule of recognition sketched in this lecture.

certain way—one that is amenable to a certain kind of game-theoretic representation of them. In this sense, the coordination convention account is too strong or demanding.

In another sense, the coordination convention account is too weak, since such conventions do not seem to capture well the kinds of reasons officials have for acting as other officials do. While it is true that the fact that judges apply certain criteria of legality can be a reason for any particular judge to do so, it is not simply the fact that others do so that explains the character of the reason that any particular judge has. A full explanation of the character of the reason any judge has to apply the relevant criteria will accommodate the fact that these criteria have been adopted as part of a plan or project (a legal system) that can serve valuable ends—though individual judges may be committed to that project for any number of different personal reasons.

In short, it is simply not plausible to suppose that all rules of recognition must be coordination conventions—even if, as positivists rightly believe, such rules are conventional. If such rules are conventional, but not necessarily coordination conventions in the game-theoretic sense, what can be said about the kind of conventional rules they are?

Let us take a moment to frame this question in terms of the broader argument. The positivist project demands an account of the normativity of the rule of recognition. This is because the capacity of almost all legal rules to *govern* conduct depends on their bearing a certain relationship to another rule—the rule of recognition—whose capacity to govern the behavior of those to whom it is addressed (namely, officials) depends on its *guiding* their behavior. A rule guides an individual's behavior only if it is his reason for acting in compliance with it. A philosophical account of the very possibility of governance by law, then, rests on the possibility of a philosophical account of how the rule of recognition can be a reason for action. I have suggested that, contrary to prevailing wisdom, the internal point of view is perfectly well suited to an explanation of how convergent practices can be norms of conduct. Providing this sort of account of the normativity of the rule of recognition meets a burden incumbent on those who maintain that the conventionality thesis can explain the possibility of legal authority. However, the conventionality thesis—which I am defending, and which Hart also endorsed—entails the further claim that the rule of recognition can be a duty-imposing rule. While the argument just summarized may explain how practices can become norms—how social rules can be reasons— it falls considerably short of explaining how a social rule can impose duties.

Two aspects of the claim that the rule of recognition is a duty-imposing rule cannot be explained by the internal point of view. First, a duty-imposing rule cannot normally be extinguished unilaterally, whereas rules that are reasons solely in virtue of one's commitment to them can, in the typical case, be unilaterally extinguished. Second, the particular kind of duty one has under a rule of recognition is to act in a coordinative way with others to achieve certain ends, and in doing so to be responsive to the interests, intentions, preferences, and actions of others. Nothing in the internal point of view addresses either of these features of the duty imposed by the rule of recognition. Many forms of social life, not just the legal practices of officials, have these features. The general problem is to offer a philosophical explanation of such practices. This is a problem in social theory, not in jurisprudence as such; nonetheless, a general philosophical explanation of the structure of such practices might help us understand the nature of the practice of legal officials.

A general philosophical analysis of exactly this sort has been proposed by Michael Bratman, who identifies a class of practices that he calls "shared cooperative activity" (SCA).[30] SCA is something we do together—taking a walk together, building a house together, and singing a duet together are all examples of SCA. I would like to suggest that the practice of officials of evaluating conduct in the light of rules that satisfy certain criteria of legality is an instance of SCA.[31]

Bratman identifies three characteristic features of SCA:

   (i) *Mutual responsiveness*: In SCA each participating agent attempts to
       be responsive to the intentions and actions of the other . . . Each
       seeks to guide his behavior with an eye to the behavior of the other,
       knowing that the other seeks to do likewise.
  (ii) *Commitment to the joint activity*: In SCA the participants each have an
       appropriate commitment (though perhaps for different reasons) to
       the joint activity, and their mutual responsiveness is in pursuit of
       this commitment.
 (iii) *Commitment to mutual support*: In SCA each agent is committed to
       supporting the efforts of the other to play her role in the joint activ-
       ity . . . These commitments to support each other put us in a position
       to perform the joint activity successfully even if we each need help in
       certain ways.[32]

The practice of officials of being committed to a set of criteria of legality exhibits these features. Judges coordinate their behavior with one another

---

[30] Michael E. Bratman, "Shared Cooperative Activity" *Philosophical Review* 101/2 (Apr. 1992) 327–41 and "Shared Intention" *Ethics* 104 (Oct. 1993) 97–113.

[31] The argument that follows was heavily influenced by Scott Shapiro, who suggested that it might be illuminating to think of the rule of recognition as a shared cooperative activity in Bratman's sense. Shapiro develops this idea far beyond my limited purposes here. I introduce the idea largely to provide a philosophical grounding for several of the claims I have made elsewhere concerning the conventionality of the rule of recognition—in particular, that the rule can be conventional yet controversial, and that controversy regarding either its content or its application can be resolvable by substantive moral argument.

[32] Bratman, "Shared Cooperative Activity" 328.

through, for example, practices of precedent, which are ways in which they are responsive to the intentions of one another. The intention of an appellate court is that its decisions be binding on lower courts. Lower-court judges typically respond to these intentions by treating higher-court judges' decisions as constraints on their own behavior. The best explanation of judges' responsiveness to one another is their commitment to the goal of making possible the existence of a durable legal practice (though judges may have different reasons for thinking that a durable, sustained legal practice is desirable). Abiding by a practice of precedent is one way in which each judge helps the other do his part in fulfilling the aims of a legal practice.

While Hart was right to identify the normative structure of the practice of officials, he was wrong (as was I and Gerald Postema as well) to conclude that the rule of recognition represents, in effect, a Nash equilibrium solution to a game of partial conflict. The practice of officials necessary to create and sustain law is a more general form of social coordination, a form that is otherwise familiar to us. Bratman has a plausible and attractive account of such practices and of their possibility conditions.

Among the possibility conditions of SCA are what Bratman refers to as "shared intentions".[33] Despite the name, a shared intention is not actually a kind of intention at all. Intention (as Bratman notes at the beginning of his essay) is an *attitude*; by contrast, he writes,

shared intention, as I understand it, is not an attitude in any mind. It is not an attitude in the mind of some fused agent, for there is no such mind; and it is not an attitude in the mind or minds of either or both participants. Rather, it is a state of affairs that consists primarily in attitudes (none of which are themselves shared intentions) of the participants and interrelations between those attitudes.[34]

The particular form of interrelated responsiveness constitutive of shared intentions is not important for my purposes. It is important, however, that shared intentions function in our practical lives by helping to "coordinate our intentional actions", to "coordinate our planning", and to "structure relevant bargaining".[35] In the latter case, our shared intentions "will tend to provide a background framework that structures relevant bargaining"[36] between us about how the joint activity is to proceed. In other words, when we participate jointly in SCA, we must share an intention that converges on a common goal—even if our reasons or motives for doing so are importantly different. The content of our shared intention is not fully specified, and indeed is specified more fully by the course our activity takes.

Moreover, carrying on together may require a continuous process of "give and take", as increasingly specific actions are required of us. Thus, we

---

[33] Michael Bratman, "Shared Intention".   [34] Ibid. 107.   [35] Ibid. 99.   [36] Ibid.

negotiate or bargain with one another in a particular way—that is, within a particular framework. The framework itself creates the parameters of reason that are recognized as appropriate or good ones, and so on.

The distinctive, though by no means unique, normative structure of SCA can be seen as conceptually necessary elements of the practice of constituting a rule of recognition, a point that Ken Himma explicates in discussing my view of the rule of recognition,

> What is conceptually essential to the social practice constituting a conventional rule of recognition . . . is that it has the normative structure of an SCA. It is a conceptual truth about law that officials must coordinate their behavior with one another in various ways that are responsive to the intentions and actions of the others; what a judge, for example, does in a particular case depends on what other judges have done in similar cases. Similarly, it is a conceptual truth that officials be committed to the joint activity and to supporting one another; officials responsible for promulgating law require an assurance of continuing support from officials responsible for enforcing and executing those laws . . .[37]

Bratman's notion of an SCA also makes intelligible the claim that the rule of recognition can be a duty-imposing rule. To quote Himma again:

> While the point of Coleman's analysis of the rule of recognition as an SCA is to make explicit the normative structure of the supporting social practice . . . the notion of an SCA might contribute to an explanation of how a social practice can give rise to obligations. The notion of an SCA involves more than just a convergence of unilateral acceptances of the rule of recognition. It involves a joint *commitment* on the part of the participants to the activity governed by the rule of recognition . . . And there is no mystery (at least not one that a legal theorist is obliged to solve) about how joint commitments can give rise to obligations; insofar as such commitments induce reliance and a justified set of expectations (whether explicitly or not), they can give rise to obligations.

Bratman's account of SCA thus helps to make intelligible the rule of recognition as a duty-imposing rule, as well as providing philosophical insight into the normative structure of judicial practice. In doing so, his account helps to discharge the remaining burden positivists face concerning the normativity of the rule of recognition.[38]

In addition to making explicit the way in which the conventional rule of recognition can be duty-imposing, Bratman's analysis provides a unified philosophical framework from which I can defend several controversial claims I have made about the conventionality of the rule of recognition.

[37] Kenneth Einar Himma, "Inclusive Legal Positivism" in Jules Coleman and Scott Shapiro (eds.), *The Oxford Handbook of Jurisprudence and Legal Philosophy* (Oxford: Oxford University Press, 2001).

[38] I am grateful to Michael Bratman for his comments on a previous draft of this section of the lecture, and to Scott Shapiro for formulating many of the ideas pertaining to the rule of recognition that have been outlined in skeletal form here.

Many of these claims have been controversial among my positivist allies as well as among my critics. Until now I have defended them in a more or less ad hoc fashion. Bratman's account of SCA enables me to defend these claims in a more unified and systematic way. Let me explain.

Beginning with "Negative and Positive Positivism," I have argued that while the conduct of participants is an existence condition of a conventional rule of recognition, the content of the rule is not determined by their behavior. Second, and relatedly, I have argued that conventional practices or conventional rules can—indeed almost certainly must—admit of the possibility of disagreement. Moreover, I have argued that such disagreements may take either of two forms: disagreements about how to apply the rule, or disagreements about its content. Whereas others have claimed that the latter kind of disagreement is not compatible with conceiving of the rule as conventional, I have argued not only that disagreement about content is possible in a conventional rule, but also that there is no reason to believe that such disagreement must be reserved for the "penumbra" case.[39] Finally, whereas no one else, to my knowledge, has allowed that appeal to substantive moral argument to resolve disputes in the rule of recognition can be compatible with conceiving of the rule as a convention, I have steadfastly asserted that compatibility.[40] There can be general and widespread appeal to moral principle to resolve controversies about the rule of recognition, I claimed—if the rule itself specifies that controversies about its content are to be resolved that way.[41]

I have defended these positions, until now, simply by responding to particular objections to them. As I said, there has been something philosophically unsatisfying about this strategy of response. Though I am satisfied that I have adequately met individual challenges to my claims as those challenges have arisen, I have not done so in a way that expresses or yields a unifying account of the conventionality of the rule of recognition. Conceiving of shared intentions and the SCAs they make possible as frameworks for bargaining provides such an account, and reinforces each of the positions I have taken about the conventionality of the rule of recognition. The framework is created and sustained by the behavior of participants, but the content of the rules that constitute the practice is not. The rules are the result of ongoing negotiations. Thus there may well be disagreement about their content—disagreement, moreover, that is substantive and important, and which, given the framework, might well be settled by an appeal to substantive moral argument about how one ought to proceed, and that may invite discussion about the point of the practice.

[39] I take this issue up again in more detail in Lecture 11.
[40] The objection is that if the proper interpretation of the rule's content depends on moral argument, the rule itself has to be a moral rule, not a conventional one.
[41] See "Negative and Positive Positivism".

Dworkin has rightly argued that in a mature legal practice, disagreement about the content of the criteria of legality will exist, and that such disagreement is likely to invite discussion about the best interpretation of the practice. The best interpretation, in turn, will invoke discussion of the proper point or purpose of the activity. Where Dworkin goes wrong—as I have argued here and elsewhere—is in inferring that such disagreement and the means available to its resolution are incompatible with the criteria of legality being conventional in the way positivists claim they are and must be. Positivism—as I have argued—is compatible with everything Dworkin says about the possibility and character of disagreement in legal argument. More importantly, in characterizing judicial practice as SCA, positivists have an explanation of the sense in which law is a social or conventional practice—an explanation that is unavailable to Dworkin, given the structure of his theory.

My views about the conventionality of the rule of recognition have also been criticized, at least implicitly, by other positivists. For example, Andrei Marmor appears to believe that we must appeal to a novel kind of convention—what he calls a constitutive convention—in order to accommodate the facts of disagreement and the relevance of appeals to evaluative argument.[42] The implicit objection is that a view like mine cannot have it both ways: it cannot claim that the rule of recognition is a convention *and* that disputes about its content are subject to resolution by moral argument. I have responded that there is no contradiction in holding such a position, since it could be part of the conventional practice surrounding the rule of recognition that individuals resolve disputes about its content by appealing to certain kinds of moral arguments. Though obviously coherent, this response, I admit, has always struck me as somewhat ad hoc. I am now in a position to provide a far more satisfying response. Since the rule of recognition is itself a framework for bargaining about how to go on, there is nothing at all ad hoc in supposing that such bargaining might involve moral or political arguments about the point of the practice. In short, positivism never needed a new kind of convention—for example, constitutive conventions. It only needed a better philosophical account of conventional practices.[43]

3. Before concluding, I would like to consider an objection that will allow us to revisit the question with which this lecture began, the question of how to explain law without appealing to law. The objection is along the following lines.

The rule of recognition, we are told, exists only when officials act in a certain way; but whether or not individuals are *officials* in the relevant sense

---

[42] See Andrei Marmor, "Legal Conventionalism" *Legal Theory* 4/4 (Dec. 1998) 509–31.
[43] This is Shapiro's characteristically pithy way of expressing the point.

seems to depend on the existence of a rule of recognition. After all, persons are officials in virtue of the laws that create officials. But those laws, we are told, are valid only if they are validated by the rule of recognition, which leads us back to where we started. So it appears that the conventionality thesis has not solved the original problem. It explains law in terms of law after all.

This is indeed a clever objection, but there is a clear and decisive response. We must differentiate between two distinct roles that the same group of individuals plays in the conventionalist story. First, some group of individuals—we do not call them officials and we need not identify them by reference to laws—choose to have their behavior guided by a certain rule. In other words, they take the rule as giving them good reasons for action. If that rule takes hold in the sense of establishing membership criteria in a system of rules, and if those rules are complied with generally, and if institutions of certain types are then created, and so on, it is fair to say that a legal system exists. If a legal system exists, then that rule which guides the behavior of our initial group of individuals is correctly described as the rule of recognition for that legal system. And those individuals who guide their behavior by that rule are thus appropriately conceived of as "officials". They are, in a sense, officials in virtue of that rule, but they are not officials prior to it (in either the factual or the logical sense). Their behavior makes the rule possible; but it is the rule that makes them officials.

In this chapter I have offered a distinctive account of the positivist claim that legality is conventional—what I have called the "conventionality thesis". In this account, the rule of recognition expresses a conventional practice among officials in virtue of which (though only together with certain other necessary conditions) a legal system can be said to exist. The possibility of legal rules purporting to govern conduct depends on the existence of a rule whose claim to govern conduct depends on its being practiced from an internal point of view. As Shapiro puts it, legal rule governance is made possible by rule guidance.

In explaining how legal governance is possible we have not explained *how* law governs; nor have we determined the conditions, if any, under which legal governance is or can be morally legitimate. The legitimacy of legal authority will no doubt depend on the value of the ends law serves. These ends may be heterogeneous—they may include personal security, an efficient cooperative system of production and exchange, or the creation of conditions under which individuals can be responsible for the lives they lead. Any or all of these are possible functions of law, but none is necessary to the concept of law.

Whatever ends it serves, however, the distinctive feature of law according to most positivists is that it serves these ends through rules that purport to guide conduct. Law guides conduct by offering reasons for action. The question before us now is whether this conception of legal governance imposes constraints on the criteria of legality; in particular, can a norm be law simply in virtue of its moral merits? The form of positivism that claims that morality cannot be a criterion of legality is commonly called exclusive legal positivism. The version of positivism that denies that constraint on the criteria of legality is inclusive legal positivism. I turn my attention in the next lecture to delineating the respective claims of these two main branches of positivism as part of the larger project of defending the latter.

Lecture Eight—
Inclusive Legal Positivism

In the previous lecture I identified a variety of issues surrounding the conventionality thesis. To say that the criteria of legality are conventional is at least to claim that their existence depends on practice. It is a further question whether the conventionality of the criteria of legality implies the existence of a rule of recognition; and if it does imply that, there are yet further questions about the relationship of the rule to the practice. The conventionality thesis is thus a special instance of the general claim that the criteria of legality are conventional.[1] Other legal positivists have developed alternative versions or interpretations of this basic commitment.

Despite their differences, the shared emphasis on the conventionality of law distinguishes legal positivism from a family of views that claims that the existence and content of criteria of legality are not a matter of convention or social fact, but of substantive moral argument instead.[2] Ronald Dworkin is the leading contemporary advocate of this kind of view. I consider and respond to some of Dworkin's criticisms of my version of positivism at the end of this lecture,[3] but I begin with some of his earlier criticisms of Hart, because these have been so important in provoking the defining theoretical developments in positivism in the last several decades. Indeed, the most fundamental divisions within positivism can be seen as stemming from alternative ways of responding to Dworkin's initial objections to Hart.

In "The Model of Rules I" Dworkin advances an extensive critique of Hart's positivism, taking as his point of departure the observation that judges appear to treat at least some moral principles as binding legal sources, and not merely as discretionary standards. The natural conclusion to draw from this observation, he maintains, is that such standards in fact *are* binding law, and that judges treat them as such for that reason. Dworkin takes this conclusion to imply that legal positivism—or at least Hart's version of it—must be abandoned. Dworkin's argument turns on his particular characterization of legal positivism.

---

[1] The general claim that the criteria of legality are conventional is itself an instance of the even more basic social fact thesis.

[2] Dworkin invariably characterizes the positivist claim that legality is a matter of convention or social fact as the very different claim that legality is a matter of "hard facts", by which he means uncontroversial or noncontestable facts. While there is a sense in which every positivist endorses the former claim, no positivist need be committed to the latter.

[3] I present a fuller response to Dworkin in Lecture 11.

According to Dworkin, there are four fundamental tenets of positivism: (1) the rule of recognition—the claim that wherever there is law there is a "master rule" that specifies the conditions necessary and sufficient for membership in the category "law"; (2) the model of rules—the claim that every norm that falls within the category "law" must be a rule; (3) the separability thesis—the claim that the substantive value or moral merit of a norm cannot be a condition of its legality;[4] and (4) the discretion thesis—the claim that in a wide range of so-called hard cases there are no right answers compelled by the applicable law, and that judges in such cases exercise a limited "lawmaking" or quasi-legislative power.[5]

The argument is that countenancing moral principles as binding legal sources—and not merely as discretionary standards—undermines each of these tenets. If moral principles can be legally binding, then they are legal standards; but principles are not rules, and so the model of rules—the claim that all legal standards are rules—cannot be sustained.[6] If certain moral principles are legally binding, they are binding as principles, and therefore in virtue of their status as principles, which is to say that their claim to legal authority depends on their substantive merits; but if the substantive morality or merit of a principle is (or can be) a condition of legality (at least for some legally binding norms), then the separability thesis—the claim that morality cannot be a condition of legality—must likewise fall.[7] So too the rule of recognition—the claim that all and only rules that satisfy the criteria set forth in a master rule are law—since at least some norms are binding as law in virtue of their substantive merits, and not in virtue of the fact that they satisfy conditions set out in any master rule. Finally, the need and opportunity for discretion is reduced as the

---

[4] The "separability thesis" is a proper name, and I guess one can stipulate what proposition one means it to refer to. However, if it is to refer to any tenet of positivism, then Dworkin's formulation is wrong. As I have used the term, the separability thesis is the claim that there is no necessary connection between law and morality. That claim does express a tenet of positivism; however, it is also perfectly compatible with the morality of some norms counting as a condition of their legality.

[5] In saying that judges are necessarily authorized to exercise a legislative role, one is not saying that their authority to do so is regulated in the same way the authority of legislatures is, or, in other words, that their actions are free or constrained in just the way legislatures are.

[6] Many commentators continue to emphasize Dworkin's reliance on the claim that moral principles can be binding legal standards as the linchpin of his critique of positivism. The crucial point, for these commentators, is that, unlike rules, principles have a dimension of weight, and so, even if they can be identified as binding legal standards, there is no formal procedure for identifying the exact weight they are to be accorded in legal argument. As the discussion of this lecture—and especially the argument in Lecture11—should make clear, I don't find this interpretation of Dworkin to be accurate or illuminating. I argue in Lecture 11 that Dworkin's objections to positivism are based on its commitment to various forms of conventionality.

[7] This is true only for the formulation of the separability thesis that Dworkin imputes to positivism, not the one positivists actually hold. For a fuller discussion, see Lecture 11.

number of legally authoritative standards is increased; in the limiting case it evaporates altogether.[8]

Although (for reasons I will come to soon) no one nowadays considers this argument convincing, it would be hard to find an essay that has been more influential in the development of contemporary jurisprudence. The importance of "The Model of Rules I" lies in its having provoked alternative explanations of the place of moral argument in legal discourse. Legal positivists have been forced to explain, in a way that is consistent with positivism's basic tenets, the apparent fact that moral principles can sometimes be binding legal sources. I will not rehearse here the range of explanations that have been offered in this regard; suffice it to say that nearly every conceivable response has found an advocate. I want to focus on the responses that have come to characterize the two main competing camps within the legal positivist tradition: exclusive legal positivism and inclusive legal positivism.[9]

The central tenet of exclusive legal positivism is the claim that the criteria of legality must be *social sources*. Membership in the category "law" cannot depend on a norm's content or substantive merit. Something's being a law cannot depend on its being the case that it *ought* to be the law. The question is how and in what ways exclusive legal positivism can accommodate or respond to Dworkin's observation that at least some moral principles are binding law in virtue of their substantive merits and *not* their social source. Can exclusive legal positivism explain cases in which morality is apparently incorporated into law?

The first thing to note is that what Dworkin has offered by way of a challenge to legal positivism is not a fact, but an interpretation of a fact. The relevant fact that needs to be explained or interpreted is that moral norms often figure as standards to which judges appeal in resolving legal disputes. Dworkin's interpretation is that judges appeal to these norms because they are binding on them, binding as law, and law because of their merits—because, in other words, they express an appropriate dimension of justice or fairness. It is not incumbent on legal positivism to provide in its

---

[8] Of course, even as discretion owing to the availability of legally binding resources decreases (as the set of available resources increases), the possibility of discretion owing to vagueness increases (as the set of controversial moral predicates legally binding on officials increases). The same predicates that reduce discretion on one front increase it on another: a consequence of Dworkin's own view that moral predicates are controversial and contestable. To defeat the positivist view of discretion, Dworkin has to do more than show that the set of available legal resources on which a judge can draw goes beyond rules. Of course, no positivist really limits the set of resources binding on officials in the way Dworkin claims positivist do. The debate, then, has to be resolved on grounds having more to do with the structure of legal justification than with the set of binding legal sources.

[9] As I have already noted (Lecture 6 n. 3), "Incorporationism" seems to me the more apt term for the latter position; but I accede here to common usage in the interests of not multiplying terms.

own terms an account that embraces these interpretive claims of Dworkin's; for example, the legal positivist need not show (though doing so would be one possible way of answering Dworkin) how moral principles can be binding law in virtue of their merits. What legal positivism must account for in terms of its own basic commitments is simply the fact that moral norms figure importantly in adjudication.

In considering the range of strategies available to an exclusive legal positivist, we should begin by noting that he need not claim that every time a judge appeals to a moral principle she is doing so for the same reason. In other words, moral principles can figure in legal argument in different ways at different times. Thus, it is always open to exclusive legal positivism to claim that at least sometimes when judges appeal to moral principles, they are exercising discretion in the strong sense: appealing to standards that—contra Dworkin—are not binding on them, that are instead optional. This is not the only resource available to the exclusive legal positivist, however. He could argue that when moral principles figure in law, they are sometimes (or always) binding law—just as Dworkin claims they are. However the exclusive positivist would deny Dworkin's claim that such principles could be binding *law* because of their merits. Exclusive legal positivism is committed to the view that if moral principles are law, it is in virtue of their pedigree or social source, not their content.

By employing an important distinction of Joseph Raz's, the exclusive legal positivist can also argue that sometimes moral principles can be binding on officials without being part of the law of a community. Raz distinguishes between standards that are *binding on officials* and standards that are *part of a community's law*. Every standard that is part of the community's law is binding on officials, but not every standard that is binding on officials is part of the community's law. In a conflicts-of-law case, for example, a judge in the United States may be required to apply the law of another country. He may have no freedom to do otherwise. Yet the fact that the law of the other country—say, France—might be binding on an American official is not a reason for claiming that the law of France is part of the law of the United States, or that the law of the United States incorporates the law of France. The fact that judges of one country may be bound to apply the law of another does not eliminate the distinction between those two legal systems; nor does the legally mandated application by judges of the standards of a particular trade, business, or social group eliminate the distinction between the law and these other normative systems regulating behavior within a given society. Thus, even if Dworkin were right that moral principles can sometimes be legally binding, it would not follow that such standards are *part of the community's law*.

Raz's strategy also suggests a more sophisticated understanding of discretion. Because moral standards can sometimes be binding on officials without being part of the community's law, the positivist is not committed to the claim that whenever a judge appeals to a moral principle she is thereby applying a discretionary norm—in the sense of a norm she is free to ignore. Some extra-legal norms may be binding on officials, yet without being discretionary in the worrisome sense of being optional.

To summarize briefly: The exclusive legal positivist believes that moral standards may bind officials, but without being law (they may bind the way the law of France can be binding on US judges); that moral standards may be binding *as* law (though only in virtue of being identified by their social source); and finally, that moral standards may be nonbinding, and enter into legal argument as discretionary standards. Exclusive legal positivism thus admits of a variety of different possible roles for moral principles in legal argument. Moreover, all of these roles are consistent with the tenets Dworkin ascribes to legal positivism, with the exception of the model of rules—the claim that all legal standards are rules. This conclusion is of little concern, however, since no legal positivist has ever actually held that all legal standards are rules. This includes Raz and myself as well as Hart—who explicitly denied the claim long before Dworkin attributed it to him.

It is time to turn our attention to inclusive legal positivism. The first thing to note is that it shares with exclusive legal positivism a commitment to the conventionality of the criteria of legality. My own version of this claim encompasses the range of views detailed in the previous lecture under the rubric of the conventionality thesis. I have no reason to believe that Raz, for example, understands the conventionality of the criteria of legality along the same lines (though other exclusive legal positivists—for example, Scott Shapiro—do). All that matters at this point is that for positivists of whatever variety, the existence of the criteria of legality in any community depends on social facts—and not on moral arguments. The criteria of legality are in this sense conventional.

If what unites exclusive and inclusive legal positivism is a commitment to the conventionality of the criteria of legality, what distinguishes them is a difference over what can count as a criterion of legality. The exclusive legal positivist claims that all criteria of legality must state social sources. The inclusive legal positivist denies that, and allows that sometimes the morality of a norm can be a condition of its legality. Inclusive legal positivism thus rests on a distinction between the *grounds* and the *content* of the criteria of legality. The grounds of the criteria must be a social fact (a convention among officials), but the criteria themselves need not *state* social facts.[10] By contrast, the exclusive legal positivist claims both that the rule of recognition must be a social rule, *and* that the criteria of legality set forth in it must be social sources.

---

[10] For a fuller discussion, see Lecture 11.

Because inclusive legal positivism allows that some moral principles can be legally binding in virtue of their merits or value, not their source or pedigree, the inclusive legal positivist is prepared to accept more of Dworkin's suppositions than is the positivist who insists that the legality of moral principles depends entirely on their source.

Unlike Dworkin, however, the inclusive legal positivist holds that *whether or not morality is a condition of legality in a particular legal system depends on a social or conventional rule, namely the rule of recognition.* If the rule of recognition asserts that morality is a condition of legality, then morality is a condition of legality in that system. If the rule of recognition incorporates no moral principles, however, then no such principles figure in the criteria of legality.

The distinction between inclusive and exclusive legal positivism may now be stated succinctly: whereas both share positivism's basic commitment to the conventionality of legality, the inclusive legal positivist claims that positivism imposes no additional constraints on the content of those criteria, while the exclusive legal positivist maintains that legality must be a matter of social source, not content.[11]

It is important that we be as clear about what inclusive legal positivism is not as about what it is. Just about everybody gets right the basic premise of inclusive legal positivism, which is its rejection of the pedigree or social-source constraint on legality. On the other hand, it is a mistake to think that in rejecting the pedigree standard, the inclusive legal positivist is committed to the claim that wherever there is law, the rule of recognition makes morality a condition of legality. Inclusive legal positivism is the claim that positivism *allows* or *permits* substantive or moral tests of legality; it is not the view that positivism *requires* such tests. A legal system with only pedigree criteria of legality is surely a legal system, and inclusive legal positivists have no reason to think otherwise.

Another mistake is to think that whenever moral principles are law, the inclusive legal positivist must claim that this is because the rule of recognition in that a community makes morality a condition of legality. Again, not so. Inclusive legal positivism is the claim that positivism allows or permits such explanations of legal validity: not the view that positivism requires such explanations. It may well be that in a particular community all the moral principles that are law are law in virtue of their social sources. Such a legal community is surely possible, and again inclusive legal positivists have no reason to think otherwise.

Inclusive legal positivism is a theory of possible sources of legality. It says, in effect, that a positivist can accept not just that moral principles can

---

[11] Which is not to say that there are no constraints on the criteria of legality. The criteria are expressed in a rule of recognition that is a social rule. Thus, the criteria must be capable of supporting convergent behavior among officials. This is a conceptual constraint, imposed not by any commitment of positivism but by the concept of a social rule.

sometimes figure in legal argument; not just that such principles can be binding on officials; but that sometimes they can be binding on officials because they are legally valid or part of the community's law, and—most significantly—that they may even be part of the community's law *in virtue of their merits*—provided the rule of recognition in that community has such provisions.

All inclusive legal positivists agree that morality can be a condition of legality. However, there are notable differences between my version of inclusive legal positivism and the versions offered by various other theorists. One such point of difference concerns the theoretical motivations for inclusive legal positivism, and the criteria by which theories of law are to be evaluated. One might naturally infer from Wil Waluchow's excellent book on inclusive legal positivism that he believes part of the motivation of inclusive legal positivism to be its *descriptive accuracy*.[12] He notes that many constitutions and federal charters have clauses that on their face appear explicitly to make morality a condition of legality. The "due process" and "equal protection" clauses of the United States Constitution, and its prohibition of "cruel and unusual" punishments, are typical of the kind of moral language one often finds in written constitutions. Facially, such clauses suggest that morality can be a condition of legality. Inclusive legal positivism explicitly allows just that. Thus, Waluchow at least implicitly suggests that inclusive legal positivism is more descriptively accurate than a theory that excludes morality from the conditions of legality; and in virtue of that, inclusive legal positivism enjoys something of an epistemically privileged status.[13] To reject it would be to suffer a loss of descriptive accuracy, which we should be willing to accept only for the most compelling reasons.

I reject this line of argument. Of course, no one denies that descriptive accuracy is a virtue of a theory. But the dispute between exclusive and inclusive legal positivists cannot be resolved on descriptive grounds, for the simple reason that the dispute is not a descriptive one. It is an interpretive dispute. Any jurisprudential theory that can explain what I have called the "surface syntax" of constitutional clauses that make reference to morality can be a descriptively accurate theory. The question is not whether exclusive or inclusive legal positivism satisfies this criterion of descriptive accuracy; rather, the question is which view provides the *best explanation or interpretation* of the fact that moral language appears in constitutional clauses. Should we understand these clauses as incorporating morality into

[12] Waluchow, *Inclusive Legal Positivism*.

[13] This is surely the understanding that leads Waluchow to refer to such clauses in the Canadian Charter as "Charter Challenges". See *Inclusive Legal Positivism*, ch. 5. I am not certain that Waluchow would accept this characterization, but it is clearly the prevailing understanding of his view. Cf. Stephen Perry, "Varieties of Legal Positivism" *Canadian Journal of Law and Jurisprudence* 9 (July 1996) 361–81.

law? Should we read them as doing so in virtue of their substantive merits? These are interpretive questions and are, as I see it, to be answered in whatever way provides the best comprehensive understanding of legal practice. We cannot settle on a view about the criteria of legality without considering how that view affects the overall theory of law being developed. In this sense, any particular claim about the criteria of legality must be assessed holistically.

In fact, Raz has articulated a coherent and tenable way of understanding the relevant kinds of constitutional clauses without abandoning his exclusive legal positivist stance. His solution is to read clauses like the equal protection clause as directing officials to engage in substantive moral argument in order to determine *whether valid laws ought to be enforced* or are binding on officials. On Raz's view, enactments that come before the court to be evaluated under the equal protection standard are law, provided they satisfy the pedigree requirements; the equal protection clause does not go to the *legality* of such enactments, but rather, directs judges to engage in moral argument in order to determine whether the laws ought to be *enforced* or treated as binding.

I don't mean to defend this view as natural or perspicuous. It is neither. But our evaluation of it should be made in light of the whole picture. As we will see in the next lecture, Raz is driven to this way of interpreting clauses like the equal protection clause by his account of law's claim to practical authority. If the best account of legal authority requires interpreting these sorts of clauses as Raz does, then however unintuitive or unnatural his interpretation may seem, it may yet be part of the best overall view of the matter available to us. As we will see in the following lectures, what drives the dispute between inclusive and exclusive legal positivism concerns the way we are to understand law's claim to practical authority. The deep issue is whether that claim, properly understood, imposes constraints on the conditions of legality or not.

In denying that "morality" clauses should be interpreted as incorporating morality into law in virtue of its merits, the exclusive legal positivist is not arguing that we must trade off or abandon *descriptive accuracy* in favor of a better account of legal authority. Rather, exclusive legal positivists are arguing that we must trade off a degree of simplicity or intuitive appeal in one part of our account in exchange for a certain comprehensive understanding of law—of its conventionality and the role it plays in our practical lives. The defense of exclusive legal positivism rests on the claim that the most attractive comprehensive understanding available to us precludes interpreting "morality clauses" in a way that credits the surface syntax.

Similarly, in defending inclusive legal positivism, I am arguing that it too can provide a comprehensive understanding of law, its conventionality, and the role it plays in our practical lives; and that it can do so in a way that credits the surface syntax. Allowing for the possibility that morality can figure in legal practice in the way it appears to do is indeed a reason to prefer inclusive legal positivism—but only if the understanding of law it provides is otherwise compelling. It is not, on its own, the basis of a "challenge" that has to be met by exclusive legal positivists. Crediting the surface syntax has nothing to do with descriptive accuracy, and is thus inadequate to ground an "epistemically privileged" status for inclusive legal positivism.[14]

I differ from other inclusive legal positivists not only about the motivations of the inclusive legal positivist project and the criteria for assessing its success, but, more importantly, about how to understand the nature of the objections exclusive legal positivists have made to that project. On a certain natural reading of Hart's discussion of the relationship between primary rules and the rule of recognition, the *function* of the rule of recognition is to solve a problem of "dissensus".[15] In a regime of primary social rules of obligation, there is likely to be disagreement about which social rules are those to which one ought to conform, and (on this reading of Hart) the rule of recognition exists to solve this problem of disagreement. Imagine, for example, living under a system of custom in which everyone is committed to acting according to custom, but where there are disagreements about what the custom *is*. To coordinate our behavior in a way that would enable us to secure the benefits of social life, we might well need a meta-rule to pick out or identify what the custom is. In the case of such a system of primary social rules, dissensus may require a "legal solution" in the form of the rule of recognition: a rule that creates a mark distinguishing those primary rules to which one ought to conform from other putative rules. Thus, the rule of recognition must be understood as existing in order to solve a problem of *inadequate consensus*.

Some inclusive legal positivists have interpreted the objections of exclusive legal positivists in the light of this rather natural reading of Hart. If the point of a rule of recognition is to solve a problem of dissensus, then no rule of recognition can impose criteria of legality that re-create that same problem. If the rule of recognition requires that individuals appeal to their beliefs about what morality requires in order to determine whether a putative norm is law (and thus constitutes the standard of conduct to which they are to comply) then the rule of recognition merely re-creates the problem it was designed to solve.

This reading of the exclusive legal positivist objection is bolstered by a similar, but in the end mistaken, interpretation of the well-known "arbitrator" example: Two people disagree about what fairness requires of them

---

[14] I do not mean this as a criticism of Waluchow. I do not, however, want the debate to turn on principles of descriptive accuracy, and, thus, am anxious to make clear that my own view rests on no such claims.

[15] The passages that give rise to this misreading are to be found in ch. 5 of *The Concept of Law*.

in their dealings with one another, and so they submit their dispute to the judgment of an arbitrator. If the arbitrator just tells them, "Do what is fair", then the arbitrator has only re-created the original problem. Some advocates of inclusive legal positivism have understood the problem to be that like the arbitrator, a rule of recognition that makes morality a condition of legality threatens simply to re-create a problem of dissensus or disagreement that the rule of recognition is designed to solve. Because it is the function of the rule of recognition to facilitate or create consensus about what ought to be done, it must set forth criteria of legality that are up to that task. This means it must set forth criteria that make the legality of a norm a matter of its social source, not its content.

Having interpreted the example in this way, it has struck some as natural to respond in the following way: to be sure, a rule of recognition must be capable of resolving dissensus to an extent sufficient to facilitate social cooperation. This constraint may be enough to rule out certain robust forms of inclusive positivism—those, in particular, that allow morality to be a sufficient condition of legality. Since sufficiency clauses merely direct individuals back to their divergent beliefs about how they ought to act, such clauses cannot facilitate or create consensus within a group about how its members are to act. On the other hand, there is no reason to suppose that less robust inclusive clauses preclude coordination or cooperative activity. In particular, necessity clauses—which require a more modest application of moral argument—may nevertheless be compatible with the rule of recognition's coordinating function. Thus, necessity clauses can withstand the exclusive legal positivist challenge (as these theorists understand it), and this has led them to defend what I take to be a truncated version of inclusive legal positivism.

We can enumerate three components in this line of response to exclusive legal positivism: (1) an interpretation of the role of a rule of recognition as designed to solve a problem of dissensus or controversy about what the obligation-imposing primary rules are; (2) a related understanding of the exclusive legal positivist objection, according to which no criteria of legality are permissible unless they are capable in principle of solving the problem of controversy or inadequate consensus; (3) the claim that this constraint rules out only certain more robust forms of inclusive legal positivism (in particular, sufficiency clauses of the sort my version of inclusive legal positivism permits). At the same time, the relevant constraint does not preclude less demanding moral criteria of legality—in particular those represented by necessity clauses.

Though each of these claims has a surface plausibility, none withstands scrutiny. The rule of recognition can of course solve a problem of dissensus, in this or that legal system, about what the obligation-imposing rules are. It does not follow, however, that this is its essential function—that in order for there to be law, there must be a rule of recognition that solves a problem of controversy. We can imagine, for example, a situation in which everyone agrees about what morality requires, but desires to have their shared moral–political commitments expressed in concrete legal institutions, as a way of fully expressing or realizing those commitments—and as a way of making those abstract commitments more concrete. In order that there be law, there must be a rule of recognition that states the criteria of legality; but the rule need not exist to solve any problem at all, let alone one of dissensus.

Turning to the second claim in the above line of argument—namely, the interpretive claim that the exclusive legal positivist objects to moral criteria of legality because such criteria merely re-create the problem the rule of recognition is designed to solve—we see that this claim too is mistaken. This interpretation is grounded in a misunderstanding of the arbitrator example, the point of which is *conceptual*. The "arbitrator" who tells us to do what is fair is not just failing to resolve our dispute, and thus failing to perform his putatively essential function—rather, the "arbitrator" is failing to *arbitrate*. His failure is not, in other words, practical or pragmatic—it is conceptual. He exercises no practical authority because he does not create reasons for acting, but merely directs us back to the dependent reasons for acting we already have. In order for him to *be* an arbitrator, he must provide us with reasons that replace—not merely ones that *restate*—the dependent reasons that apply to us.

To see in greater relief how the point of the arbitrator example differs from the way many inclusive legal positivists have understood it, we need only consider what an exclusive legal positivist would say about a case in which there is no disagreement about what morality requires. Here the rule of recognition that says, "X is law if and only if it expresses a requirement of morality" does not (indeed, cannot) re-create a problem of dissensus (there is no dissensus to re-create). Nevertheless, an exclusive legal positivist like Raz would have the *same* objection to inclusive legal positivism he has always had: moral criteria of legality vitiate law's claim to authority, because they cannot create reasons for acting that replace the ones we already have. Raz claims that the function of law is to mediate between persons and reasons. The problem with an inclusive rule of recognition, as he sees it, is that law valid under it cannot, as a conceptual matter, perform its function. This has nothing to do with matters of degree or the extent of the dissensus.

Turning finally to the third claim above, we see that it represents a version of inclusive legal positivism that is in fact unconnected to the critique that is supposed to motivate it. If the point of defending the possibility of necessity clauses only (among morality conditions of legality) is to accommodate the exclusive legal positivist's objection, then this is a misguided retreat, based entirely on a misunderstanding of the objection. Moreover, since it robs inclusive legal positivism of its ability to answer Dworkin's original objection, this truncated form of positivism strikes one as both unhelpful and unmotivated.

Moreover, this line of argument on behalf of necessity clause only versions of inclusive legal positivism confuses a conceptual argument with an empirical one. If there is widespread agreement about what we morally ought to do, then a sufficiency clause should be possible, by these theorists' own lights. By the same token, it is easy to imagine social facts that are as likely to confound, confuse, and generate controversy as is any morality clause; such social-source criteria would have to be excluded. Whether or not a given set of criteria can solve a problem of dissensus for a given society, in other words, is logically independent of whether the criteria are social facts, or specify morality as a necessary or sufficient condition of legality. It is an *empirical* question what a given society happens to find confounding, confusing, or controversial. It is simply a mistake to base a conceptual claim about possible criteria of legality on an empirical generalization (no matter how well founded) about how controversial morality usually is. The question is whether there are criteria of legality that are *in principle* incapable of guiding conduct; not whether under particular conditions— even ones we might regard as typical—certain criteria would be sufficiently controversial to prevent coordination.

Finally, even if the rule of recognition exists to solve a problem of dissensus, this should not be understood as a problem of the *degree* of dissensus. That, of course, is precisely why I emphasize the conceptual difference between the *existence* conditions of a rule of recognition (and of law and legal authority more generally) and the *efficacy* of this or that rule of recognition, or of a legal practice based upon it. I fear that alternative understandings of inclusive legal positivism are the result of a misdiagnosis of the problem—if any—law exists to solve, a misunderstanding of the concerns many exclusive legal positivists have had about the available remedies, and a prescription for a return to health that treats the wrong problem, if it treats anything at all.

Controversy is *not* the issue for the exclusive legal positivist; only natural but serious confusions have led some inclusive legal positivists to think otherwise. The issue is one of the compatibility of certain criteria of legality with the *conceptual possibility* of legal authority, not the *de facto* possibility of legality.[16] And that is why I have continued to defend the most "robust" forms of rules of recognition, in which morality can be a sufficient condition of legality. If such clauses can withstand what are in fact the objections Raz and others have made—and not merely the objections that have been wrongly attributed to them—then any weaker version of the rule of recognition will withstand criticism as well.

[16] For a fuller discussion of these issues, see my "Constraints on the Criteria of Legality" *Legal Theory* 6/2 (2000) 171–83.

While inclusive legal positivism is able to accommodate a claim like Dworkin's that our actual legal system incorporates morality into the criteria of legality, inclusive legal positivism is *not* the view that this is *in fact* the most apt characterization of our existing legal system—or of legal practice generally. It is simply the view that if such criteria of legality ever, often, or even always figure in legal practice, positivism can provide an explanation that is coherent and plausible. Inclusive legal positivism thus makes no claim as to the underlying merits of Dworkin's "observations" concerning the most apt way of characterizing the role of morality in adjudication, nor is it committed to a particular interpretation of our actual legal practice. Positivism can *grant* all of Dworkin's observations; however, it must maintain that the criteria of validity are criteria of validity in virtue of the practice among officials; that is, it must uphold some version of the conventionality thesis.

It is here that Dworkin wants to exert pressure. If the concern of the exclusive legal positivist is not morality's controversiality, that certainly is Dworkin's concern. By allowing morality to be a condition of legality, he argues, inclusive legal positivism is rendered incompatible with the conventionality thesis. The conventionality thesis is, I have argued, the central tenet of all plausible forms of legal positivism—including my own. Thus, it is especially important that we be capable of responding to Dworkin's objection that inclusive legal positivism is inconsistent with it.

In "The Model of Rules II" Dworkin argues that if there is a rule of recognition, it must be a "normative", not a social, rule.[17] The difference is a matter of existence conditions. Normative rules need not be practiced in order to impose obligations; their existence as regulative rules depends on the substantive arguments that can be mustered on their behalf. In contrast, the existence of social rules depends on their being practiced. Inclusive legal positivism—at least in the form I have developed it, which includes the version of the conventionality thesis outlined in the last lecture—requires both that the rule of recognition be a social rule *and* that the rule may incorporate principles that impose substantive moral criteria of legal validity. Dworkin argues, in effect, that these two requirements are incompatible.

[17] While the distinction between normative and social rules is clear enough, it is misleading to refer to one kind of rule as normative and the other as social. Both after all are normative rules in the only important sense: that is, they both purport to provide reasons for action and to impose obligations. One has to be careful not to be misled into thinking that social rules cannot be normative. They surely can be, as I have argued in the previous lecture.

Dworkin has shifted among a variety of related but distinct positions. At times he denies that the concept of law entails the existence of anything like a rule of recognition; other times he allows that there might well be a rule that sets out criteria of legality (a broadly speaking rule of recognition), but asserts that such a rule must be a normative rule, not a social rule. In the end I think the best interpretation of his view is this: he does not deny that there are criteria of legality. Like Raz, he sees no reason to think that the existence of such criteria must be explained in terms of a duty-imposing rule (of any sort) that sets them out, that makes them criteria of legality. Unlike Raz, who thinks that these criteria are conventional and depend on the practice of officials, Dworkin thinks they are normative in that they figure in the best interpretation of the practice of judges.

The argument is this: Moral principles are inherently controversial. Judges will disagree about which principles satisfy the demands of morality, and about what the principles require. Since the rule of recognition is a social rule, it is partially constituted by or supervenient on a convergence of behavior—the convergence is an existence condition of the rule of recognition. Convergence, however, is undermined by the disagreement that would attend any rule that makes morality a condition of legality. Thus, inclusive legal positivism is incompatible with the conventionality thesis.

As I have emphasized elsewhere, Dworkin's argument misses the important difference between what the rule is and what falls under it. Judges may agree about what the rule *is* but disagree with one another over what the rule *requires*. They could not disagree in every case or even in most cases, since such broad and widespread disagreement would render unintelligible their claim to be applying or following the same rule. Nevertheless, judges can disagree in some significant set of controversial cases, without in the process abandoning their agreement about what the rule is. It hardly follows from the fact that judges disagree about some of the demands of morality that they also disagree about whether the rule governing their behavior requires that they resolve disputes by determining what morality demands. In short, some disagreement about a rule's requirements is not incompatible with the rule's conventionality.

Dworkin has responded to this argument by labeling the distinction between content and application "doubtful". While this is clearly intended to disparage the argument, it is not obvious what point Dworkin means to make. It is plainly wrong to suggest that there is in general no meaningful distinction between application and content. Sometimes you and I may disagree about what the rule we are supposed to be following is; at other times we know perfectly well what the rule is, but disagree about what it requires of us. Dworkin's only substantive point seems to be that we can always describe the same disagreement alternately as a disagreement about the rule or a disagreement about its application. But even that seems to presuppose, rather than to undermine, the legitimacy of the distinction. Does Dworkin mean that the distinction can do no work? That is simply false. Even if it did turn out to be logically possible to describe any disagreement about a rule as a disagreement either about its content or about its application, it hardly follows that the two kinds of descriptions would be equally apt all the time.[18]

Law's conventionality does not, of course, require that every disagreement about the rule of recognition is most aptly characterized as a

---

[18] Sometimes the context will reveal to us which description is apt and why. Sometimes there may be no way of knowing independently of offering theoretical considerations on behalf of one interpretation or the other. For my part, I nowhere claim that all disagreements are best understood as disagreements in the application of the rule of recognition.

disagreement in application. Some disagreements are best thought of as disagreements about how the law should be extended.[19] But the best or most apt way of characterizing a disagreement is not simply up for grabs. Which characterization is most apt is a determination to be made on the basis of our intuitive grasp of the case, on grounds of theoretical coherence, simplicity, consilience, and the like, or (when these kinds of considerations are in conflict) on the proper balance of all of these factors.

It is as though Dworkin were to insist that in every case, no matter what the circumstances or how far-fetched it would be, we must exercise the option (supposing it really is one) of interpreting disagreements as disagreements of content. If there were some reason to do that, we should certainly have to grant Dworkin his conclusion that the rule of recognition must be a "normative", and not a social, rule. But there is no reason to do that; or at least none that Dworkin has proposed. So not only does he apparently presuppose a distinction he has labeled "doubtful"—he also chooses the side of the distinction that supports his position, and does so without offering any theoretically motivated reason for doing so.

On the other hand, if we accept this perfectly natural and common distinction, by treating some disagreements concerning the rule of recognition as "application" rather than as "content" disagreements, we gain many theoretical advantages. We may coherently maintain both that moral principles can be law in virtue of their merits, and the conventionality thesis; this in turn, I have argued, offers the noteworthy advantage of enabling us to explain the possibility of law by appealing to social facts. Again, I insist that one has to choose among incompatible but equally coherent interpretations by appealing to the norms that govern theory construction, which are themselves grounded in the theoretical interest in securing as full and comprehensive an understanding of legal practice as possible.[20]

Dworkin's argument cuts no ice against the conventionality thesis; there is no reason to think that a social rule cannot also be controversial in some of its applications.[21] However, we might reformulate the objection so that it no

[19] I would never say, and did not say, that the disagreement in the rule of recognition evidenced by *Madison* v. *Marbury* S U.S. (I Cranach) 137 (1803) was a disagreement in the application of the rule.

[20] I nowhere deny that Dworkin can offer such considerations on behalf of his own interpretation of disagreement in the rule of recognition. He has not done so, however, whereas I have; and thus his choosing his interpretation of disagreement over mine—a choice, I reiterate, that implicitly acknowledges a distinction he simultaneously labels "doubtful"—is doubly unwarranted: unwarranted both because he fails to offer the requisite theoretical reasons for his interpretation while I have offered such reasons in favor of my view; and because in choosing one interpretation of disagreement over the other, he acknowledges the very distinction he elsewhere dismisses.

[21] Indeed, the argument of the previous lecture is intended to establish that the kind of conventionality involved in the rule of recognition anticipates controversy. For the rule of recognition represents shared cooperative activity that is itself a framework of coordination and bargaining about how participation in it is to proceed. Such bargaining invites, rather than precludes, certain forms of moral argument.

longer makes a conceptual point about the consistency of inclusive legal positivism and the conventionality thesis, but rather, a practical point about the effectiveness of a rule of recognition that incorporates morality into law's validity conditions. Arguably, law is of practical significance because it guides or purports to guide human conduct. It might be thought that the motivation for insisting on the conventionality of law is to explain how law can perform this function. But the more controversial the rule of recognition, the less able it is to provide guidance—how can individuals conform to the law's demands when they cannot determine reliably what behavior those demands require? If the rule of recognition invites dispute and controversy, the motivation for insisting on its conventionality evaporates. We are left with the more natural explanation of any test that makes morality a condition of legality: namely, that a rule that imposes moral criteria is itself a normative or moral rule.

This formulation of the objection fails to grasp the theoretical purpose of the conventionality thesis. The point of the conventionality thesis is to explain how law is possible; it is motivated by the need to explain law's *existence*, not its *efficacy*. Of course, law must exist if it is to be efficacious; but there is a special problem in explaining law's existence, and the conventionality thesis purports to solve it. The claim that law is made possible by a rule of recognition that supervenes on convergent behavior accepted from an internal point of view is a conceptual claim. It does not matter, for this purpose, whether or not the rule of recognition is controversial, as long as it is a rule. The positivist will, of course, readily grant the point that a rule of recognition's *efficacy* diminishes with its controversiality, and no positivist denies that controversy matters in this way. But the conventionality thesis is unaffected by the possibility (or actuality) of controversial provisions in the rule of recognition, provided at least some of these are plausibly understood as what I have called "application disagreements". Even if Dworkin is right and we could (logically) treat all application disagreements as content disagreements (and vice versa), there are strong theoretical reasons for not doing so.

Philosophy helps us understand the practices in which we are engaged, largely by clarifying the concepts that figure importantly in them. The distinctive philosophical method is conceptual analysis. A philosophical account of a concept is a contestable conception of it that is responsive to a set of interests or concerns. Depending on the concept at issue, these concerns can be either practical or theoretical; often they are both. In the method adopted and developed here conceptual analysis aims to produce the *thinnest* conception that is adequately responsive to the theoretical and practical concerns that motivate inquiry. At the beginning of Part II I argued that our concept of law should help us understand at least two central concerns about legal practice: the possibility of legal authority and the kind of normativity that is distinctive of it, while providing a plausible interpretation of the role of moral principle in legal argument.

Of course, a variety of theories of law, or conceptions of the concept, can be responsive to these concerns. Differing accounts must be evaluated against the relevant norms of theory construction: elegance, simplicity, and, most importantly, the breadth and depth of the understanding each provides. This means that a theory that can provide a single answer to both of the two fundamental questions of jurisprudence is, other things equal, a stronger theory than one whose answers are consistent but not mutually confirming. (Either kind of theory, of course, is preferable to one whose answers are inconsistent, or which leaves the central questions and concerns unattended to.)

Properly understood, inclusive legal positivism of the sort I advocate— and the sort I take Hart to articulate as well—claims that a very thin conception of law—one that posits only the conventionality thesis—is adequate to explain the possibility of legal authority. The absence of further substantive constraints on the conditions of legality does not undermine the possibility of law resting on conventional practice—that is the point of meeting Dworkin's controversiality objection. It remains to answer the exclusive legal positivist who claims, in effect, that the conventionality thesis is not enough, and that we must add a social-source constraint on the conditions of legality in order adequately to explain law's distinctive normativity.

The remainder of this part of the book is devoted to showing that the conventionality thesis is indeed adequate to account for law's distinctive normativity. Of course, this presumes some account of what law's distinctive normativity consists in. In the next two lectures I argue that my version of inclusive legal positivism is compatible with a *range* of possible accounts of law's normativity. In Lecture 10 I articulate and defend one such account; to a large extent, however, my defense of inclusive legal positivism is more general, and does not depend on my own conception of the normativity of law. Thus, we begin with the Razian account of how to understand that normativity, and respond to the claim that inclusive legal positivism is inconsistent with it.[22]

---

[22] Henceforth, unless otherwise noted, when I refer to inclusive legal positivism, I am referring to my own version of it, and not to other accounts which, I have argued, misunderstand both my account and the powerful objections offered up against it.

Lecture Nine—
Authority and Reason

In its broadest sense, legal positivism is the view that the possibility of legal authority is to be explained in terms of social facts. Most legal positivists, including myself, take this to mean that legal authority is possible in virtue of a conventional practice among officials: norms are legal just in case they satisfy the conventional criteria of legality, which are expressed in the rule of recognition. Thus, a rule's claim to govern conduct as law rests on the fact that it satisfies the conditions expressed by the rule, and not on its content as a rule. In this sense, the reasons for acting that legal rules valid under a rule of recognition purport to create are content-independent. They are thought to be consequences not of a norm's content, but of its bearing the mark of legality. Similarly, if the rule of recognition provides reasons for acting, then the reasons it provides depend not on the moral arguments—if any—that can be mustered on behalf of the rule's content, but rather, on the fact that it is practiced by officials. Thus, the rule of recognition's claim to govern conduct is also independent of its content. It governs if it guides, and it guides only if it is practiced.

There is nothing particularly problematic in the notion of a content-independent reason as such; we do, after all, recognize all sorts of reasons for action that are independent of content. For example, if my daughter requests that I help her with some task, the fact that it is a *request* of my daughter's may give me a reason for action that is independent of the content of the request. Or suppose I promise you that I will do any reasonable thing you ask (say because you have just saved my life). If you ask me to do X, then my promise gives me a reason to do X, regardless of its content.

While we do not need a philosophical theory to explain how certain requests and promises can create reasons for acting independent of the content of the request or promise, there is no comparably transparent fact about the relationship between the individual and the state that would underwrite the law's claim to provide content-independent reasons.[1] The problem is made all the more urgent by Hart's claim that legal reasons are not only content-independent; they are "peremptory" as well. To say that the reason created by a directive is peremptory is to say not only that it is a first-order reason for acting, but that it is a reason not to deliberate on the

---

[1] Philosophical justifications of the state have long sought to cast the state into the mold of one of the more straightforward sources of content-independent reasons. Thus, in the *Crito* Socrates likens the law to a parent; social contract theorists ground law's reasons on a promise or agreement; and so on.

basis of the directive's merits. Peremptory reasons "foreclose deliberation" on the merits. Since legal reasons are both content-independent and peremptory, the law purports to govern our conduct by telling us that we have an obligation to act in a certain way for no reason other than that the law commands it.[2] Taken together, and in the absence of a philosophical explanation, the combination of content independence and peremptoriness appears to render law's reasons mere demands of *power*, and not the expressions of a legitimate normative authority that could impose genuine duties and responsibilities or confer rights and privileges. In short, the conventionality of legality, which renders positivism such a plausible interpretation of the sense in which law is a normative *social practice*, raises concerns about the interpretation of the claim that it is a *normative* social practice.

The idea that laws purport to create content-independent, peremptory reasons for action is, along with the internal point of view, another of Hart's extraordinary contributions to legal theory. Their content independence and peremptory status mark the distinctive way in which law's reasons are, for Hart, capable of guiding conduct. Seeking, no doubt, to emphasize the special nature of legal normativity, Hart goes so far as to hold that moral terms employed in law—terms such as obligation, duty, and right—have a special sense that is not necessarily connected to their use in moral discourse, but which is instead appropriate to the content-independent and peremptory nature of legal reasons. This claim of Hart's has led to some perplexity. For if legal reasons imply not only a distinctive normativity, but an entirely different normative sense, then how is the fact that a course of conduct is required by law to figure in our deliberations about what we ought to do? How are we to compare law's reasons with the reasons that otherwise apply to us, law's obligations and rights with those we otherwise have? These concerns have prompted the worry that, as Scott Shapiro has put it, legal reasons stand to reasons in the same way that kosher pizza stands to pizza. The kosher pizza is not a kind of pizza, but a different thing from pizza altogether; and on Hart's characterization, it seems as though legal reasons are similarly not genuine reasons at all, but something altogether different from reasons. Reasons are the kind of thing that by their nature can figure in our rational determination of what it is we ought to do. The worry is that it is not at all clear that legal reasons are that kind of thing.

One of Joseph Raz's greatest contributions to legal and political philosophy is his theory of authority, which includes among its elements an account of the conditions under which the content-independent reasons of law can be genuine or moral reasons. Raz begins with the idea that there is a set of

[2] Whether or not that reason is our motivation for complying with the law is beside the point: thus the distinction emphasized throughout this section of the book between having a reason for acting and acting on that reason.

reasons for action that apply to each of us, the proper balance of which constitutes what he calls "the demands of right reason". Right reason thus includes moral reasons, but is a much broader category. It includes whatever it is that we should do in a given case, taking into account all the reasons that apply to us. The question then is what relationship can legal reasons have to the demands of right reason? If the law requires of us a different course of action from the one required by right reason, then acting on the basis of law's reasons would be irrational. On the other hand, if law's directives require the same course of action as that required by right reason, then law's reasons are otiose; they add nothing to the reasons we already have.

In solving this puzzle, Raz looks to a familiar class of content-independent reasons—namely, reasons of practical authority. It is rational to accept a practical authority whenever one would do better in satisfying the demands of right reason by acting on the reasons that the authority provides than one would do by acting on the basis of one's own assessment of the requirements of right reason directly. This is what Raz calls the normal justification thesis, and he believes that when an authority satisfies it, the authoritative directive creates a moral reason for action. Typically, the law's content-independent reasons can be moral reasons when the law reflects certain kinds of special expertise, or when the demands of right reason are most effectively met by coordinated activity that the law is better able to organize by authoritative directives than are individuals acting each on his own initiative, or jointly. Because the legitimacy of legal authority depends on the capacity of legal directives to enable individuals more fully and satisfactorily to meet the demands of right reason that apply to them, Raz's conception of legal authority is a *service conception*.

This analysis is a great advance over Hart's. For Raz shows how distinctively legal reasons can be genuine reasons, and how legal obligations, duties, responsibilities, and their corresponding rights can also bear a moral signification. Law's reasons can be genuine because as a practical authority, law may reflect special expertise or may serve to coordinate individuals' actions, enabling them better to satisfy the demands of right reason; at the same time legal normativity is distinctive in that its reasons are content-independent and, on Raz's account, "exclusionary" or "preemptive". In other words, law's reasons preempt and replace the dependent reasons that would justify its commands.

Unlike Hart's notion of peremptory reasons, preemptive reasons do not foreclose *all* deliberation on the balance of reasons for action; rather, law's authority precludes appeal only to those reasons that the law purports to replace. A peremptory reason is a reason *not* to *deliberate* on the underlying merits of complying with a directive. Preemptive reasons, in contrast, do not preclude deliberation on the merits of compliance. Instead, they preclude deliberating on the basis of the dependent reasons they replace. Thus, while Raz and Hart both treat legal reasons as content-independent, they differ with regard to the way legal reasons can bear on our deliberations about what we ought to do.

It is essential to note, though the point is often missed, that neither Hart nor Raz is claiming that the legal reasons must *actually* figure in an individual's deliberation in any particular way. The essential point in the case of each theorist is that the law must be *capable* of figuring in deliberation in the appropriate way in order to create genuine obligations. Recall the distinction between and *obligation* and *guidance*.[3] To say that the law can guide behavior is to say that it can offer reasons—content-independent and (depending on the account) peremptory or exclusionary—that are capable of figuring, in a particular way, in our deliberations about what we ought to do. If those reasons are strong enough, or conclusive, then we can say that the law obligates us to act in a certain way. The obligation rests on the possibility of guidance, but is independent of whether or not law's reasons actually guide us. In order for us to meet the obligation, we need not be guided by the law—we merely have to do whatever it is the law requires of us.[4]

We began by worrying that Hart's characterization of legal reasons as content-independent raised a serious doubt about how legal reasons could be reasons at all. Ironically, one implication of Raz's account is that practical authorities can provide moral reasons *only* because their status as law is content-independent. Rather than positivism's commitment to content-independent reasons for action being a *bar* to law's capacity to provide reason for action, it is, on Raz's view, the sine qua non of that capacity.[5]

[3] See Lecture 6.

[4] Put another way, the law can impose real obligations on us only if it is capable of being an authority. It is capable of being an authority only if it is *capable* of guiding our behavior in a certain way. It is capable of guiding our behavior only if it can create genuine reasons for acting (the other features of the reasons it creates—preemptive or peremptory—are inessential to this part of the argument, to individual accounts of the character of the guidance law purports to provide). If the law in fact creates reasons sufficiently strong to obligate, then what the law demands is compliance—nothing more. Guidance goes to the case for the claim that law's reasons can obligate. It does not go to the question of what is required in order to comply with the law's demands. The exception is the rule of recognition—it is capable of imposing obligations on officials only if it is the reason for their compliance with it.

[5] Even if there is an important sense in which Raz's account of authority is an advance on Hart's, it is not at all clear that Hart or a Hartian could avail himself of it. There are many reasons for this; I mention two. First, Raz's entire account is based on seeing law in relationship to the demands of right reason. Law's authority is connected to its capacity to enable individuals to do what morality requires of them. Second, it is part of Raz's understanding of law itself that it functions to mediate between persons and reasons. Hart holds neither of these views. For Hart, law helps us answer the question of what we ought to do, and not necessarily the question of what we ought to do if we desire to do what right reason demands. Law may, for example, answer the question of what we ought to do in order to be able to coordinate our activities in such a way as to enable us to share in the benefits of a collective life. The function of law is to guide through reasons—hopefully in a way that enables us all to promote whatever interests the existence and persistence of law is connected to—but in Hart there is simply no connection between the claims of legal authority and the demands of right reason. Nor does Hart hold the view that law must mediate between persons and reasons.

Raz's account of authority is intended to be a conceptual claim about law. His view is that it is a necessary feature of law that it claims legitimate authority; and he infers from this—by a subtle argument that also employs other premises—that law must be the kind of thing that *can have* legitimate authority. Whether or not any given legal system has such authority is an empirical and contingent matter; it is a conceptual and necessary truth, however, that law is *capable* of having legitimate authority. Moreover, for Raz, the claim to authority is a claim any norm must make in order to be law, and is a claim that must be capable of being true for each legal norm.

I do not intend to subject Raz's argument to close scrutiny. Viewed broadly enough, the claim that law must be capable of being an authority is independently plausible at this point. The things law can do for us—like providing expert guidance and coordinating individuals' actions for common and collective ends—can at least strongly motivate the view that, in principle, law must be capable of legitimate authority. I do not agree, however, that law's claim to authority imposes a constraint on particular rules. That is, I reject the idea that no rule can be law unless it is capable of being a practical authority.[6] Nor do I accept Raz's particular account of authority.

Having registered these caveats, what remains to be said is that Raz's account is brilliant both in the depth of its problematic and in the perspicuity of its solution, and that it is certainly the most fully developed, sophisticated, and influential doctrine of legal authority to date.[7] As such, any challenges it raises must be taken seriously. In what follows, I will be *assuming* the Razian account of authority for the sake of argument, in order to dispute what Raz takes to be one of its consequences. Specifically, Raz believes that his account of legal authority entails the sources thesis; the sources thesis, in turn implies that inclusive legal positivism must be rejected.

Raz's argument against inclusive legal positivism is as follows. A rule that is an authority preempts or replaces the dependent reasons that would justify it. In this sense, authorities mediate between persons and the reasons that apply to them. If, in order to identify the law or its content, one must appeal to the dependent reasons that the law replaces, law is disabled from mediating between persons and reasons, and its claim to authority is vitiated. Law's claim to authority entails, therefore, that one cannot determine the law's identity or content by appealing to the dependent reasons that would justify it. A rule of recognition that allows morality to serve as a condition of legality appears to require that one investigate the dependent reasons the law replaces or preempts, in order to determine what the law or its content is; and this would vitiate law's claim to authority.

---

[6] This point is developed in the next lecture.

[7] We will revisit some of the concerns registered here about Raz's account—briefly at the end of this lecture, and in detail in the next.

To state the argument in slightly different terms, a norm's legality can either (*a*) be a natural fact; (*b*) depend on its content; or (*c*) be determined independently of its content—that is, by its source—its form, or manner of enactment. On the reasonable assumption that legality is not a natural fact, legality can depend on either its content or its form and manner of enactment—its source. Raz's claim is that law must claim to be a legitimate authority, and the fact that this claim must be the sort of claim that could be true entails that legality must depend entirely on social source. If a norm's legality must always depend on its social source alone, then it can never depend on its content. Inclusive legal positivism claims that legality can sometimes depend on a norm's content, and so if Raz is right about law's authority, inclusive legal positivism must be abandoned.[8]

Before taking up the argument in earnest, I want to make it clear what is and what is not at stake. First, as the reader will recall from the previous lecture, no one denies that morality figures in legal discourse. All the parties to the debate, including Dworkin and the proponents of both inclusive and exclusive legal positivism, agree that there is, as it were, a "surface grammar" of moral language in law that needs to be explained. The differences among the competing views are to be found in the kind of explanation each gives. Second, and more importantly, the particular explanation each offers will invariably be driven by other commitments of the theory.

Now that we have had a chance to consider Raz's account of legal authority and its motivations, we can see that it is his view about authority that leads him to reject inclusive legal positivism, and which thus drives his view about the status of morality clauses in the rule of recognition.[9] When he argues that such clauses direct judges to determine whether valid laws should be enforced, and do not actually constitute conditions of legality, that is not

---

[8] In Lecture 7 I noted the differences between the Razian account of law's conventionality and my own. This lecture highlights the most basic difference between us, which concerns how to interpret the ways in which moral principles can figure in legal argument. He is committed to the sources thesis and I am not. He thus believes that the content of morality cannot be incorporated into law. I believe that it can, or at least that legal positivism is not precluded from believing that it might. Like Dworkin, Raz believes that legal positivism is committed to pedigree- or source-based, and thus non-contentful, criteria of legality. While they understand this aspect of positivism in a similar way, however, their reasons for doing so are very different. We saw in the previous lecture that Dworkin's arguments are based on two claims: (1) that moral criteria of legality are incompatible with the separability thesis; and (2) that moral criteria of legality are incompatible with the conventionality thesis. As we saw, neither of these claims can be sustained. The separability thesis (in the sense that positivists are actually committed to it) claims simply that morality is not *necessarily* a condition of legality, not that morality *cannot* be a condition of legality, as a contingent matter. As for the conventionality thesis, we have seen that there is no reason why a conventional rule cannot set forth moral criteria for legality. Unlike Dworkin, however, Raz claims neither that moral criteria of legality violate the separability thesis, nor that moral criteria of legality are incompatible with the conventionality thesis. His reasons for rejecting inclusive legal positivism rest entirely on his claim that such criteria are incompatible with law's claim to legitimate authority.   [9] See Lecture 7.

because Raz supposes this is the most natural or perspicuous way of characterizing how such clauses operate in our legal discourse; rather, it is
because alternative understandings that might on the surface seem more
natural are thought to be incompatible with the claim to authority.

Thus, it is at the level of the theory of authority that the debate between
inclusive and exclusive legal positivism is joined. The argument that morality cannot be a condition of legality rests on two premises: first, that if
morality is a condition of legality, then it would be necessary to appeal to
the underlying dependent reasons in order to determine what the law and
its content is; and second, that if one were required to appeal to the dependent or justifying reasons in order to identify the law or its content, then the
law could not be an authority.

The expression "is a condition of legality" seems to cover both necessary
and sufficient conditions. There is, however, an important distinction
between a rule of recognition that makes morality a *necessary* condition of
legality and one that makes morality a *sufficient* condition of legality. To
illustrate the distinction, a rule of recognition that claims that no norm can
be law *unless* it is fair appears to treat morality as a necessary condition of
legality. A rule of recognition that claims that certain norms are law *because*
they express a dimension of justice or fairness treats morality as a sufficient
condition of legality.

Clauses like the equal protection clause of the 14th Amendment to the
United States Constitution or similar provisions in the Canadian Charter
are, arguably, instances of rules of recognition that treat certain features of
the morality of a norm as a necessary condition of its legality. On the other
hand, the principle "No man should profit from his own wrongdoing"
might be thought to be law because it expresses a dimension of justice or
fairness, in which case its doing so appears to be sufficient for its legality.

The distinction is an important one because in at least some cases of
necessity clauses, the moral principle that is a condition of legality need not
direct us to the underlying dependent reasons for a law. For example, consider a rule of recognition specifying that only rules that satisfy certain
requirements of fairness and equality—like whether or not the law offers
fair opportunities for appeal, whether or not it is fairly administered, and so
on—can be legally valid. Here is a clause in which the morality of a norm is
a necessary condition of legality, and so the rule is an evaluative test—just
the sort ruled out by the sources thesis. Nevertheless, the evaluative test
does not direct us to the dependent reasons that would justify any particular
legal rule. The kinds of moral considerations the fairness clause expresses
are not part of the justification for laws prohibiting murder, for example.
These considerations are not part of the reasons why it is morally good or
desirable to have such a law, and thus they are not among the dependent
reasons that the law would replace. In general, *the evaluative considerations*

that go to the legality of a rule need not coincide with those that go to the merits of the rule. Such clauses are therefore consistent with the Razian view of authority.

Inclusive legal positivism is incompatible with Raz's account of authority only if the former entails that officials must appeal to the dependent or justifying reasons that legal rules are thought to replace or exclude. But there is no reason to suppose that every evaluative criterion of legality functions in that way. In fact, many possible evaluative clauses in a rule of recognition clearly do not; and very likely most, if not all, evaluative clauses that express necessary conditions of legality do not.

We have been considering the case of clauses that make substantive morality a necessary condition of legality. However, to explain in a natural and perspicuous way how moral principles such as "No man shall profit from his own wrongdoing" can be legally binding standards, inclusive legal positivism must be prepared to claim that sometimes it is possible for moral principles to count as law merely in virtue of their expressing a requirement of fairness. In other words, we must defend the possibility of "sufficiency clauses" in the rule of recognition.

It should be apparent immediately that the argument I just offered in defense of necessity clauses won't work. In the case of sufficiency clauses, I can no longer claim that the evaluative criteria that figure as conditions of legality direct officials not to the justifying reasons for the rule, but to other more general reasons. A clause that makes morality a sufficient condition of legality states that a norm is law just *because* it has certain moral features, and so its legality is completely dependent on precisely the justifying reasons its legality is supposed to exclude or preempt. I therefore need a different argument to establish the consistency of legal authority with sufficiency clauses.

Let us look more closely at what is entailed by the theory of legal authority Raz has proposed. It entails a certain metaphysical claim about the nature of law: a constraint on the kind of thing law must be. Stated precisely, law must be the sort of thing that in principle is capable of having its identity and content determined without recourse to moral argument, because, otherwise, law could not mediate between persons and reasons in the appropriate way.[10] We might say that this metaphysical or conceptual constraint requires something *like* a sources thesis: it requires that the criteria by which the members of a community identify the law and its content must be social sources.[11] But this does not entail the sources thesis as a constraint

---

[10] For ease of exposition, I will use the phrase "without recourse to moral argument" to mean "without recourse to moral argument about what the law should be".

[11] Obviously there are other conceivable sources of law besides moral argument and social sources; for example, aesthetic argument. The point is that moral argument and social sources are the only sources of law that anyone defends.

on the conditions or criteria of *legality*. It requires rather a constraint on modes of *identification*. The criteria of legality may also be employed as modes of identification, but they need not be.

That is the crucial point, and it is one that I have long emphasized in drawing distinctions among identification, validation, and existence conditions. The rule of recognition sets out validity or membership conditions. It may, but need not, serve an epistemic role; it may, but need not, provide the vehicle through which individuals identify the law and its content. If law is to be capable of being an authority, there must be some way of identifying it and its content without recourse to morality; but there is no reason why that vehicle must be the rule of recognition, and no reason, therefore, why the rule of recognition should not be capable of imposing morality conditions, even as sufficient conditions of legality. (Of course, this conclusion is quite general, and bears on necessity clauses as well.)[12]

Does this secure the consistency of inclusive legal positivism and the theory of authority? It might be argued that it does not. The argument is this. If law is to have authority, it must be possible that the law be in principle identifiable without recourse to moral argument about what it should be. Since law's claim to authority covers all those to whom it is directed or applies, law must in principle be identifiable by each person over whom the law claims authority without recourse to moral argument about what it should be. This condition cannot be met by a rule of recognition that incorporates morality as a sufficient condition of legality, however. For even if everybody else learns the law by asking the "legal–moral expert", the expert himself cannot learn the law without engaging in moral reasoning about what the law should be. Therefore, it is not true for him that he can learn the law in the appropriate way. Thus, such a rule of recognition would be incompatible with the epistemic constraints imposed by the theory of authority. Only a rule of recognition in which the conditions of legality are social sources can satisfy the in-principle identifiability condition. Thus, the sources thesis is vindicated.

This is an intriguing argument, but, not, in the end, persuasive. Suppose I am the legal–moral expert who learns the law by investigating what the law should be. Strictly speaking, even for me, the law is something which is *in principle* determinable without recourse to moral argument about what it should be. The law is that sort of thing. It is just that *as it happens*, that is not how I determine what the law is, because as it happens, I am the expert. This

---

[12] The argument from authority concerns the criteria by which those to whom the law is directed determine what the law is; it does not concern the criteria by which the law is made determinate. In other words, the argument from authority bears on matters of identification, not validation. The rule of recognition, in contrast, sets forth criteria of validity. This is just the difference between the criteria that make something *determinate* and those that bear on *determining* that something is of that sort: the difference between existence and epistemic conditions.

does not entail that the law is not in principle identifiable for me without my engaging in the prohibited form of reasoning: in principle, somebody else could be the expert. The fact that someone has to be the expert does not mean the law is the kind of thing that cannot, in principle, be identified by each person over whom the law claims authority without appealing to the underlying moral justification of the law.

It might be objected that while it is true that the law is in principle iden- tifiable by each person over whom the law claims authority without her having to engage in moral argument about what it should be, it does not appear to be the case that every person over whom the law claims authority can in fact identify the law in that way. Someone will have to engage in the prohibited moral argument. Thus, even if the law is in principle capable of being identified without recourse to moral argument about what it should be, the law cannot in fact be identified by everyone in this way.

It is not obvious why that should matter if the constraint imposed by the theory of authority is that the law can in principle be identified without recourse to moral argument about what it should be. The law can in prin- ciple be so identified by everyone, even if it cannot in fact be so identified. Without further argument, this point seems uninteresting.

The objection might be pursued in the following way, however.[13] First, we need to draw a distinction between something being an authority and its being a successful authority. For the law to be a successful authority for a given individual, she must have identified its content without recourse to the dependent reasons that it replaces. Otherwise the rule would fail to mediate between her and the dependent reasons that apply. The idea is that a particular law may be an authority in the sense of being capable in prin- ciple of mediating between reasons and persons, but may fail nevertheless in practice to perform that role. A rule that is an authority for everyone may nonetheless not be a successful authority for a given individual at a given time. Any time someone learns what the law is by consulting the reasons that it purports to replace, then the law is not a successful authority for that person—even if the law is as much an authority for her as for everyone else to whom it is directed. Thus, there is a kind of agent-relativity in the idea of successful authority that is not part of the concept of authority itself. Presumably law can be an authority over all those to whom it purports to apply without being *successful* with respect to all of them.

So one thing an exclusive legal positivist could argue is that the law must in principle be capable of being a successful authority for everyone. The need for a legal–moral expert precludes the law from performing a mediat- ing role for everyone. Thus, whenever a rule of recognition makes morality

[13] I am not sure that this is the kind of argument that Raz would advance in response. It was suggested to me in a very illuminating, helpful, and fruitful exchange with Ruth Chang, and she believes that it is the kind of response Raz would make. The argument is, in any case, worth pursuing on its own merits.

a sufficient condition of legality, there will be at least one person for whom the law cannot, even in principle, serve as a successful authority.

The exclusive legal positivist should now be understood as maintaining that the law must be the sort of thing that at least in principle is capable of being a successful authority for everyone to whom it is directed. It looks as if an inclusive rule of recognition cannot satisfy this requirement. Indeed, only a rule of recognition that satisfies the sources thesis can. Thus, properly understood, the theory of authority entails the sources thesis.

Even this argument won't do the trick of undermining inclusive legal positivism, however. If we accept that in order for law to be capable of being an authority it must be capable of being a successful authority for everyone, there is no reason to think that this requirement cannot be satisfied by an inclusive rule of recognition.[14] Consider such a rule for some political domain, say, the United States. If the rule incorporates morality as a sufficient condition of legality, that means that at least one person must identify its content by appeal to the moral considerations about what law ought to be. But there is no reason to suppose that that person must be someone over whom the law of the United States claims authority. In deference to my friend Frances Kamm, let me suppose that the legal–moral expert is a Swede. The law could not serve the mediating role for the Swede; but then again, it does not claim authority over the Swede. So every individual over whom the law claims authority could learn the law from the Swede. Thus, it would in fact be true that the law is a potentially successful authority over all those to whom its authority is directed.

One response to this objection is that it is not enough to learn the law from the Swede, who is a social source. One must, in principle, be capable of learning the law from the law's source, that is, from the rule of recognition. That response simply begs the question. It has the consequence of entailing the sources thesis; but why must it be the case that one must be able to learn what the law is from the rule of recognition? Almost no one ever does; and the authority of a law does not depend on how one learns what the law is or what its content is, but on how the law can affect one's deliberations. How one learns the law or its content matters only in so far as that bears on its capacity to mediate between persons and reasons. Any other constraint is unmotivated by the theory of authority.[15]

---

[14] I will use this expression in the present discussion to mean a rule of recognition that incorporates morality as a *sufficient* condition of legality.

[15] May I add, the claim that the theory of authority entails that law must have the capacity to be a successful authority for everyone seems to me completely unmotivated. It is not clear why it should be inadequate to say that something can be an authority provided: (1) its identity and content is in principle determinable without recourse to moral argument about what it should be; and (2) it can in principle be a successful authority for at least one person. It wouldn't make any sense for the law to claim authority if it could not succeed even for one person; but if it could succeed as an authority for one person, then the claim is perfectly intelligible. In any case, as I have just argued, there is no reason to think that an inclusive rule of recognition could not satisfy even this unmotivated constraint.

Consider one final objection a Razian might have to my efforts to render the Razian theory of authority compatible with inclusive legal positivism. The key to this objection is the claim that in order for law to be an authority, its directives must be graspable as authoritative directives by those subject to them. According to the objection, this implies that no matter how one actually learns what the law is, one could have learned it directly—that is, from its source—because to do so is what it means to experience the law as an authoritative directive. In principle this is something one could do for all legal rules validated by source-based criteria of legality. It is not something one could do for legal rules valid under an inclusive rule of recognition, since in determining what the law is under such a rule, the subject of the directive would be engaging in just the sort of deliberations that vitiate the law's claim to authority.

This line of response is reminiscent of the argument I have been considering to the effect that law can be an authority only if it is capable in principle of being a successful authority for all those individuals at whom it is directed. The point of each objection is to motivate the requirement that one be able to identify the law without recourse to moral arguments about what it should be. In the first objection, the inability to do so implies that the rule cannot mediate between reasons and persons. In the present objection, failure of a cludes one's being able to experience the norm as an authoritative directive.

The objection fails, however. Since it is not true as a general rule that in order to be an X, something must be graspable or experienceable as an X, we might require that some reason be given for thinking that for a directive to be authoritative it must be graspable as such. Even granting that, there seems to be no reason to suppose that it is a necessary condition of grasping or experiencing a directive as authoritative that one be able to identify it as a directive by its source. Even if being able to do so is a *sufficient* condition for being able to experience a rule as an authoritative directive—and there are ample reasons of doubting that it is—it is surely not a *necessary* condition for experiencing a directive as authoritative. Recall that directives are authoritative in Raz's sense *not* in virtue of how they are created, but in terms of how they are to figure in practical deliberations. Authoritative directives preempt the dependent reasons they replace. It follows rather straightforwardly that as long as someone subject to a directive can treat the law's directives as preemptive reasons in his deliberations about what to do, he is capable of grasping or experiencing them as authoritative directives. Thus, it simply does not follow that in order to grasp or experience a law as an authoritative directive, one must be able to identify it as a directive by its source. It is enough to be able to employ it in one's deliberations in just the way authoritative directives must be capable of figuring.[16]

---

[16] I would have thought that to experience a legal directive as authoritative is to act for the reason the directive provides for the reason that the law provides it.

The exclusive legal positivist does not claim that the rule of recognition must be an epistemic rule any more than I do. What the exclusive legal positivist claims is that because the rule of recognition (on his understanding of it) sets out a sources test of legality, it is always possible for the law and its content to be identifiable without recourse to moral argument by consulting the rule of recognition. The debate between inclusive and exclusive legal positivists, on my reading of it, is not about whether the rule of recognition must serve an epistemic function; nor is it about the ways in which, as an empirical matter, ordinary folks come to learn the law of their community. Neither Raz nor I supposes that ordinary folks learn the law and its content by consulting the rule of recognition. Our disagreement concerns the constraints that the theory of authority imposes on the conditions of legality, not the constraints it imposes on the criteria of identification.

It has been said by some proponents of exclusive legal positivism that the argument I have just presented fails to take account of the fact that Raz's claims about the epistemic role of the rule of recognition have implications that are conceptual, and thus which bear on the criteria of legality. It is a conceptual point that the law must be able to make a practical difference by mediating between reasons and persons. I have simply failed to note the fact that Raz's argument is conceptual, not epistemic. I am always baffled when I hear this sort of objection; but perhaps a few disclaimers will help to resolve the confusion. I nowhere deny that Raz's argument from authority is designed to make a conceptual point about the nature of law—namely, that law must be the sort of thing that is capable of making a practical difference by mediating between reasons and persons. I have allowed even that the theory of authority imposes certain epistemic constraints. I have *argued*—not assumed—that this conceptual claim about law entails no constraints on the conditions of legality. Raz's argument from authority takes as a conceptual claim that law must be capable of legitimate authority, and it purports to derive from it constraints on the criteria of legality. I have argued that those constraints follow only if the criteria of legality are also criteria of identification. The entire point of my distinction between ontological and epistemic uses of the rule of recognition is aimed at showing that the conceptual claim about law entails a kind of "sources thesis" as a constraint on identification only, and not on legality, whereas the point of Raz's argument was that it imposed constraints on legality conditions.

The dialectic between Raz's theory of authority and inclusive legal positivism is, I believe, a fertile and illuminating one. It forces us to confront the deepest issues concerning the role of morality in our legal discourse, and reveals what is really at stake in the difference between the two main branches of positivism. I do not pretend that Raz or other defenders of his theory of authority will have no further response to my argument, or that all the deep issues here have been laid out in plain view. I do wish to note in conclusion, however, that the debate has been prosecuted entirely on Raz's home ground. I have granted his theory of authority in order to argue that it is consistent with inclusive legal positivism. But even if the two turned out not to be consistent, inclusive legal positivism would remain a coherent and tenable position. It would be coherent for the simple reason that it is not wedded to Raz's theory of authority. And it would be tenable because that theory of authority is by no means uncontroversial.

Indeed, I am inclined to be suspicious of it on a number of counts. First, I am not convinced that it is a conceptual feature of law that it necessarily claims *morally* legitimate authority. The fact that law can serve a variety of legitimate human interests may ground the claim that law must be the sort of thing that can possess a normative power to create genuine duties and responsibilities or confer genuine rights and privileges. From this it hardly follows that that normative power represents a moral authority.

Secondly, I am not convinced that legal authority must function exactly as Raz says it does, namely by preempting the reasons that justify a law. I hardly mean to deny that laws can, or even that some do, function as authoritative directives in that way; but the authority of law may sometimes lie elsewhere, for example in its making clearer what the demands of morality are. In general, it does not seem necessary that every law must be authoritative in the same way.

Finally, granting that as a conceptual matter law must claim authority of some sort, I am not convinced that this is best understood as meaning that each law must be able to make a practical difference in our reasoning about what to do. Of course a legal system as a whole must be capable of serving valuable human interests. It may very well do so through rules the vast majority of which can and do guide conduct by offering reasons. Still it is not obvious that as a conceptual matter all rules—in order to qualify as law—must be capable of guiding conduct, let alone of doing so in just the way Raz's theory claims they do.

Lecture Ten—
Practical Difference

Law can promote valuable human interests, and in doing so can serve a variety of legitimate aims. One of Hart's important claims is that what is distinctive about law is that it promotes these aims through rules that guide conduct by offering reasons for action (many of which are duties). Raz's theory of authority, discussed in the previous lecture, is the leading account of the way in which law purports to guide conduct by reasons. One element of his account is that the reasons law purports to create replace the dependent reasons that go to the merits of the law, and that otherwise apply to those governed by law. On that basis, Raz argues that inclusive legal positivism must be rejected, because a norm that is law in virtue of its moral merits cannot guide conduct without requiring those to whom it is addressed to evaluate its merits by consulting the reasons it is supposed to replace. Requiring that would vitiate law's claim to authority. Against this line of argument, I have suggested that it does not follow from the fact that a norm can be law in virtue of its substantive merits that those to whom the law is addressed must have recourse to substantive moral argument about its merits to identify or to be guided by it.

One need not embrace all the particulars of Raz's view to be sympathetic to the underlying claim that law is the kind of thing that must be capable of guiding conduct by reasons. At a very general level, we might say that if a law is to be capable of guiding conduct, it must be able to make a practical difference as law: that is, a difference in the structure or content of the practical deliberations of those to whom the law is directed. Call this the "practical difference thesis".[1] Raz's account of legal authority would then be one way of formulating the practical difference thesis. Even if, as I suggested in the previous lecture, inclusive legal positivism were compatible with the Razian account of authority, it might yet fail to be compatible with other formulations of the practical difference thesis.

In a recent article Scott Shapiro argued that rules valid under an inclusive clause of a rule of recognition cannot guide conduct, in the sense that they cannot make a practical difference. If in order to be law a rule must be capable of guiding conduct, rules validated by inclusive clauses cannot be real laws. Or if they are laws, it cannot be the case that law necessarily has a guidance function. In either case, inclusive legal positivism is incompatible

[1] This is a "working" formulation of the practical difference thesis. It is made more precise later in this lecture.

with law's having a necessary guidance function.[2] In developing the argument, Shapiro draws a distinction, which he finds implicit in Hart, between *epistemic* and *motivational* guidance. "Someone is motivationally guided by a legal rule when his or her conformity is motivated by the fact that the rule regulates the conduct in question . . . To be motivated to conform to a legal rule by the rule itself is to believe that the rule is a legitimate standard of conduct and to act on [that] belief."[3] In contrast, "a person is epistemically guided by a legal rule when the person learns of his legal obligations from the rule . . . It is not necessary that the agent be motivated to follow the rule *because* of the rule".[4]

Shapiro notes that in Hart's account legal rules provide epistemic guidance by mediating between rival standards of conduct. "*Qua* law, they eliminate the problems that arise when nonofficials must answer all normative questions and resolve all social controversies by themselves."[5] We live amidst rival views about what ought to be done—conflicting standards, each claiming to express some aspect of how we ought to organize our affairs with one another. One thing the law does is to mark a certain set of these standards with the authoritative designation "law". That designation picks out the standards with which we must comply.

The difference between epistemic and motivational guidance is helpful in illuminating Hart's distinction between primary and secondary rules. As we saw in Lecture 7, the internal point of view is an existence condition for the rule of recognition. But to say that officials adopt the internal point of view toward the rule of recognition is (at least) to say that they are motivationally guided by it. Necessarily, they take the rule as their reason for acting. By contrast ordinary folk need not necessarily take the internal point of view toward the laws valid under the rule of recognition. They may do so; but the primary function of these subordinate rules is epistemic guidance. This means that their bearing the mark "law" should be enough to pick them out as the rules with which one must comply.

The practical difference thesis interprets the thought that law matters in our practical lives. As Shapiro understands it, the practical difference thesis implies that in order to be a law, a norm must be capable of guiding conduct either motivationally or epistemically. Primary rules valid under a rule of recognition must be capable of epistemic guidance. The rule of recognition itself must be capable of motivational guidance. But what test can we apply

[2] Scott Shapiro, "On Hart's Way Out" *Legal Theory* 4/4 (Dec. 1989) 469–507.
[3] Ibid. 490.   [4] Ibid.
[5] In fact, Shapiro notes that legal rules serve two distinct epistemic mediating functions in Hart's account. In addition to mediating between rival standards, they also mediate between officials and nonofficials: "*Qua* rules, they eliminate the need for officials to issue particularized orders." However, the latter is not the kind of epistemic mediation that concerns us in this discussion.

to determine in a given case whether a rule is capable of guidance? The test Shapiro proposes is counterfactual:

To know whether a rule makes a practical difference, we must consider what would happen if the agent did not appeal to the rule. The rule makes a difference to one's practical reasoning only if, in this counterfactual circumstance, the agent *might* not conform to the rule. If, on the other hand, the agent were fated to conform to the rule even though he or she did not appeal to it, we would have to conclude that the rule does not make a practical difference.[6]

With these distinctions in hand, Shapiro argues that inclusive legal positivism is incompatible with the practical difference thesis. As we saw in the previous lecture, inclusive rules of recognition incorporate morality through either necessity or sufficiency clauses. In claiming that inclusive rules of recognition are incompatible with the practical difference thesis, Shapiro must therefore advance four arguments: one that establishes that rules valid under a sufficiency clause cannot guide motivationally; another establishing that such rules cannot guide epistemically; a third showing that rules whose morality is a necessary condition of their validity cannot guide motivationally, and finally a fourth to establish that such rules cannot guide epistemically. Let us take these in turn, beginning with clauses that make morality a *sufficient* condition of legality.

The possibility of such clauses is of special interest because they would accommodate in the most straightforward way Dworkin's observation that in at least some cases, certain moral principles are law and thus binding on officials *because* the principles express a dimension of justice or fairness. The question is whether a law valid in virtue of its morality could provide either epistemic or motivational guidance to those to whom it is addressed. Shapiro argues that it cannot.

First, he shows that if one is motivationally guided by an inclusive rule of recognition, then one cannot be motivationally guided by rules valid under its sufficiency clauses. Take an example of a rule of recognition in which the morality of a norm is thought to be a sufficient condition of its legality: "A rule is a legal rule provided it is a moral rule."[7] Rules that are law under such a rule of recognition purport to govern as law solely in virtue of being moral rules. At the same time, anyone who is guided by the relevant rule of recognition is *already* committed by reason to acting in conformity with any moral rule; no particular rule of morality can add anything in the way of motivational guidance to what the rule of recognition itself provides.[8] Thus, rules valid under the relevant rule of recognition cannot motivationally

---

[6] Scott Shapiro, "On Hart's Way Out" 495–6.

[7] This rule is for illustration only. I nowhere ever suggest that such a rule is practicable; only that it is conceptually possible.

[8] Though particular rules can add greater specificity to what the rule of recognition requires.

guide those already guided by it. Since it is a condition of law's possibility that some group of individuals (officials) be motivationally guided by the rule of recognition, it follows that there is necessarily some group to whom the law is addressed and who cannot be motivationally guided by rules valid under a sufficiency clause. A nice way to sum up Shapiro's argument is to say that all the reasons for action given by rules validated by such a clause in the rule of recognition are already contained in the rule of recognition itself; because such rules cannot add any reason for action, they are not capable of motivationally guiding those whose reason for action is the rule of recognition.[9]

Rules valid under sufficiency clauses are not capable of epistemic guidance either. Epistemic guidance mediates among conflicting standards of conduct, all of which purport to demand conformity on the merits. The guidance is provided by an official marking that designates certain standards as those to which one must conform. This *authoritative marking* obviates the need to deliberate on the merits of competing norms. If we have to deliberate on the merits of competing norms in order to determine which standard bears the requisite mark, then the "mark" cannot serve its epistemic guidance function.

This does not mean that a legal norm valid under a sufficiency clause cannot guide conduct—simply that it cannot guide conduct in virtue of its *legality*. The norm can, however, guide conduct by its *content*. The important point, of course, is the practical difference thesis requires that a law be capable of making a practical difference *in virtue of its legality*. Since rules whose morality is sufficient for their legality are capable of providing neither motivational nor epistemic guidance *as law*, Shapiro concludes, they cannot make a practical difference.[10]

Shapiro's argument against the possibility of epistemic guidance by rules valid under a sufficiency clause applies equally to the possibility of epistemic guidance by rules valid under a necessity clause: in either case, the need to inquire into the merits of a norm in order to discern the mark of law defeats the mark's ability to mediate between conflicting norms. Again, laws valid under a necessity clause are not precluded from guiding conduct—but they are precluded from guiding conduct epistemically *as law*, that is, in virtue of their legality. This is an important point to which I shall soon return.

[9] Ordinary folk need not be guided by the rule of recognition, nor does the rule of recognition purport to govern their behavior. Still, there is nothing incoherent in an ordinary citizen treating the rule of recognition as her reason for action. In that case, rules valid under the rule of recognition cannot motivationally guide her behavior either.

[10] Strictly speaking, Shapiro has not shown that primary rules valid under an inclusive rule of recognition cannot motivationally guide conduct. He has shown only that they cannot guide those who are motivationally guided by the rule of recognition.

This leaves remaining the question whether rules valid under necessity clauses can guide motivationally. Here Shapiro cannot employ the same argument as the one he used to show that rules valid under a sufficiency clause cannot motivationally guide those already guided by the rule of recognition. In the case of sufficiency clauses, all the relevant reasons for acting that the subordinate rule could create are already contained in the rule of recognition. That follows from the fact that the sufficiency clause makes those very reasons the grounds of legality. In the case of necessity clauses, the moral reasons already captured in the rule of recognition need not capture all the reasons that would justify rules valid under it. That is a logical implication of the fact that such clauses state necessary conditions only. Thus, Shapiro needs a new argument to show that rules valid under a necessity clause could not guide motivationally.

Central to the argument he offers is Hart's claim that legal reasons for acting are content-independent and *peremptory*. In Hart's view, a law guides an individual motivationally when she complies with the law because it is the law, independent of its content and without deliberation on the merits of compliance. Rules valid under an inclusive clause that makes substantive morality a necessary condition of legality cannot be peremptory reasons in this sense. In order to act on the basis of the reason the rule provides, one would have to deliberate about the rule's substantive merits; and that vitiates its claim to being a peremptory reason for action. Again, the claim is not that such rules cannot guide conduct; rather, they cannot guide conduct in the way that legal rules must, on Hart's account, be capable of guiding conduct—as peremptory reasons. If Shapiro is right, inclusive legal positivism is incompatible with the practical difference thesis.[11]

Shapiro's objections to inclusive legal positivism are powerful, straightforward, and sustained. It is therefore no surprise that they have provoked a number of responses defending the compatibility of inclusive legal positivism with the practical difference thesis. Most of the respondents concede Shapiro's argument that sufficiency clauses in a rule of recognition are incompatible with the practical difference thesis, and focus instead on establishing the compatibility of that thesis with necessity clauses.[12] I have not been persuaded by the efforts I have seen, nor am I sympathetic to this strategy of defense, which has the unfortunate consequences of being inadequately motivated while conceding too much.[13] Of greater interest and promise are those efforts to respond to Shapiro that take him on at just those

---

[11] Or at least it is incompatible with any version of the practical difference thesis committed to legal reasons as peremptory reasons.

[12] See W. J. Waluchow, "Authority and the Practical Difference Thesis: A Defense of Inclusive Legal Positivism" *Legal Theory* 6/1 (Mar. 2000) 45–81; see also Matthew Kramer, "How Moral Principles can Enter into the Law" *Legal Theory* 6/1 (Mar. 2000) 83–108.

[13] See my essay "Constraints on the Criteria of Legality" and Lecture 8.

points where others are prepared to admit defeat. Working our way through at least some of these responses will, I believe, deepen our understanding of the issues.

I begin with Shapiro's argument that primary rules valid under sufficiency clauses cannot guide motivationally. What Shapiro shows is that such rules cannot motivationally guide all those who are also guided by the rule of recognition; notably (but not necessarily exclusively) judges. Against Shapiro, Kenneth Himma argues that the practical difference thesis does not require that a judge be capable of being guided by both a rule of recognition and rules valid under it.[14] Quite correctly, Himma notes that the practical difference thesis requires that all rules be capable of guiding those *to whom they are addressed*. He then argues that whereas the rule of recognition is addressed to officials, primary rules are addressed to ordinary folk. The rule of recognition must guide officials motivationally, while primary rules must be capable of guiding ordinary folk epistemically. There is no reason, Himma maintains, to think that an inclusive rule of recognition cannot guide judges motivationally, while at the same time validating primary rules that can guide ordinary folk epistemically.

A rule of recognition does two things. First, it makes determinate which rules bear the mark of legality. Second, it creates a duty for a certain class of individuals—officials—to evaluate conduct under the set of primary rules that bear that mark. Officials have a duty under the rule of recognition to evaluate conduct on the basis of the standards set forth in the rule of recognition. This is the sense in which the rule of recognition is addressed to judges, and not to ordinary folk. It imposes a duty on officials, but not on the rest of us.

While the rule of recognition is addressed to officials, the primary rules are addressed to ordinary folk. This is not to say that the primary rules have no impact on judicial behavior: they are, after all, the rules that judges must apply in evaluating conduct. When a judge adjudicates or evaluates conduct by primary rules, however, he conforms to his responsibilities under the rule of recognition. He does not, thereby, conform to the primary rules themselves—any more than does an ordinary citizen, in complying with the primary rules, thereby conform to the rule of recognition.

The first part of Himma's response, then, is to give content to and make plausible the claim that the rule of recognition is addressed to officials, whereas primary rules are addressed to ordinary folk. Himma then reasons: (1) The practical difference thesis requires that in order to be law a norm must be capable of guiding those to whom it is addressed. (2) The rule of recognition is addressed to officials, i.e. judges. (3) It must be capable of

---

[14] A really good example of this line of argument is to be found in Kenneth Einar Himma, "H. L. A Hart and the Practical Difference Thesis" *Legal Theory*, 6/1 (Mar. 2000) 1–43.

guiding them motivationally. (4) Primary rules valid under the rule of recognition are addressed to ordinary folk. (5) They must be capable at least of guiding them epistemically. (6) inclusive legal positivism is compatible with the practical difference thesis if the rule of recognition is capable of motivationally guiding officials and primary rules are capable of epistemically guiding ordinary folk.

Having thus identified ambiguities in Shapiro's formulation of the practical difference thesis, and having reformulated it, Himma goes on to argue that an inclusive rule of recognition can motivationally guide officials, while at the same time the primary rules valid under its inclusive clauses can epistemically guide ordinary folk. To see how the argument goes, consider again our old standby the inclusive rule of recognition: A norm is law if and only if it satisfies the demands of morality. The judge's duty under the rule of recognition is to evaluate conduct by its morality. Ordinary folk are required by law to act morally.

Understood in this way, the only constraint the practical difference thesis imposes on primary rules subordinate to the rule of recognition is that they be sufficiently clear and precise to allow ordinary folk to be guided by them and judges to evaluate conduct under them. Though morality is controversial, most moral requirements are not. Many people actually are guided by morality, so there is no reason to suppose that they cannot be guided by legal rules that are coextensive with the demands of morality. Similarly, we are generally capable of evaluating conduct as moral or immoral, and so there is no reason to suppose that judges will be incapable of evaluating conduct under laws possessing moral content. Thus, there is no reason to think that an inclusive rule of recognition cannot satisfy the requirements of the practical difference thesis, once that thesis is properly understood. Those who would deny that primary rules valid under an inclusive rule of recognition could epistemically guide conduct are simply too skeptical about morality, or otherwise overstate its controversiality.

The notion of epistemic guidance is difficult and we need to avoid a certain confusion about it. No one but the most skeptical among us—and neither Shapiro nor I are among them—denies that moral rules can guide conduct by their *content*. The problem is that the practical difference thesis requires that law be capable of guiding conduct in virtue of its *legality*. Epistemic guidance must be content-independent. That primary rules are clear and precise enough to guide by their *content* is irrelevant for these purposes. The real question is not whether legal rules that are valid in virtue of their moral content can guide conduct; rather, it is whether primary rules can guide epistemically in the sense the practical difference thesis claims they must—in virtue of their legality, and thus independently of their content. The point of epistemic guidance is to mediate among conflicting standards of conduct. The mark of legality is to signify which of the conflicting standards are legitimate, in the sense of being those to which individuals are to conform. The problem with an inclusive rule of recognition is that in order to determine which standards bear this mark, one must engage in deliberation about which standards are morally legitimate—precisely the kind of deliberation the mark of legality is supposed to make unnecessary. Epistemic guidance is not about clarity of content; it is about mediation by authoritative marking. If one has to deliberate in order to discern the marking, the mark cannot mediate, and thus cannot guide epistemically.

We need a different kind of argument to defend the claim that rules subordinate to an inclusive rule of recognition can nevertheless provide epistemic guidance. As long as ordinary folk can determine which norms bear the mark of legality without engaging in the prohibited form of deliberation, those rules can in principle guide them epistemically. The primary rules valid under inclusive clauses cannot epistemically guide those who consult the rule of recognition in order to determine which norms are law— in other words, those rules cannot guide officials; but if Himma is right, the primary rules are not addressed to officials, and so the fact that officials cannot be epistemically guided by them is of no moment. As long as ordinary folk can determine the law without needing to consult the inclusive rule of recognition, the rules that are addressed to them can guide them epistemically. But this possibility has already been secured by my response to the Razian objection in the last lecture: ordinary folks need not deliberate about the merits of a rule in order to determine that it is a binding legal rule. They need merely consult the Swede. If they do, the rule maintains its capacity to guide them epistemically. Shapiro's objection seems vulnerable to my distinction between criteria of validity and criteria of identification, and to the general line of argument I develop based on that distinction.

Suppose ordinary folk learn what the law requires of them not by consulting the inclusive rule of recognition, but by consulting the now infamous Swede. Recall that in my argument the Swede determines what the law is by consulting the rule of recognition itself. That rule is an inclusive rule in which whether or not something is law depends on its moral value or merits. Thus, the Swede must deliberate on the balance of reasons in order to know whether or not a norm is a law. The key to my argument was that even if this fact means that the rules valid under the rule of recognition cannot epistemically guide the Swede, there is no problem because they are not addressed to him because (we can assume) she lives and remains outside the jurisdiction.

I take it Shapiro's response would be this.[15] If the Swede determines which norms bear the mark of law (apropos Shapiro's objection) or what

---

[15] The present response was expressed by Shapiro in conversation. I do not know if it remains his considered view on the topic, but it is an illuminating response, whether or not he continues to defend it.

the balance of dependent reasons require (apropos Raz's) by deliberating on the moral merits of a norm, then the Swede—and not the rules valid under the rule of recognition—is the real practical authority. It is the Swede who mediates between reasons and persons, or who adjudicates between conflicting standards or norms; and that is what it means to be a practical authority. It is not the fact that a rule is "valid" under the rule of recognition that makes it law, but, rather, the fact that such a rule is judged by the Swede to express what the balance of reasons demands. The Swede, in other words, is not merely *reporting* what the law is; she is *determining* what the law is. The law is what the Swede says it is. Thus, we secure the possibility of guidance by, in effect, disabling the inclusive rule of recognition in favor of the Swede. To make matters worse for the inclusive legal positivist, the Swede— whatever else she may be—is a social source. If the Swede is the practical authority, then all those to whom the law is addressed determine its content and identity not by moral argument, but by appealing to a social source.

Shapiro is not claiming that whenever someone learns from someone else what the law is, the latter person is by that fact alone the actual practical authority. Shapiro's objection covers the special case in which the person from whom one learns the law must engage in substantive moral deliberations about a rule's underlying merits in order to determine whether a rule is valid law. Neither Shapiro's nor Raz's arguments require that individuals determine what the law is only by appealing directly to the rule of recognition. Rather, the rule of recognition must be the sort of thing that can guide *indirectly*, by making it possible for ordinary folk to determine what the law is by way of some authority-preserving chain of intermediary steps. Only rules of recognition that make legality depend on social sources can be authority-preserving. Any other kind of rule of recognition breaks the chain of authority by substituting the deliberator's authority for the rule of recognition's.

This line of argument, if sound, undermines the force of my now well-known and widely followed distinction between criteria of validation and identification. In doing so, it not only renders Shapiro's objections to inclusive legal positivism invulnerable to my response, it appears as well to save the Razian objection from the response I offered to it in the last lecture. I have not formed a settled judgment on the merits of what I take to be Shapiro's reply, but if I had no other response to Shapiro and Raz, I would be very worried indeed. However, there is a powerful avenue of defense open to an inclusive legal positivist, and to which I now turn.

If Shapiro and Raz are right, the conventionality thesis, the practical difference thesis, and inclusive legal positivism form an inconsistent set, and the only way to save the latter would be to abandon one of the others. Since the conventionality of the criteria of legality is the core of positivism, the only alternative would seem to be to abandon the practical difference thesis. In a previous essay I pursued this strategy in a tentative way, and sketched a version of inclusive legal positivism without the practical difference thesis.[16] However, I now believe that there is no need to abandon the practical difference thesis in order to save inclusive legal positivism.

Both Raz's and Shapiro's objections to inclusive legal positivism are based on an interpretation of its claims that is unsupported by the arguments they have so far presented. Instead of abandoning the claim that law must be capable of making a practical difference, all we need give up is the claim that this is a conceptual constraint on *each* law. Surely it does not follow logically that because *law* must be capable of being an authority, no norm can count as *a law* unless it is capable of being an authority in the requisite way; moreover, I see no good reason to accept the latter claim as a conceptual truth in its own right. In the remainder of this lecture I outline my view about the nature of the claim to authority law makes, and about the relationship of that claim to the constraints it might impose on particular legal norms.

Law is a human artifact. It is designed by humans, presumably because it can serve a variety of our interests. Many of these are legitimate—for example, allowing individuals to coordinate their activities with one another for mutual advantage; giving concrete institutional expression to principles of political morality while at the same time making more explicit what those principles require; and facilitating institutions that enable each individual to take responsibility for how his or her life goes. In so far as law can serve interests like these, it is in principle the sort of thing that is capable of possessing a normative power to confer rights and privileges and to impose genuine duties and responsibilities.[17] It doesn't follow that the duties and rights thereby created are necessarily moral rights, nor does it follow that having an authority to create rights and duties of this sort entails or requires moral legitimacy.

In saying that the rights and duties to which law can in principle give rise are genuine or real, I mean to say that even if they arise within the context of an institution, they are not tied to the institution in the way, for example, many of the rights and duties created by the rules of a game are—for example, the right a chess player has to move his piece in a certain way or the duty a tennis official has to call a ball that lands beyond the court "out". Legal duties arise in law, but they are duties that figure in our determination of what we ought to do generally and not just in our deliberations about what we ought to do in playing the game "law".

[16] That particular line of defense would not be available to Hart, whose version of positivism is the target of Shapiro's critique.

[17] I am not presenting a complete argument to support this claim. Some anarchists might deny it, but I regard it as plausible on its face.

Law necessarily claims a normative power to create genuine rights and obligations. That law is capable of being an authority in this sense is, in my view, a conceptual truth about law. It is a version of the claim that law guides conduct by providing reasons, distinct from Raz's interpretation of that claim (that law necessarily claims legitimate authority); and distinct as well from Shapiro's (that law must be capable of motivational or epistemic guidance). Having said that, my primary objection to both Raz and Shapiro is not that mine is the better account of how to interpret the claim to practical authority made on behalf of the law. The point I want to emphasize, rather, is that no matter how the general conceptual claim is best analyzed, it simply does not entail any claims about what must be true of any *particular* law. Law can claim authority in any of these senses without it following that a norm could not be law unless it was capable of being an authority in that sense. What is or must be true of *the law* need not be true of *a law*. Without further argument, the claim that each law must make a practical difference in order to be law seems to be an instance of the fallacy of composition.

It might be thought that, as a conceptual matter, each law must be able to make a practical difference because laws are a species of command. Commands are prescriptions to action and must be analyzed accordingly. Thus, commands are to be analyzed in terms of act guidance. Laws are commands and commands must in principle be capable of guiding conduct. This argument has the advantage of not relying on an apparently unwarranted inference from what must be true about law to what must be true about *each* law. The problem with this strategy, however, is that even if commands must be analyzed in terms of act guidance, not all laws are commands. This, of course, was one of Hart's great insights and the basis of many of his devastating objections to Austin. Rather than commanding action or forbearance from action, many laws confer powers, and in doing so articulate recipes individuals are to follow in order to give legal effect to their actions.

There thus remains a logical gap between what must be true about law, and what must be true about *each* law; and so far there appears to be no conceptual argument that would bridge that gap. I would like to suggest further that there is some reason for skepticism about its ever being bridged. The reason for skepticism is to be found in a consideration of the deeper aims of analytic jurisprudence, as Hart himself understood that enterprise.

The argument begins with a reassessment of one of Hart's most controversial claims. Hart notes not only that law can serve a variety of important and legitimate human interests, but that it does so in a distinctive manner: through rules that guide conduct. The vast majority of commentators understand Hart to claim thereby that guiding conduct by rules that create reasons is law's *essential function*. Seizing on this interpretation of Hart, Stephen Perry argues that it is contestable what law's function is, and that Hart has no option but to defend this claim on grounds of substantive political morality.[18] The choice apparently is to read Hart either as a metaphysical essentialist about law, or else as engaged in normative jurisprudence of a kind seemingly inimical to positivism. Neither option is attractive, of course. Hart is explicitly skeptical of all essentialist–functionalist projects, while the last claim an interpreter should want to give up about Hart's project is that it is thoroughly positivist.[19]

There must be a better way than this to read Hart, and Shapiro himself has been developing one. On this view, Hart is making neither a metaphysical claim about law's essential function, nor a normative claim that must be defended by invoking controversial moral premises. Rather, he is offering a kind of social-scientific explanatory hypothesis. What needs to be explained is why legal systems arise, why they persist, develop in the ways they do, and acquire the features or shape characteristic of what Hart regarded as their "mature" form. His explanatory hypothesis is roughly this: law serves a variety of human interests (that is part of the explanation of why they arise and persist) and does so through rules that guide conduct through reasons (that is part of the explanation of why they evolve in certain ways and have the shape they do in mature legal systems). If we posit law as an institution that serves human interests by rules that guide conduct, then we can explain why it exists and persists and how it responds or adapts to a variety of social and historical pressures and eventually comes to take a certain shape in mature legal systems. In other words, we can explain why, regardless of the diversity of their aims or purposes, the shape and structure of mature legal systems are similar in the ways Hart claims they are: that is, as consisting in primary and secondary rules, including especially a rule of recognition, rules of change, and rules of adjudication.[20]

It is this explanatory sociological project that animates the conceptual analysis and makes it continuous with the social sciences.[21] This is one interesting and particularly illuminating way in which we might come to understand Hart's claim that his project of analytic jurisprudence is a kind of descriptive sociology. On this reading, the claim that law must be capable of guiding conduct is not to be taken as a bare conceptual truth that is

[18] See Perry, "The Varieties of Legal Positivism."

[19] For further argument on this topic, see Lecture 12.

[20] Shapiro is especially drawn to this characterization of Hart's project and believes that it provides the best explanation, internal to the body of Hart's work, for the claim that law's function is to guide conduct.

[21] He hints at the argument in "On Hart's Way Out" and in "Law, Morality and the Guidance of Conduct" *Legal Theory* 6/2 (June 2000) 127–70. My characterization of the argument is drawn from several discussions with him about it.

discovered by reflecting a priori on our concept of law; nor is it merely a part of what I call our "folk theory" of the concept of law—our pretheoretical conception of the kind of thing law is or must be. And it is certainly not a moral–political claim about the best or proper function of law. Rather, the concept of law with which we are working is part of an explanatory picture that answers to a range of theoretical concerns as central to social science as they are to philosophy. Positing law as conduct-guiding and reason-giving is part of an explanation of why law exists, persists, and takes the shape it does in its mature form.

It might be thought that viewing the concept of law in the light of this kind of social-scientific explanatory project provides just the sort of resource needed to bridge the gap between what must be true about law and what must be true about each law. In any case, the argument for the claim that each law must be able to guide conduct need no longer be made on a priori conceptual grounds; instead, it could perhaps be defended by an argument of a more general holistic kind, to the effect that such a constraint might figure in the best explanation or picture of law's existence, persistence, evolutionary pattern, and shape.

In fact, I believe these kinds of considerations cut the other way. Even if the best explanation of the existence, persistence, and shape of law involves positing guidance through rules as the function of law, it is not obvious why each rule must be conceived of as contributing to the guidance function in the same way. Traditional functional explanations of systems—biological or other—do not suppose that every component part of the system contributes to the overall function in the same way.

Absent a reason to think otherwise, I reject the claim that in order to be law a rule must be capable of making the kind of practical difference law itself must be capable of making. If I am right, there is no reason to worry about the compatibility of inclusive legal positivism and the practical difference thesis. This makes the strategy of retreat advocated by certain inclusive legal positivists even less appealing than it might otherwise be. No positivist need accept the practical difference thesis in a form that creates problems for inclusive legal positivism.

There remains, however, the question of whether inclusive rules of recognition are compatible with *law's* (rather than every particular law's) capacity for practical authority. Here I see no obstacles. Giving concrete institutional expression to a shared political morality is surely among the legitimate ends law might serve. A rule of recognition for such a legal system might well have an inclusive clause—in which the morality of the norm would be a condition of its legality—as a way of insuring that legal practice embodied moral ideals. Legal rules under such a rule of recognition would render explicit the demands of political morality, or would see to it that otherwise source-based rules were not inconsistent with those demands. There is no reason to think that such a legal system could not possess a normative power to create rights and impose duties; this, in spite of the fact that if either Raz or Shapiro is right, at least some rules valid under the rule of recognition would be incapable of guiding conduct as law, or constituting a practical authority.

In rejecting the familiar, strong version of the practical difference thesis I am not denying that the law as a whole must be capable of making a practical difference, nor am I denying that most laws govern by creating reasons for actions. I accept that the distinctive feature of law is that it serves the interests it does by guiding conduct through rules that create reasons. I am denying only that a rule cannot be a legal rule unless it is capable of making a practical difference. Moreover, without that premise the view I have defended of law, its fundamental conventionality, and the role of morality within it is fully consistent with any plausible understanding of law's role in our practical lives.

In maintaining that norms valid under an inclusive rule may be law despite their not being able to guide conduct, I have emphasized that they may serve the role of embodying political morality and making its demands more explicit. They cannot independently guide as rules by creating reasons, but they can make more concrete the requirements imposed by the reasons in the inclusive clauses. In this sense, legal rules may not necessarily guide conduct, but they can, and often do, elaborate and make more concrete the demands of more abstract moral principles. That of course was one of the claims advanced in Part I of this book. The view I have defended about how to think about tort law in relationship to both corrective justice and fairness is of a piece with my jurisprudence.

In this part of the book I have defended a version of inclusive legal positivism according to which the morality of a norm can be a condition of its legality. Time and again I have advanced the view that the law can legitimately give expression to a shared political morality. This could give the impression that I am not a positivist at all—but a good old-fashioned natural lawyer instead. Any such impression is of course mistaken. In defending inclusive legal positivism, I am not maintaining that law is *necessarily* the institutional embodiment of political morality. As I emphasized in Lecture 8, inclusive legal positivism accommodates a range of possible roles that moral principle can play in legal practice. It does not assert that law *must* embody morality; nor that when law does embody morality, it must do so in virtue of a clause in the rule of recognition making morality a condition of legality. Finally, inclusive legal positivism is not committed to the view that Anglo-American legal practice must be explained in terms of an inclusive rule of recognition. It leaves open a wide range of possible ways of accounting for that practice. The point is that a positivist gets to be an inclusive legal positivist for free.

The central claim of this part of the book is that legal authority is to be explained in terms of a social convention. That is the distinctively positivist commitment at the root of the position I have been articulating. As it turns out, that commitment is consistent with the possibility of the law's embodying political morality; it is also consistent with the law's failing to do so. While fully committed to the conventionality of the criteria of legality, I have argued that legal positivism imposes no additional constraints on those criteria. If this means that some legal rules are incapable of guiding conduct, we need infer neither that the law lacks authority nor that the rule of recognition that makes law possible is itself incapable of imposing duties on officials.

Part Three

The Methodology of Jurisprudence

Lecture Eleven—
Legal Content, Social Facts, and
Interpretive Practice

It is common to characterize legal positivism in terms of two basic tenets: the social fact thesis and the separability thesis. Of the two, the separability thesis is more familiar, more closely associated with positivism, and more contested—all of which strikes me as somewhat mystifying. The separability thesis is the claim that there is no necessary connection between law and morality. Interpreted as a claim about the relationship between substantive morality and the content of the criteria of legality, the separability thesis asserts that it is not necessary that the legality of a standard of conduct depend on its moral value or merit.[1] Thus, the claim it makes is true just in case a legal system in which the substantive morality or value of a norm in no way bears on its legality is conceptually possible. The truth of this claim seems so undeniable as to render it almost entirely without interest; the claim it makes so weak, no one really contests it.[2]

If the separability thesis is thought to be controversial, that is because it is often mischaracterized or confused with a different claim. On one mistaken interpretation, the separability thesis denies that legal validity can depend on the practices of conventional morality, or on the moral beliefs of officials. This is an odd claim to associate with positivism. That people treat this or that sort of conduct as right or morally obligatory is an empirical fact about them. Positivism should not be interpreted as denying that the legality of standards of conduct could depend on empirical facts of any sort. If legal positivism denies anything, it denies that legality must depend on what *is* right or obligatory, not on what people believe or treat as right or obligatory.

Others interpret the claim that law and morality are not necessarily connected as the claim that they are necessarily not connected. This is just the difference between external and internal negation in the modal context, which is, of course, all the difference in the world. The separability thesis asserts that it is *not* the case that morality is *necessarily* a condition of legality, whereas the claim with which it is here confused asserts that *necessarily*

---

[1] Below I suggest an alternative interpretation of the separability thesis as a claim not about constraints on the content of the criteria of legality, but about the grounds of the criteria themselves. I hinted at this interpretation before, at the beginning of Lecture 7.

[2] The claim the separability thesis makes is, therefore, so weak that it is hard to see how it could represent a central tenet of positivism, let alone its most fundamental commitment. See "Negative and Positive Positivism".

morality is *not* a condition of legality. To be sure, many positivists defend
the latter, stronger claim; it is a corollary of the sources thesis—the distinctive claim of exclusive legal positivism. However, no one who defends the
claim that necessarily morality is not a condition of legality ever confuses it
with the separability thesis. Only positivism's critics—most notably among
them, Dworkin—make that mistake.

We cannot usefully characterize legal positivism in terms of the separability thesis, once it is understood properly, because virtually no one—
positivist or not—rejects it. Neither can we characterize positivism in terms
of the sources thesis or the corollary claim that necessarily morality is not
a condition of legality—because many positivists reject those claims. If
we are looking to characterize legal positivism as a distinctive and interesting jurisprudence we should focus instead on what I call the "social fact
thesis".[3] It makes an interesting claim about law, and it serves to distinguish positivists on the one hand from natural lawyers and interpretive
theorists of Dworkin's school on the other. Both of the latter reject the
social fact thesis, while positivists all accept it.

Whereas the separability thesis makes a claim about the *content* of the
membership criteria for law, the social fact thesis makes a claim about their
grounds, or *existence conditions*. It claims that the grounds of the criteria of
legality in every community that has law are a matter of social fact. Austin
provides a useful illustration of the difference between the content and the
grounds of the criteria of legality. Roughly, for Austin, law is the command
of the sovereign-properly-so-called. Having the property of being a command of a sovereign is both necessary and sufficient for legality, and thus
states the test or criterion of legality. The form of the criterion is invariant
across legal systems—wherever there is law, a norm is a law if and only if
it has the property of being a command of the sovereign. However, "the
sovereign" might be analyzed as a sort of elliptical indexical expression,
whose meaning could be "the sovereign here" or "the sovereign in that
jurisdiction". Thus, while the form of the criteria of legality is invariant, its
content varies across jurisdictions. What makes "being the command of
a sovereign" the criterion of legality in every community that has law are
certain *social facts*—specifically, the fact that there is general and habitual
obedience to the sovereign, who, in turn, is not in the habit of obeying
anyone else. These facts constitute the grounds, sources, or existence
conditions of the criteria of legality.[4]

Hart's view invokes an analogous distinction. In every community that
has law, the norms that are law are those that satisfy the criteria set forth in
the rule of recognition. The content of the criteria may vary with different

[3] Of which the conventionality thesis developed in Lecture 7 is a particular instance.
[4] Except for variations based on the delegation of sovereign powers to subordinates.

rules of recognition. However, that these are the criteria in a community depends on a set of social facts. The rule of recognition exists because it is practiced by the relevant individuals in the appropriate way (that is, accepted from an internal point of view by the bulk of officials).[5] These social facts are the grounds of the criteria of legality. Their existence does not depend, for example, on whether the norms that satisfy them contribute to human flourishing or enhance well-being; nor does it depend on whether the criteria themselves state requirements of justice or fairness. In the end their existence as criteria of legality in a given community depends only on their being adopted and practiced by the relevant officials.

The social fact thesis expresses the sense in which positivists are committed to the view that legality is ultimately a matter of fact, not value. In whatever form it takes—Austin's or Hart's, habits of obedience or conventional practices—it is the core claim of legal positivism. It cuts across all positivist positions—for example, it is shared by both exclusive and inclusive legal positivists. It is, moreover, distinctive and interesting in a way that the separability thesis is not. Both natural lawyers and Dworkinians can accept the separability thesis, properly understood; neither can accept the social fact thesis. Indeed, the claim that the criteria of legality in a particular community are conventional or that their existence as the criteria of legality for that community depends on their being practiced is thought by Dworkin to raise insurmountable difficulties for the positivist project.

Roughly, the objection is this. To say that a practice is conventional is to say that there exists a certain shared understanding of what it means to engage in it. There can be disagreements about whether this or that pattern of behavior is an instance of the practice, as well as disagreements about how the practice ought to proceed; but there can be no basic disagreement about what the practice is. Broad disagreement of this fundamental sort is incompatible with the conventionality of the practice. Where the practice is one of accepting and applying certain criteria as authoritative standards of legality, this objection is that if the criteria of legality are conventional, participants in the legal practice—especially judges governed by the rule of recognition that sets out the criteria—cannot meaningfully or coherently disagree about what the criteria are. They can only disagree from time to time about whether this or that norm satisfies the criteria; or they can disagree about what the criteria *ought* to be; how they should be revised. However (the objection continues), officials can and do disagree not only about what the criteria should be and whether this or that putative legal rule satisfies them; they disagree as well about what the criteria of legality

---

[5] This is what Hart means when he says that we do not ask whether a rule of recognition is valid; only whether it exists.

(or what Dworkin calls the "sources of law") *are*. This is, in any case, their face value understanding of the nature of their dispute. Any theory of law that treats those criteria as conventional—as positivism does—lacks the resources to explain the nature and scope of this pervasive aspect of judicial behavior.

The better account, Dworkin maintains, credits the judges' view that they can and do disagree sometimes about what the criteria of legality are. These conflicting views reflect, and are explained by, more fundamental disagreements about the point or purpose of the legal practice of evaluating conduct in the light of standards that meet the criteria—disagreements about the contribution to human well-being and social solidarity a system organized around these criteria makes, and so on. Because disagreement about what the criteria of legality are can be resolved only by substantive moral argument about the value, point, or purpose of law, what the criteria of legality in a particular community *are* depends in part on what they *ought* to be. In short, the foundation, grounds, or existence conditions of the criteria of legality are not a matter of social fact alone, but rest instead on controversial moral and political judgments about how to understand those facts. The criteria of legality depend not simply on how judges behave, but rather on the best *interpretation* of their behavior.

One cannot fully understand Dworkin's own project without appreciating that his most fundamental and enduring objections to positivism revolve around the various forms its commitment to the conventionality of law take. This is evident in his early argument that there is no conventional "master rule"—no rule of recognition in Hart's sense—for determining legal validity; and in his corollary complaint that even if there are conventionally accepted criteria of legality, not every legally binding norm or standard of conduct depends on that convention for its status as binding law—in particular, legally binding moral principles are not dependent in that way. It shows up again when, in response to me and others who pointed out that there is in principle no reason why a rule of recognition could not incorporate morality in its criteria of legality, he argues that such a rule would be controversial in a way that precluded its being a *conventional rule*; rather it would have to be what he calls a "normative" rule. At one time or another, then, he has argued (1) that there is no conventional master rule of recognition; (2) that the status of moral principles as legally binding need not depend on such a rule; (3) that if we tried to devise a rule that incorporated the validity of such principles, the rule would be controversial in a way that would preclude its being conventional. In short, Dworkin has long maintained that invoking the idea of a convention at the foundation of law—the very core of contemporary positivist thought—is neither necessary nor helpful to our understanding of important aspects of legality. Worse, it obscures our understanding of the nature and scope of disagreement in law while providing an inadequate explanation of the possibility of, and the extent to which there are, right answers to legal disputes.

The same themes recur, in a somewhat veiled form, in *Law's Empire*, where Dworkin introduces the notorious "semantic sting" argument. In their haste to dismiss that argument most commentators have failed to appreciate that properly understood, it is simply another version of Dworkin's objection to conventionalism. To be sure, the semantic sting argument of *Law's Empire* is riddled with philosophical confusions, and most positivists—including Hart—have rightly objected to it as yet another instance of Dworkin's mischaracterizing their project in an effort ultimately to discredit it. The semantic sting attributes to positivism two theses, neither of which any positivist holds or must hold. First, Dworkin claims that positivism purports to offer an analysis of the semantic content of the term "law". Second, he claims that the semantics to which the positivist is committed is "criterial". A semantic theory is criterial if it asserts that there are criteria for the proper application of any term, and that these criteria are shared by all those who grasp it. In analyzing the concept of law, that is, in recovering or determining its content, the positivist seeks to identify what the shared criteria of legality are.

Thus, the objection to positivism becomes an objection to criterial semantics. Unsurprisingly, the objection turns on the claim that criterial theories cannot account for the nature and scope of disagreement about the criteria for the proper application of the term or concept "law".[6] People who share the same criteria can disagree about whether a particular form of governance meets the criteria; this is largely an empirical or a quasi-empirical disagreement, and is resolvable in principle without either side arguing about what the criteria are. Those who share the same criteria for applying a concept can also disagree about whether and how to revise the concept. Dworkin even suggests that a criterial semanticist could allow that those who share the same concept of law could perhaps disagree at the margins of "law". However, they cannot, he claims, disagree about the criteria for properly applying the term "law", which apparently means they cannot disagree about the core of the criteria.[7] That is because, according to criterial semantics, to have the same concept is to have the same (or very nearly the same) criteria for applying it. Thus, the semantic sting argument expresses,

---

[6] For a very fine discussion—and one sympathetic to Dworkin's overall project—of the claim that Dworkin himself has a semantics of law, see Nicos Stavropoulos, *Objectivity in Law* (Oxford: Clarendon Press, 1996).

[7] A puzzling allowance, given that disagreements at the margins of "law" are, after all, still disagreements about the criteria for properly applying the term "law." (If not, what would distinguish the "marginal" disagreements from the quasi-empirical ones and the ones about how to revise the concept?)

though in a different context, the same objection as the one Dworkin levels against the conventionality of the rule of recognition and of the criteria of legality set forth in it. In the latter case, relying on a convention at the foundation of legality leaves positivism unable to explain disagreement about the content of the criteria of legality; in this case, relying on conventionally accepted or shared criteria for the application of the concept "law" leaves positivists unable to explain disagreement about what the proper criteria of application for the concept "law" are.

Though the objection is essentially the same in both cases, Dworkin employs it to significantly different effect. The argument against the conventional rule of recognition is designed to support an interpretive account of the sources of law (the criteria of legality), and aims to show that "legality" is an interpretive concept. Because we can disagree about what the criteria of legality are, what they are cannot be a matter of convention; rather, what they are depends on the best interpretation of our practice of evaluating conduct in the light of standards binding on officials. By contrast, the semantic sting argument is designed to support a view about how legal philosophy *itself* must proceed. Analysis of our concept of law—the distinctively philosophical approach to explaining it—cannot be a *descriptive activity* of identifying the shared criteria of application for the term "law". Instead, the distinctive philosophical account of law is *interpretive*, and thus normative; it is an effort to provide the best interpretation of our linguistic practices of applying the concept of law. Legal philosophy— jurisprudence—is thus a branch of political philosophy. The sources-of-law argument is supposed to establish the claim that the concept of legality is an interpretive concept; the semantic sting argument is supposed to establish the very different claim that legal philosophy or jurisprudence is itself an interpretive activity.

At every important stage in the development of his own views, Dworkin has found it helpful to characterize positivism in some conventionalist terms, and to contrast his view accordingly. It is against the backdrop of this attribution and in contrast to it that he develops the distinctive claims that characterize his mature thesis: that what the law is, in any particular community, is not entirely a matter of social fact, but is at bottom a matter of moral argument; and that the activity of legal philosophy—or jurisprudence —is itself a branch of first-order moral and political philosophy.[8]

Though the argument Dworkin offers to establish both claims is roughly the same, the response to each need not be. Let me address each of the arguments in turn. The problem with the semantic sting argument is that it mischaracterizes what individuals must share in order to have the same

---

[8] I will have occasion in Lecture 12 to consider the semantic sting argument along with others designed to defend so-called normative jurisprudence. So my remarks here are brief, and focus only on the semantic sting argument.

concept. Individuals can share the same concept if they agree, not on criteria of application, but on a set of paradigm cases or instances of the concept. These paradigm cases, in turn, are each in principle revisable, though they cannot all or nearly all be revised at the same time. As long as the majority of competent language users agree on a sufficient set of paradigm cases, they share the same concept.[9] Sharing a set of revisable paradigms does not entail that, in picking out the paradigms, individuals use the same criteria for applying the concept; and it certainly does not entail that all would formulate the criteria for applying the concept in the same way—if, indeed, they could formulate any criteria or rule at all. This means of course that sharing the same concept does not imply for a pragmatist—and need not imply for any positivist—sharing the same application criteria. This is a standard pragmatic view of what it means to share a concept, and there is no reason whatsoever why a positivist should not avail herself of it. I surely do.

Dworkin's other argument—what I call the sources-of-law argument—maintains that if the criteria of legality in a community are determined by a convention, then officials cannot disagree about what they are. By modus tollens, if officials can disagree about what the criteria are, then the criteria are not a matter of conventional practice. Dworkin takes this to imply that the criteria of legality must depend on the best interpretation of legal practice. Since officials can and do in fact disagree about what the criteria are, Dworkin concludes that legality is an interpretive concept.

The problem with the argument is that it relies on an inappropriate and misleading conception of the conventional practice of applying the criteria of legality. As I have argued in Lecture 7, the practice of applying criteria of legality is best conceived as a shared cooperative activity in Michael Bratman's sense. SCAs are familiar ways of coordinating interaction among persons over a period of time, and admit of fundamental and penetrating disagreement about how to continue the activity—and even about its basic ends or purposes. SCAs may be characterized as a framework for ongoing negotiation about the very content as well as the aims of the practices. If the rule of recognition governs a practice that is an SCA in this sense, a framework of coordination, planning, and negotiation, it is unsurprising that individuals engaged in such a practice would have a range of disagreements about what it requires of them, what its content is, how to resolve disputes about what its point is, and how to proceed. It is not surprising that in resolving such disputes, the parties offer conflicting conceptions of the practice in which they jointly participate, conceptions that appeal to differing ideas of its point or function. In doing so, they may make substantive

---

[9] This is true even if the set of paradigm cases shifts over time—as often it is likely to do for some concepts.

moral arguments—all framed, however, by the nature of the SCA. Never-theless, the sense in which the SCA is conventional is plain. Its existence does not depend on the arguments offered on its behalf, but rather on its being practiced—on the fact that individuals display the attitudes con-stitutive of shared intentions.

Officials can and do disagree about the content of the criteria of legality; they may believe there can be obligations even in the face of disagreement, and that such disputes are resolvable by substantive moral argument. That all this is true of the practice of officials is perfectly compatible with the rule of recognition regulating a conventional social practice, and thus with the rule of recognition being a conventional rule. There is no good reason to believe that the criteria of legality are not conventional. The problem is not with the claim that the criteria of legality are conventional, but with various cramped and inadequate analyses of how to understand that claim.

In addition to enabling us to identify precisely the battleground between positivists and natural lawyers, switching the focus from the content of the criteria of legality to their existence conditions or grounds allows us to identify what is distinctive about Dworkin's position. It allows us as well to identify similarities between his position and positivism, on the one hand, and between his position and the natural lawyers on the other.

In denying that the criteria of legality are conventional, Dworkin main-tains that what the criteria of legality are in a particular community is determined not by its legal practice, but rather by the best interpretation of that practice. Interpretation is a normative activity, and the norms appro-priate to interpreting a practice of evaluating conduct or resolving disputes in ways that are subject to coercive enforcement—the practice of law—are moral and political norms. In this sense, like natural lawyers, Dworkin holds that in the end legality is to be understood in terms of moral and polit-ical theory, not social facts. This is the sense in which Dworkin is, at least with regard to this fundamental issue, a natural lawyer.

On the other hand, for the typical natural lawyer, the possibility of legal authority is to be explained in terms of regulative moral ideals that exist apart from, and are logically prior to, legal institutions—moral ideals that are typically thought to derive from a robust metaphysical view of human nature or from God. Nothing Dworkin says relies on a robust metaphysics of human nature, of course[10]—nor is his argument in any way theistic. Indeed, his position is, in a significant sense, practice-centered. Although

[10] This is not to say that Dworkin relies on no metaphysics of the person at all. For example, his claim that the appropriate norms for interpreting a coercive practice are moral norms would appear to depend on the (relatively thin and uncontroversial) metaphysical view that persons are by nature the sorts of things that should not be subject to, for example, arbitrary coercion. Metaphysical commitments of some sort are difficult to avoid; the issue here con-cerns the robustness of the metaphysics to which one appeals.

he rejects the positivist claim that the criteria of legality in a community are just those that are practiced by the relevant officials, Dworkin does not, for example, claim that the criteria of legality are those which are morally speaking the best, the most just, or the most likely to contribute to human flourishing. Rather, the criteria of legality in any community are those that fall out of the best interpretation of that community's *legal practice*. In this sense, Dworkin's account is practice-centered in a way that has misled many to see him as no more than a nicely dressed-up positivist.

In fact his is a distinctive position. Against the positivist and like the natural lawyer, Dworkin denies that the possibility of legal authority is a matter of social fact. On the other hand, against the natural lawyer, and like the positivist, he maintains that the criteria of legality in a community are not simply a matter of moral or political argument, but a matter of (interpreted) practice, and thus, in the end, a matter of the practices of interpretation. Thus, in objecting to the positivist, Dworkin never denies the centrality of practice to determining the criteria of legality.

We have focused a good deal on Dworkin's objections to legal positivism to the exclusion of the natural law position; let us remedy that. It has struck many natural lawyers that the problem with legal positivism is that it seeks to explain the normative concept of legal authority in terms of some set of social facts. But, they contend, one cannot derive an "ought" from an "is" and so, to put the matter crudely, legal positivism engages in the naturalistic fallacy by attempting to derive law's "ought" from some set of social facts.

It is an open question whether the so-called naturalistic fallacy is a fallacy at all, but that issue need not detain us. In fact, positivism is in no way committed to *deriving* law's "ought" from social facts, and so the charge that positivists engage in the naturalistic fallacy is misplaced. The naturalistic account that positivism provides by explaining law in terms of social facts does not entail any particular moral ontology of the duty that law can create; rather the naturalistic account is just supposed to show how, by appealing to social facts alone, we can see that law is in the same boat with a lot of other practices that we normally suppose are capable of creating reasons and duties. Positivism seeks to show that the way in which law can give rise to duties is no more—*and no less*—mysterious than the way in which promises, pacts, reciprocal expectations, and so on can create duties. The ontology of the duties that inhabit this class of practices is not a *special* problem for legal theory, but is rather in the provenance of meta-ethics. In so far as positivism is not wedded to any particular meta-ethical view or moral ontology, it cannot be accused of the naturalistic fallacy.

This very same approach to legal philosophy is apparent in my discussion of the claim that the rule of recognition is a duty-imposing rule. In claiming that the rule of recognition can create duties, I argue that it is important to recognize the practice it governs as a Shared Cooperative Activity. SCAs display a normative structure that enables us to show that law is a special case of a familiar class of reason- or duty-creating human activities or practices. The broader class includes pacts, promises, conventions, and SCAs (among others). All of these kinds of practices are "natural" phenomena, at least in the sense that they can be characterized without any appeal to moral facts; but the question of *how* these familiar kinds of activities give rise to duties—that is to say, the question of the nature or ontology of those duties—is a question for meta-ethics. From the standpoint of legal theory, these practices *just are the kinds of things that create duties, or that we generally suppose do so*: they are the sorts of practices for which we seek or need a meta-ethics, the kinds of things for which a meta-ethics is apt.

It is not the primary burden of a jurisprudential theory to explain how duties can be created by law.[11] What needs explanation is something else altogether, the possibility of *claiming* to impose such duties as law. We turn to a philosophical theory to make the normative language of the law *intelligible* to us. A jurisprudential theory succeeds on this account if it has the resources available to make sense of the important normative concepts of legal discourse while explaining how legal authority is possible.[12]

Thus, conceiving of the rule of recognition as an SCA provides the only kind of philosophical explanation that we have a right to demand with respect to the question of "how" a rule of recognition can be a duty-imposing rule. There is nothing else that needs to be done to defend either the social fact thesis—the claim that legal authority is made possible by social facts—or the claim that the rule of recognition can be a duty-imposing rule.[13]

---

[11] The general meta-ethical problem might be solved naturalistically, theistically, via some form of Kantian constructivism, or by appeal to a class of autonomous moral facts. We might be cognitivists or noncognitivists about the issue, and so on. In fact, it is perfectly compatible with positivism that law never succeeds—as law—in imposing any duties whatsoever.

[12] Many theories might succeed on this score; importantly, not all theories can. Thus, as Hart argues, sanction-based theories simply lack the resources to allow us to make out the differences between being obliged and being obligated.

[13] I am not claiming that a jurisprudential theory that maintains that the rule of recognition is a duty-imposing rule can *never* have the burden of explaining the source or ontology of the duty the rule creates. Theoretical problems could, in principle, always arise that would make such an explanation an adequacy condition for any such jurisprudential view. However, given the account I have offered—and absent some reason to the contrary—we have no special reason to doubt the capacity of the rule to create obligations or duties. This follows from the basic pragmatic principle that skepticism must be motivated by more than the mere possibility of falsehood.

Both in our practical lives and as meta-ethicists, we have a good deal of confidence in our assumption that contracts, pacts, promises, and certain other activities that have the structure of SCA can indeed be duty-imposing. Of course, explaining the source or ontology of the duties created by this general class of practices is no walk in the park; but on a pragmatist view, the mere fact that we have not yet settled on a fully satisfying explanation of such duties is no

I have distinguished between two sets of questions regarding the criteria of legality. The first concerns their *existence* conditions. The second concerns their content. The social fact thesis holds that the existence of the criteria of legality in any community is ultimately a matter of social fact. This, and not the separability thesis, is the core of legal positivism. The social fact thesis makes an interesting claim about the possibility conditions of legal authority—a claim that is distinctive of positivism and that is denied by the natural lawyer and the Dworkinian, both of whom believe (though in different ways) that legal authority is an expression or embodiment of political morality, and that the criteria of legality necessarily depend on substantive moral argument.[14]

It is one thing to determine the criteria of legality in a community, another to identify the standards of conduct that satisfy those criteria. It is yet another matter to determine what the rules and standards of conduct that satisfy the criteria of legality require of those governed by them. What do the rules (individually) and the law (generally) require or permit; what rights and privileges do they confer; what duties does the law impose? This is the question of *legal content*. How do we recover, construct, or determine the content of the law?

We can think of the problem in this way. The set of standards, rules, or norms that satisfy the criteria of legality in any community will be a set of abstract linguistic entities that have propositional content. These propositions constitute the set of authoritative pronouncements, but they do not constitute the law. There are at least two components to a theory of legal content. The first is the set of official pronouncements; the second is a

reason for skepticism about their existence. We need some further reason for calling such fundamental assumptions into doubt. In showing that law is in the same boat with this range of common normative practices, we do not immunize law against skepticism; rather, we simply show that any skepticism about law's claim to be duty-imposing must take the form of a general skepticism about this range of practices, and must be *motivated* by something more than the mere fact that we may not yet have a completely satisfying theoretical explanation of their source or ontology.

[14] Again, it is this fact about the criteria of legality that leads to a dispute among positivists about whether the rule of recognition can be a duty-imposing rule. Those who deny that it can be—Marmor and Raz, for example—do so because they do not see how conventions can give rise to duties. That is one reason why there is a burden on other positivists, like Hart and me, who believe that the rule of recognition is a duty-imposing rule to show how that is possible. One important consequence of thinking of the practice of officials under a rule of recognition as an SCA is that doing so makes intelligible how certain forms of conventional practices—in virtue of the role they play in coordinating expectations and structuring normative relationships among participants—can be duty-imposing. It is also important to note that this difference among positivists about whether the rule of recognition can be a duty-imposing rule is not the same difference as that between inclusive and exclusive legal positivists. That difference concerns constraints on the content of the criteria of legality, not the implications of their conventionality. Thus, some exclusive legal positivists, for example, Shapiro, conceive of the rule of recognition as purporting to be duty-imposing, whereas many others, like Raz and Marmor, do not.

function that operates on those pronouncements to generate the content of the law. Content is determined both by the set of official or authoritative rules, standards, and acts, and by the function that enables us to construct the law's content from them.[15] Thus, the content of the law will differ in different legal systems based on differences in the nature, number, scope, and content of authoritative resources, as well as differences in the practices adopted for constructing the law's content from the available set.[16]

To his credit, Dworkin has done more than anyone else has to develop a general theory of legal content. On his account, legal content is a function of *constructive interpretation*, an activity that Dworkin understands as having two elements: fit and value. An interpretation operates on the set of authoritative legal pronouncements as the "data points" of the interpretation of the law of a community. The interpretation must fit its authoritative pronouncements (and history) in roughly the same way that an interpretation of a novel must fit the themes, plot lines, and characters of the novel. By contrast, the value dimension of the interpretation invokes the norms appropriate to the kind of object being interpreted. Because law invokes the coercive authority of the state, the norms to which an interpretation of law must turn are those governing the political morality of coercive authority. The object of the interpretation is to show the law of a particular community "in its best light"—to understand it as adhering to and embodying the norms of the relevant institutional political morality to the greatest extent it can, consistent with the official pronouncements the interpretation must fit.

I have been persuaded by Mark Greenberg that the best way to understand the fit requirement is as an aspect of the justification or value dimension, and not as an independent aspect of interpretation. If we interpret an Agatha Christie novel as the story of Hamlet, for example, we may seem to be treating it as embodying to the greatest possible extent the norms governing the value of a work of fiction; but in fact, a work of fiction

---

[15] To say that the content of the law is a function of authoritative pronouncements is to say that for any given individual at any given time, there is a function that takes as its input the set of authoritative pronouncements and produces as its output the set of legal requirements to which that person is subject at that time. In terms of adjudication, this means that for each case, there is a function that takes as its inputs the authoritative pronouncements and produces as its output a decision. This is not to say that for every legal system and for each action A, there is a determinate answer to the question whether or not the law permits or requires A; nor is it to say that for every legal system and for each case C, there is a single right answer to the legal question posed by C. The output of the legal content function may sometimes be undefined, and when it is, then cases must be decided on some basis other than the content of the law. See below for an important distinction between what I call "guidance content" and "adjudicatory content".

[16] It should be clear that the content of the law cannot be simply the *sum* of the contents of particular authoritative pronouncements. A theory of legal content must also allow for relationships among those pronouncements. Thus, we need a theory of precedent; an account of the relationship between legislative and judicial pronouncements; an account of how conflicts among different pronouncements are to be resolved; and the like. All are essential to determining the law's content.

whose content has no connection with its themes, characters, events, and so on is actually a very bad work of fiction. The requirement that the interpretation fit the "data points" of the object under interpretation is thus a *part* of showing it in its best light, and not an independent threshold requirement that we then supplement by appeal to the governing norms.[17]

These are the main building blocks of the Dworkinian theory of legal content. There are, however, a couple of subsidiary elements that are also important to the theory. One such element is Dworkin's view that the officials whose task it is to determine the content of the law claim that the authority they exercise is legitimate. This amounts to the claim that their exercise of the coercive authority of the state is justified. A second subsidiary element of the account is Dworkin's view that the principle of charity requires that we treat the majority of these claims to legitimacy as true. When these elements are conjoined with the fit and value constraints, we have Dworkin's full theory of legal content. The content of the law is determined by the interpretation that best justifies a community's authoritative pronouncements; to justify them the interpretation must fit them, as well as showing them to be as morally attractive as they can be. This means that the interpretation will at least prima facie justify the exercise of political authority, and in doing so will reveal the majority of officials' claims to be legitimately exercising authority to be true.

A function operates on a set of inputs to yield a determinate outcome or answer to a question. In a case involving truth-values, for example, a function can yield the outcomes "true," "false," or "indeterminate" ("undecidable"). As long as it yields one or the other of these outcomes, it is a determinate function in the formal or logical sense. Translating this idea to law, we can roughly associate a function with the values "plaintiff wins", "defendant wins", and "the law is indeterminate as to who wins".[18] A

---

[17] This topic is also addressed above in Lecture 3 n. 10. Most commentators take the fit requirement to imply that Dworkin is a coherentist about legal justification. However, as I understand it, the fit requirement is *not* a coherence requirement; and Dworkin is not to be interpreted as a coherence theorist. The fit requirement does not mean that the law must be made to cohere. It means that the law must be recognizable or identifiable as the law of the community.

[18] This characterization focuses on legal content from the perspective of adjudication—which is the perspective from which Dworkin's account is articulated. This does not necessarily provide the appropriate analysis of the content function from the perspective of guidance, however. Adjudication can be analyzed as applying a binary function analogous to a truth function; but I am not sure we can analyze the question of what the law requires of a given individual at a given time as a binary function—since for each action, the law can forbid, permit but not require, permit but be undecided about whether it requires or not, require, or be undecided altogether. In other words, we seem to need a sequence of two binary functions applied to each action A (individuated in terms of a particular individual at a particular time): f_1 will take as its inputs the authoritative pronouncements along with A, and yield as its output that the law either forbids or permits A (or is undecided); f_2 will operate on actions that the law permits and will tell us, for each, whether the law requires or does not require that action (or whether the law is undecided).

distinctive feature of Dworkin's account is that the function that operates on the inputs yields in all but the most unusual cases either the answer "plaintiff wins" or the answer "defendant wins". There is, in his view, not just a determinate answer, but a right answer as a matter of law that supports one of the litigant's claims authoritatively and decisively. It is also a feature of his view that the determinate answer is unique.

We might put these points by saying that there are a series of corollary claims that are not, strictly speaking, part of the theory of legal content, but are important aspects of its orientation. Among these are that there are right answers as a matter of law to nearly all disputes; that the legitimacy of the activity of adjudication depends in part on seeing adjudication as oriented toward determining that answer, and that the content of law is ultimately a matter of political morality (because of the normative aspect of the theory of interpretation). Central, then, to Dworkin's overall theory is the claim that the legitimacy of adjudicatory authority depends on adjudication as a practice oriented toward determining or identifying the existence of right answers to even the most difficult disputes.

It is natural to ask what the relationship is, in Dworkin's view, between this feature of his theory of legal content and Hercules. Hercules, as most readers will know, is a judge endowed with "superhuman intellectual power and patience" and who, moreover, is committed to interpreting the law according to Dworkin's theory of legal content.[19] The suggestion is plain that Hercules gets the right answer to any dispute he takes under consideration.

We can distinguish at least three different accounts of the relationship between Hercules and the doctrine of the unique right answer. First, we might think that on Dworkin's account, the fact that X is, or would be, Hercules' answer constitutes the unique rightness of X. His reaching an answer, in other words, is a right-making characteristic of that answer. This gives Hercules a metaphysical role within the theory, while it renders Dworkin something of an internal realist about the nature of objectivity and truth in the legal domain.[20] Alternatively, we can view the role Hercules plays in the theory as epistemic, rather than metaphysical. Legal content or the right answer to legal disputes is not constituted by Hercules' judgment; it's just that by judging the way he does, Hercules manages invariably to reach the right result. From time to time I have been drawn to

[19] *Law's Empire*, 239.

[20] In other words, a statement that so-and-so is the law, or that the law requires that P, is true if and only if that is the judgment that an ideal observer (Hercules) would come to under appropriate epistemic conditions (the various ideal conditions under which Hercules, according to Dworkin, decides cases). For a discussion of this view, see Jules Coleman and Brian Leiter, "Determinacy, Objectivity and Authority" *Pennsylvania Law Review* 142 (Dec. 1993) 549–637.

both of these interpretations of the role Hercules plays in the Dworkinian theory of content.

In the end, however, I am inclined to regard Hercules as playing a role that is neutral between these alternatives. He is a useful heuristic device for illustrating the components of the theory of content and their relationship to one another, highlighting the idea that there are right answers to legal disputes, and that legal content can be fully determinate (or nearly so). He thus illustrates and makes intelligible the idea that the behavior of judges is oriented toward unique and determinate legal content, without representing any particular ontology of that content.

While I have no developed theory of legal content to oppose to Dworkin's, I do have certain reservations about his account, as well as some thoughts about the way in which any positivist theory of content is likely to differ from his. In setting out these observations, I can only sketch the kind of account I hope in the near future to develop more fully. I merely want to take a wide-angle lens photo of the battleground.

On Dworkin's view, authoritative pronouncements are the data points that constrain the interpretive theory. The theory is no good unless it fits them in such a way that they can be seen as contributing to the "legal themes" by which the theory fleshes out the content of the community's law. Official legal pronouncements thus enter primarily as *constraints* on the interpretive theory. For positivists, by contrast, the rules or standards that satisfy the criteria of legality are not merely data points or parameters on which, or within which, an interpretive theory is to operate. These pronouncements are, in the first instance, potential guides to human conduct.[21] This is one important reason why positivists might object to thinking of legal content as analogous to literary or artistic content. It is plausible to assert that in order to grasp the content of a work of fiction, for example, we must view the themes, plot line, events, and characters holistically; none of these discrete elements can plausibly be said to have an artistic meaning independently of the work of which it is a part. Particular authoritative pronouncements in law, however, often do seem to play a discretely analyzable role in guiding conduct. Positivists focus on this role in conceiving of legal rules as creating reasons for action.

There appears to be no evidence that Dworkin sees legal rules as having the function of offering those governed by them reasons for action. Indeed, we might even read him as denying that rules constitute any part of the law's content; rather, legal content resides in the principles, to which the

---

[21] It would be impossible to understand the debate between inclusive and exclusive legal positivists without grasping the significance of authoritative pronouncements as potential guides to conduct.

rules are transparent.[22] Thus, authoritative pronouncements are insignificant in the Dworkinian picture beyond the role they play as constraints on the interpretive theory, whereas these pronouncements are essential to the positivist picture.

This difference is extremely important in several ways. The first concerns the role that the set of authoritative pronouncements plays within the theory. In both Dworkin's account and the positivist's the binding legal standards are linguistic entities that have propositional content. So we need a way of determining their content, regardless of the role they ultimately must play in the theory. For Dworkin, however, these pronouncements have no guidance function. Thus their status as binding, and their content, are altogether provisional and revisable in the light of the theory of content. That theory, in turn, is oriented toward determining right answers to particular disputes and not toward guiding the conduct of ordinary folk. Thus, for Dworkin, the only point of identifying the authoritative pronouncements and ascribing content to them is to construct legal content. The authoritative standards at this juncture in the argument are no more than raw material for a theory of content. That theory itself then provides all the warrant one needs to revise the set of authoritative pronouncements. In Dworkin's theory the actual set of binding legal standards—or authoritative pronouncements—falls out of the theory of content.

When Dworkin's view is understood in this way, several familiar objections to his account are seen to be misplaced. For example, the claim that Dworkin is himself committed to a rule of recognition for identifying the set of binding legal standards on which the theory of interpretation operates is misleading in several ways. First, of course, the rule of recognition for a positivist is always conventional, and Dworkin rejects conventionalism of all kinds and at every turn. Second, and much more important in this context, the provisional set of authoritative pronouncements are not, in the end, the binding set of legal standards. They are the raw materials for the theory of content. Once the theory of content is constructed, the set of binding and authoritative pronouncements falls out of that theory. This is the sense in which it is both accurate and illuminating to see Dworkin as, in effect, developing a theory of law from a theory of adjudication.

While the above objection to Dworkin is misplaced, Dworkin's approach does leave him open to the charge that, in his account, there never really

---

[22] This is not to say that Dworkin does not see the law from the perspective of those governed by it. Quite the contrary; he sees it primarily from the point of view of litigants claiming rights against one another, and against the state, to have disputes resolved in one way rather than another. Nor is it to say that Dworkin attributes no guidance function to the law; for he believes that the law guides officials in determining what it requires. However, they are guided not by particular rules, but by the content of the law, which must be determined holistically.

are binding authoritative pronouncements, only provisional ones. Those standards that are provisional at time t_1 allow us to construct a theory of content, from which fall out the "binding" legal standards at t_2. But there is no meaningful or interesting sense in which those standards are binding. Because of the way the theory is constructed, they are no more than the set of provisional standards at t_2, on which the theory of content operates. This is a feature of Dworkin's emphasis on what I am calling "adjudicatory legal content": the set of authoritative standards are relevant in his view only for the purposes of determining legal content, but not for the guidance of conduct. The rules are not seen from the perspective of governing the conduct of ordinary folk, but rather as the raw materials for the theory of legal content that guides judges in resolving disputes. One effect of this picture of legal practice is that the notion of a binding legal standard has to be rethought or eliminated. The difference between binding and provisional is lost.

The problem is deeper, however. It is not just that such a view cannot make sense of the ordinary distinction between binding and provisional standards—the theory cannot even get off the ground. For we cannot infer that a determinate answer to a legal dispute is, for that reason alone, a statement of the *law*. Here is the problem. Suppose one holds that it is a conceptual truth about law that something is law only if it is capable of guiding conduct, and a norm, decision, or rule is capable of guiding conduct only if those to whom the law is addressed can know in advance what it requires of them. On this view, determinate answers to disputes state the law only if they are knowable in advance.[23] Thus, even a decision reached by applying authoritative sources and those to which one is authoritatively directed, and doing so in an appropriate or authorized way, need not state the *law*. That depends on what one's theory of *law* is.[24]

In entertaining this view I am not defending it, nor am I asserting that the determinate answers derivable from the Dworkinian account will fail to meet this conceptual constraint on legality or legal content. The point I am making is more general. Dworkin attempts to derive a theory of what *law* is from a theory of determinate *adjudicatory* content. The point of the example is to express doubt about this strategy. Adjudicatory content is not, by that fact alone, legal content. Because it is not a theory of *legal content* without a theory of law, we cannot derive a theory of *law* from a theory of adjudicatory content. And if we cannot derive a theory of legal content from a

---

[23] I picked up this objection from Ken Himma, who in typically modest fashion did not let on how devastating it is.

[24] Scott Shapiro has suggested to me that this can be seen as another way of making Raz's point that there is a difference between norms or decisions that are law and norms or decisions that are legally valid or binding. Thus, absent a theory of law, a theory of adjudicatory content is at best a theory of legal validity.

theory of adjudicatory content, we cannot derive an account of what is to count as binding legal standards or authoritative pronouncements from the Dworkinian theory of content.[25]

My remaining concerns about the Dworkinian theory of legal content have to do with the way in which the principle of charity—which Dworkin takes from Donald Davidson—is thought to apply holistically over the range of authoritative legal pronouncements. In the first place, it is not obvious that the set of legal pronouncements or standards are sufficiently similar to a single person's set of beliefs for the Davidson theory of ascribing content to beliefs to provide a ready-made argument in the legal context. One main reason for applying the principle of charity in the belief context is as a precondition of being able to interpret human behavior—including linguistic behavior. The principle of charity is an a priori constraint on interpreting human behavior as rational. What the principle of charity requires in this context is that contradictions be resolved, beliefs constructed so that the basic rules of logic are satisfied, and the bulk of the beliefs are treated as true. In the Davidsonian view, the principle is applied holistically over the set of all of a person's beliefs.

Now it is not at all clear that even in the belief context, the principle of charity must be applied holistically, as opposed, say, to locally. By "applied locally", I mean applied only to the subset of beliefs that have to be rendered consistent and generally true in order to understand the agent's behavior as rational. This approach has the additional advantage of phenomenological accuracy, since it leaves open the possibility of tension or inconsistency between various components of a person's set of beliefs— a phenomenon that is psychologically all too familiar.

The law, moreover, is not a set of beliefs of any single cognizer, but the product of the activities of many agents over a period of time. Understanding what the law is or means is not the same kind of project as understanding an individual's behavior—linguistic or otherwise. In order to attribute content to law, we do not have to treat all of the law as consistent or as satisfying all the basic rules of deductive logic. Again, local rationality may be enough. Local rationality certainly fits better with the phenomenology of judging. Even if Dworkin is right that judges must posit the working hypothesis that there are right answers to legal disputes, judges find themselves, more often than Dworkin acknowledges, adopting the view that in fact there is no determinate legal answer to the case at hand. Judges regard the law as warranting inconsistent answers more often than one would expect were we to apply the principle of charity holistically.

---

[25] A different way of making the point would be to say not that Dworkin's theory cannot get off the ground; rather, it can get off the ground only by assuming that adjudicatory content is legal content. Of course this would be to beg some important questions.

Finally, in the belief context, applying the principle of charity implies treating all or the majority of an agent's beliefs as true. In the legal context, the analogue would seem to be treating as justified all or the majority of instances of the legal use of coercive authority. Thus the theory of content will have a political–moral dimension in which the principles that render the law the best version of the kind of thing it is will do so in a way that is likely to make the claim to legitimate authority true. The obvious problem is that while it is impossible to interpret a person's behavior as rational without assuming both the logical consistency and the truth of at least a relevant subset of his beliefs, it is by no means clear that law is not rationally comprehensible unless its claim to legitimacy is rendered true.

Though a positivist must allow that the set of binding legal standards is revisable—in many ways, including, of course, as a consequence of the theory of content—authoritative pronouncements are not merely provisional, nor is their role to be explicated entirely in terms of their being the resources on which an interpretive theory for deriving legal content operates. These norms or rules typically purport to guide conduct. Of course, positivists can disagree about what this implies by way of constraints on *the legal rules'* content. Raz believes that the action-guiding nature of legal rules implies that substantive argument cannot figure in a determination of their content. Thus, whereas the Dworkinian holds, in effect, that legal rules are transparent to the principles that justify them, the Razian believes that law's guidance precludes exactly that. On the other hand, all positivists at a minimum deny that the legal content of authoritative standards must depend on moral argument; all deny that legal rules must be transparent to the principles that would justify them.

Thus, there are any number of ways, consistent with legal positivism, to determine the content of individual authoritative statements. Perhaps the most obvious and familiar is to identify the content of a particular rule with its "plain meaning" (or in the case of technical predicates with their stipulated meaning). Or the positivist might avail himself of semantic holist strategies of interpretation, such that the content of the terms in individual authoritative pronouncements derive their semantic content holistically. So, for example, in order to interpret a rule imposing tax burdens on families, the concept of a family will in part depend on what sort of associations count as families in other parts of the law and in our social, political, and economic practices generally. The content of a rule can also make reference to the legislators' beliefs about the point, purpose, or value of such a rule. I am advancing no view in particular at this time. There may be no uniquely positivist approach to determining the content of a legal rule or other authoritative pronouncements; though if Raz is right, there may be constraints on interpretive strategies—specifically, the constraint that no appeal can be made to moral argument about what the law should be.

Just as there may be many accounts of the content of individual rules, there may be many accounts of the law's content that are consistent with positivism. Against the Dworkinian, all positivists would claim at least that legal content need not rely on substantive moral or political argument. Beyond that, my guess is that any positivist theory of content will be conventionalist and relativistic in ways that Dworkin's is not. Most importantly, in my account anyway, the principle of charity applies locally. This preserves the possibility of broader conflicts and contradictions in the law, a greater degree of indeterminacy, and no sense at all that the claim to legitimacy of officials is true—generally, or at all.

I would not want to leave the reader with the impression that any positivist theory of content is going to be satisfactory or less worrisome than is Dworkin's. Far from it. Still there are some features of Dworkin's theory that could stand further scrutiny than I have been able to give them in this context. Setting aside various worries about the application of the Davidsonian principle of charity and its scope in the context of ascribing content to legal utterances, the more important concerns seem to me these. In the first place, the theory of what law is cannot fall out of a theory of adjudicatory content, just because we first have to determine what are, if any, the conceptual truths about law. This means, for example, that even if there are unique and determinate right answers to legal disputes—answers that are arrived at by applying only authoritative legal sources (along with any extra-legal standards to which officials may be directed by the legal sources)—we have no grounds for asserting that those answers are the law's answers, or that they state what the law is on that issue. Whether or not these determinate answers state the law depends on what must be true of law. I think Kenneth Himma is absolutely right about this very deep point. For if it is a conceptual truth about law that it must be capable of guiding conduct, then it will not follow that every determinate right answer is the law's answer. Himma's point is general, and does not presuppose that the law actually must guide conduct. As I understand the point, it is that we must first know what is true conceptually about law before we can figure out whether a determinate answer is a legal answer; and so we cannot infer backwards that the set of binding legal standards are just those that figure in determining the unique answer to disputes that arise under the law. The only way to meet this objection is to presuppose that adjudicatory content is identical to legal content, and that just begs the question about the nature of law.

A second important problem seems to me to follow on the heels of this one. For Dworkin, we draw a distinction between the provisional and revisable set of legally authoritative standards from which the content of the law is constructed, and those binding legal standards that fall out as authoritative in the light of the content of the law. The problem, of course, is that given the structure of Dworkin's argument, and the resources at his disposable, there are literally no grounds whatsoever for treating the legal propositions that fall out of the theory of content as any more secure than is the set of provisional and revisable standards with which we begin. They have no role in the theory other than to be the data points on which the law's content is to be constructed when another legal dispute arises: when another question comes up about what the law is on a particular matter. So there is, within the confines of the theory, no meaningful sense to be made of the expression "binding legal standards". Or, to put it another way, if the standards that emerge after any act of constructing content are binding legal standards in the Dworkinian sense, then so too are the ones with which he begins—that is, those he regards as the revisable and provisional set. Being revisable and provisional is shared by all standards: both pre- and post-interpretation, that is, both before and after the process of constructing content.

Like Dworkin, the pragmatist believes that all legal standards and rules are in principle revisable—what they require or demand of us subject to change. But we do not treat each case as, in effect, an opportunity to consider whether to revise them. Indeed, the pragmatist is committed to the principle that one ought not to consider whether to revise unless there is a problem that requires adjustment. On the face of it, Dworkin appears to have no theoretical resources for distinguishing cases that call for revision from those that do not. His only available mechanism is the existence of a dispute that triggers litigation about what the law is or requires. In contrast, the positivist has resources for determining when revision is needed—among these resources are law's guidance function and various distinctions that are corollaries of it, for example, the distinction between core and penumbra and that between application and content disagreements.

I think these points can be illuminated further by drawing out a useful distinction between Dworkin and positivists that flatters both equally and subjects both to criticism. Take Hart as a typical, thoughtful positivist. One way of looking at Hart's position is that when cases fall within the core of rules, the law guides conduct well and there are right answers as a matter of law that are unique, determinate, and by and large determinable. When there are no right answers, when there is substantial and significant dispute about what the law requires, when we are in the penumbra (these are not all the same thing for me, but they sometimes appear to be for Hart, but that is of no importance in this context), the judge must revise the law. There is no answer as a matter of law to what conduct is required, permitted, or prohibited; the law must be revised if it is to provide an answer. The problem is that positivists have no theory of revision. Hart certainly does not. He tells us only that to resolve the dispute and in effect therefore to revise the law, the judge must exercise discretion. On the other hand, discretion is a rational and not a random procedure. It is governed by norms and reason; a discretionary decision is still one that should, in this sense, be rationalized. Of course, the question is how—to which the typical positivist has no answer at all. If Hart is the paradigm, a critic could with warrant claim that positivism thus has a nice explanation of what is going on in the standard case, why things work and how they work; but no theory of any use about how to revise the law, when the law is indeterminate and needs fixing.

In contrast, if we look at Dworkin's theory of legal content as instead an account of how judges should (and do)revise the law rationally when the law needs to be revised, then it is—barring some doubts I have about applying the principle of charity globally rather than locally, and the like— a perfectly attractive and sensible theory. It probably comes reasonably close to describing what judges in fact do when they revise the law. That is, they ask themselves what the binding sources are, how best to put them together in a way that flatters the enterprise of governance by law, and then ask what decision would fit best with that larger conception. The problem with Dworkin's view is that he has no way of telling which cases call for revision. His theory of revision is his theory of law. His theory of law answers a political question: when is the coercive authority of the state legitimately imposed? It does not answer a practical question: is the law adequate to its practical purposes?[26] If positivists can be charged with offering the label "discretion" instead of a theory of revision, then what Dworkin offers is a theory of revision masquerading as a theory of law.

I have distinguished so far among three different questions in which the relationship between law and morality can arise. These are: (1) What are the possibility conditions of legal authority (or what are the existence conditions of criteria of legality)? (2) What are the constraints, if any, on the content of the criteria of legality? (3) What is the content of the law? The Dworkinian is committed to three claims: (1')What the criteria of legality are in any community is a matter in part of moral argument. (2') Morality can be, and often is, a condition of legality. And (3') the content of law is a matter of moral argument.

Whereas Dworkin's original objection to positivism was based on a particular answer to (2)—an answer that is endorsed by inclusive legal positivists—Dworkin's distinctive theses are really captured by his answers to (1) and (3). Dworkin's answer to (1) has evolved over time. It began as the claim that in legal systems in which morality is a condition of legality

---

[26] I hope I have expressed well enough this important point, which Scott Shapiro has been impressing on me (in slightly different terms) since we first began discussing these issues years ago.

the criteria of legality could not be conventional, and must instead be expressed in a normative rule. That is the argument I have taken up in Lecture 8 and elsewhere, and found wanting. Dworkin's mature view that the criteria of legality derive from moral–political argument does not depend on the content of any particular criteria of legality being controversial, but instead on the claim that disagreement about the criteria of legality—whatever their content—is an enduring and pervasive feature of legal practice in developed systems. Contrary to prevailing wisdom, what distinguishes positivists from Dworkin is not their view about (2), but rather their denial of (1) and (3). More importantly, I have also shown how Dworkin's view about (1) derives from his view about (3). Positivists not only have answers that differ from Dworkin's about (1) and (3); positivists deny as well that what counts as a binding legal standard in a particular community falls out of a general theory of legal content. Thus, in addition to rejecting Dworkin's answers to (1) and (3), they reject his view of the relationship between them.

In setting forth the arguments of this lecture, I take myself to have been engaging in analytic jurisprudence. And in representing the views of others (fairly, I hope) I have regarded them as also engaged in, broadly speaking, the same enterprise. Those who are persuaded by my arguments will come to the view that law is a social practice in which the criteria of legality are conventional, in which morality may, but need not, be a criterion of legality, and in which the content of law is generated by a function that operates on the content of those authoritative pronouncements that satisfy the relevant criteria of legality. Those moved by Dworkin's arguments will, of course, come to a different view of the nature of the law. However, the arguments on all sides of the issues addressed here are, I take it, conceptual. They make use of the tools of analytic philosophy in the hopes of uncovering necessary truths about our concept of law.

It is not difficult to understand the basis of a certain kind of skepticism about how fruitful such arguments can be in resolving important disputes in jurisprudence. For example, on each of the fundamental issues we have addressed pertaining to the relationship of law to morality, one cannot help but be struck by the fact that good arguments have been adduced on every side. Some legal theorists have taken this to mean that we cannot, by merely reflecting on our concept of law, decide whether or how morality figures in law; and if so, in what ways. They claim, therefore, that conceptual analysis can take us only so far, and that our concept of law ultimately needs to be disciplined by *practical considerations*. We should fashion or discipline that concept in whatever way is most likely to produce the best outcomes in our practical lives. On this view, conceptual analysis can be valuable, but it cannot resolve for us the most basic and important disagreements we have about law or our concept of it. We should therefore adapt or complete the concept of law in the way that best serves our political interests or needs.

Other theorists are less kind in their assessment of the role conceptual analysis can play in explaining law. They see in the disputes we have visited little more than conflicting intuitions dressed up in fancy philosophical garb. They see conceptual analysis as a fruitless activity issuing in irreducible and irresolvable battles among conflicting intuitions. For these critics, the only hope for jurisprudence lies in taking a *naturalizing* turn. Conceptual analysis is to give way to naturalized jurisprudence. Rather than supplementing conceptual analysis with practical considerations, we should abandon philosophical inquiry (or limit its scope) and replace (or supplement) it with social science. Philosophy of law needs to give way (in part or in whole) to natural and social science.

Finally, there are those who believe that conceptual analysis is not necessarily fruitless or of limited value, but that, understood in a certain way, it is in a sense impossible—at least in so far as we regard it as an analytic or non-normative enterprise. Describing our concept of law is not what the philosophy of law is about. Law is a normative predicate. Any understanding of it must at its root reflect that fact; any theory of law must therefore be at least in part an exercise in first-order moral–political philosophy. Closely related to this view is the claim that even if descriptive conceptual analysis were possible, identifying the subject-matter of inquiry requires appeal to moral or political norms. A conceptual analysis of law will be viewed as successful only if it deepens our understanding of central features of our legal practice—but how are we to determine which aspects of the law our concept must account for, and in what way? Identifying the very subject-matter of a conceptual analysis of law is itself an activity regulated by norms of moral and political philosophy.

Each of these objections has a certain currency and initial plausibility. The last, in particular, has nearly risen to the level of conventional wisdom. None of the objections are persuasive, however. All misconceive the philosophical project while underestimating the resources of conceptual analysis. Those who would argue that conceptual analysis is incomplete and must somehow be supplemented by practical considerations underestimate the resources available within pragmatism for conceptual analysis. The naturalist underestimates the role conceptual analysis must play even within his own project. And the project of normative jurisprudence is able to get off the ground as a serious alternative only by ascribing to theorists like Hart and myself positions neither of us hold, and by completely misunderstanding the role substantive moral and political argument can play in conceptual analysis. Or so I am about to argue.

Lecture Twelve—
Normativity and Naturalism

When he published *The Concept of Law*, H. L. A. Hart took himself to be engaged in a familiar philosophical project of conceptual analysis. He took himself to be doing the same kind of philosophical work that his peers in the philosophy of language, metaphysics, ethics, and epistemology were doing. Where others were analyzing the concepts of meaning, truth, the real, substance, good, and knowledge, he was offering an analysis of the concept of law. The methods and tools of analysis were essentially the same; the only significant difference was in the object of analysis.

Recently some of Hart's critics, notably Ronald Dworkin and Stephen Perry, have raised doubts about whether an analysis of the concept of law can apply the same methods and tools as those employed in the core areas of philosophy. For these critics, there is something special about the concept of law that requires that an analysis of it must proceed by invoking substantive norms of political morality; an analysis of the concept of law is, in the first instance, an exercise in political theory. Other critics of Hart take issue not so much with the very possibility of a conceptual analysis of law, but with Hart's self-understanding of his project. These critics, especially Stephen Perry, claim that Hart's analysis of the concept of law proceeds at every key turn by invoking contestable considerations of first-order political theory.

In this book I have offered a theory of the concept of law that applies the same basic tools and methods of analysis that apply everywhere in philosophy. Thus, the objections that these critics have offered against Hart should apply to me as well. If the critics are right, then either my analysis is flawed or I have mischaracterized what I have done (or both). Though many of the arguments for what has come to be called "normative jurisprudence" are interesting and worth pursuing in their own right, none poses a threat to the argument of this book or to the methodology employed here. Establishing this helps complete the project I have here undertaken.

Arguably, the most familiar and fruitful way in which legal philosophy contributes to our understanding of legal practice is by providing an analysis of the concepts that are central to it—including, of course, the concept of law itself. In the Postscript to *The Concept of Law* Hart famously defends what he calls "descriptive jurisprudence", his (as it turns out) unfortunate label for the methodological approach that he takes to conceptual analysis of law. Just as famously, Ronald Dworkin rejects the very possibility of a descriptive jurisprudence, and argues instead that a philosophical theory of the concept of law is necessarily an activity of first-order moral–political philosophy. Jurisprudence is, in large part, a branch of substantive political philosophy, and its proper method is that of "normative jurisprudence".[1] This is not—at least not on the face of it—a debate about the substantive theory of the concept of law, but rather a dispute about the methodology of theory construction in legal philosophy in particular, and perhaps in philosophy more generally. While there may be no issue more prominent in the recent literature than this dispute between the proponents of descriptive and of normative jurisprudence, it is difficult to frame the debate in a way that would justify the attention it has received, or the passions that have arisen on both sides of the divide.

In characterizing his project as descriptive, Hart intended to make a very narrow and, to his mind, unobjectionable claim—that a jurisprudential theory need not warrant the inference from legality to moral legitimacy. By his lights, any other approach to analyzing the concept of law runs the risk of begging the question of the legitimacy of law, and so in describing his project as descriptive, he takes himself to be doing no more than what is necessary to avoid begging that question.[2] Nothing Hart says rules out the possibility that some or all forms of governance that fall within the concept's extension are morally legitimate, worthy of endorsement, or capable of generating moral obligations to obey; he meant only to rule out the inference from legality to legitimacy.[3] Correctly or not, Hart takes Dworkin to be imposing the constraint that an adequate theory of the concept of law is one in which its instances are at least prima facie morally legitimate or worthy of endorsement. Thus, in calling himself a descriptive jurisprudent, Hart means to emphasize several differences between his

---

[1] It is not clear who is responsible for introducing the expressions "normative" and "descriptive" in order to characterize alternative approaches to the analysis of the concept of law. Hart explicitly calls his method "descriptive", and in doing so clearly aims to distinguish his view from Dworkin's, which by implication is "normative" in the relevant sense. Stephen Perry explicitly characterizes Dworkin's approach as normative and Hart's as descriptive. Perry also calls descriptive jurisprudence "methodological positivism". Whoever is responsible for the labels, it is now clear that there are two apparently different takes on the project of conceptual analysis of law: what is less clear is what the difference between them consists in, and why it matters. One aim of this lecture is to explore both of these concerns.

[2] In calling his jurisprudence descriptive, Hart says only that it has no justificatory or endorsement ambitions. See *Concept of Law*, 241–3. At other places he is quite clear that his approach to the concept of law has a normative dimension. For example, he argues that positivism would do a better job than natural law of promoting moral criticism of the law. See ibid. 210.

[3] We can distinguish between two senses of the expression "an inference from legality to legitimacy". In one sense, the inference is from the legality of a particular legal norm to its legitimacy; in the other sense, the inference is from the law of a community taken as a whole to its legitimacy. It is clear that Hart meant to deny both inferences; still, the primary focus of his discussion is the inference from the law of a community taken as a whole to its legitimacy. It is clear that he takes Dworkin's interpretivism to warrant precisely that inference, and Hart's concern is to dissociate himself from any such view.

approach to jurisprudence and what he takes to be the Dworkin's. First, he is explicitly denying that normative jurisprudence is methodologically inevitable or unavoidable. Second, he is implicitly rejecting the view that it is the best methodological approach. Third, and most importantly, he is drawing attention to the fact that his is an altogether different enterprise from Dworkin's.

In a series of interesting and valuable papers Stephen Perry has argued that—his protestations to the contrary notwithstanding—Hart is indeed engaged in normative, not descriptive, jurisprudence. Perry begins with Hart's provocative remark, in the preface to *The Concept of Law*, that his project of analytic jurisprudence might also be characterized as "descriptive sociology". While it is a phrase that Hart nowhere repeats, it has nevertheless puzzled theorists and commentators since. Many commentators (Perry among them) maintain that there is little evidence that Hart was actually engaged in a social-scientific inquiry of any sort: he seeks to uncover no law-like regularities that would support counterfactuals, nor does he measure his project by the norms usually governing such inquiry—for example, by its predictive accuracy.[4] If Hart is not engaged in social science as such, then what else might he mean by referring to his project as "descriptive sociology"?

One possible answer is that like J. L. Austin, Hart believed that we could secure knowledge of the world by exploring the way we talk about it. So a descriptive sociology in this context turns out to be a sociological study of the use of language—in particular, of the use we make of the expression "law". The job of the descriptive theorist—or the conceptual analyst, in this sense—is to investigate usage and to report his findings. So conceived, descriptive jurisprudence is little more than an investigation the primary aim of which is to identify shared criteria for applying the predicate "law" to schemes of governance.[5]

The apparent problem is that Hart has a good deal more in mind than this. Indeed, conceptual analysis—whether of "law" or of any other concept—is never descriptive in this narrow sense. Hart's aim is not to report on usage, but to analyze the concept of law—to offer a theory of the concept. Theories of concepts are normative both in their construction and

---

[4] As I noted in Lecture 10, Scott Shapiro argues that there is ample evidence that Hart did have certain social-scientific ambitions. In particular, Shapiro takes Hart to be committed to a functionalist account of law that is very much social-scientific in its aims and methods. See Lecture 10 n. 20 and the discussion below. Shapiro's account has influenced my thinking, and his influence is apparent in Lecture 10 and in the discussion of law's function that follows. For my part, I have argued in Lecture 10 that Hart did have a scientistic account of law's function that plays an important explanatory role in his theory of the concept. I revisit this line of argument below.

[5] This is, of course, a different sense of "descriptive jurisprudence" from the one Hart explicitly intends in the Postscript.

ambition. They are responsive to the norms governing theory construction, and aim not merely to report on linguistic behavior, but to discipline use and to structure thought. This is in the very nature of philosophical inquiry into concepts. But if this is what conceptual analysis applied to law amounts to, then it is normative through and through. It could not be otherwise.

There is nothing in these claims about the normative dimensions and ambitions of conceptual analysis generally, or about the analysis of "law", that Hart must reject or that he does reject. Indeed, there is nothing in these claims that anyone could plausibly reject. While the meaning of a term or of the concept it expresses is of course intimately bound up with its use, that subtle relationship could never be captured by a simple reporting project aimed at tabulating commonalities of shared usage. Such a project could in most cases yield only a vague and ambiguous notion. To provide a theory of the concept of law is, among other things, to rationalize the concept by articulating criteria for its use that enable us to be more precise than we could otherwise be in using the expression "law". If this is the sense in which we are to understand the claim that jurisprudence must be normative, then that claim amounts to little more than the assertion that jurisprudence is, or entails, a project of conceptual analysis. And on this interpretation, descriptive jurisprudence is not an alternative form of philosophical inquiry into the concept of law—for the simple reason that it is not really a form of philosophical inquiry at all. Any theory of the concept of law is indeed normative in this sense, but that is hardly a revelation, and certainly not something Hart or anyone else would contest. In short Hart can, and surely would, accept the normativity of conceptual analysis of law while insisting—quite rightly—that his is a project of descriptive jurisprudence—by which he means only that it is not undertaken with the goal of warranting an inference from legality to legitimacy. If such an inference is warranted, it will be on substantive, and not conceptual or logical, grounds.

We cannot make progress unless we can formulate the debate in a way that at least joins recognizable issues. To that end, the formulations I have considered to this point on both sides of the debate are unhelpful. If normative jurisprudence asserts no more than that the analysis of the concept of law is a norm-governed activity and aims to regulate use and discipline thought, then normative jurisprudence is the rather vacuous claim that jurisprudence is, or involves, conceptual analysis. On the other hand, if we accept Hart's formulation, a jurisprudence is normative if and only if it warrants an inference from legality to legitimacy—or takes warranting such an inference as an adequacy condition. Any other methodology is descriptive. On the first formulation it is impossible for jurisprudence not to be normative, whereas on the second formulation it is virtually impossible not to be a descriptive jurisprudent. One would be hard-pressed to say that the issue has been adequately joined.

If we are to make progress, we have to look elsewhere for an illuminating and philosophically respectable formulation of the distinction—one that not only is consistent with plausible characterizations of the projects and methods of conceptual analysis generally, but that explains the motivations of those who advocate a normative jurisprudence as well as those who reject it. The aim of conceptual analysis is to retrieve, determine, or capture the content of a concept in the hopes that by doing so, we will learn something interesting, important, or essential about the nature of the thing the concept denotes. On the classic understanding of it, the aim of conceptual analysis is to identify an interesting set of analytic truths about the concept that are discernible a priori. These truths enable us to identify necessary or essential features of instances of the concept; these features in turn orient the analysis of the concept. Normative jurisprudence would then be the claim that among the necessary or essential features of law are certain properties that necessarily orient the analysis of the concept toward principles of political morality.

One can have doubts about analyticity generally or about whether all analytic truths must be discernible a priori. If one has doubts about analyticity, as pragmatists, for example, do, then conceptual analysis cannot consist in searching for analytic truths about the concept that reveal essential features of its instances. Instead, conceptual analysis would consist in uncovering the most salient features of the concept: those that figure most prominently in an explanation of the kind of thing it is the concept of—that are central to our understanding and appreciation of it. Normative jurisprudence in this sense would make a very different kind of claim about the role of moral and political argument in conceptual analysis. Here the claim would be that in order to identify the most important or explanatorily fundamental features of the concept of law it is necessary to invoke substantive norms of political morality.

Dworkin is the most important proponent of normative jurisprudence, and his most famous argument for the claim that jurisprudence must be normative is the semantic sting argument, discussed in the last lecture. To state that argument again briefly, Dworkin holds that law is an "essentially contested" concept—competent language users disagree not only about whether this or that is an instance of law, and about what the concept of law ought to be; they also disagree about what the concept of law is—or in other words, they disagree about the criteria of application for the expression "law". It follows that we cannot retrieve the content of the concept of law simply by identifying shared application criteria (which is what Dworkin mistakenly believes positivists seek to do), and so Dworkin concludes that jurisprudence must take the form of "constructive interpretation".⁶

Before we can consider how the semantic sting argument is supposed to lay the groundwork for a normative jurisprudence, we must first attend to a fundamental confusion at the heart of the argument—a confusion that undermines it and that reappears in Dworkin's defense of normative jurisprudence. This is the confusion between *the content of the concept of law* and *the content of the law of a particular community*. Dworkin cannot fail to understand the difference between these two notions; yet he fails to attend to this difference in his argument—with disastrous results.

The semantic sting argument begins with a characterization of a particular semantic theory ("criterial semantics") to which Dworkin takes positivists to be committed. According to this theory of meaning, "we follow shared rules . . . in using any word: these rules set out criteria that supply the word's meaning".⁷ Thus, the "very meaning of the word 'law' makes law depend on certain specific criteria, and that any lawyer who rejected or challenged those criteria would be speaking self-contradictory nonsense."⁸ Of course, the meaning of the word "law" may depend on specific shared criteria even if the law of a particular community does not depend on shared criteria of any sort. And thus a lawyer who challenged what the criteria of legality were in his community could hardly be accused (even by a criterial semanticist) of speaking "self-contradictory nonsense".

In developing his critique of a criterial semantics of "law", Dworkin runs together two distinct notions: the first is the meaning or application conditions of term "law" (or the semantic content of the concept of law); the second is the criteria of legality in a particular community. Dworkin claims that if we adopt a criterial semantics of law, we cannot explain the possibility of disagreement about the concept's application criteria—at least not in the case of important and central, or what he calls "pivotal", disagreements. "If legal argument is mainly or even partly about pivotal cases," he writes, "then lawyers cannot all be using the same factual criteria for deciding when propositions of law are true and false. Their arguments would be mainly or partly about which criteria they should use."⁹ He concludes, "if two lawyers are actually following different rules in using the word 'law',

⁶ Mark Greenberg has suggested to me an alternative understanding of the semantic sting argument in which its point is not to establish the necessity of a normative jurisprudence, but rather to clear the way for an argument to the effect that law is an interpretive concept. On this reading, we do not infer normative jurisprudence from the semantic sting. Rather, if criterial semantics is the correct way to think about law, then it cannot be an interpretive concept. On this reading, interpretivism is not established by the semantic sting; the semantic sting makes interpretivism about law viable. This is an interesting suggestion, and though I have my doubts about whether it is supported by the structure of the argument of *Law's Empire*, accepting Greenberg's interpretation has no effect on the argument that follows.
⁷ *Law's Empire*, 31.   ⁸ Ibid.   ⁹ Ibid. 41.

using different factual criteria to decide when a proposition of law is true or false, then each must mean something different from the other when he says what the law is."[10]

The conclusion of the argument reveals just how deeply embedded Dworkin's confusion is. The syntax of the sentence—and everything else in the argument that leads up to the conclusion—suggests that Dworkin takes the first two clauses—"If two lawyers are actually following different rules in using the word 'law' " and "using different factual criteria to decide when a proposition of law is true or false"—to come to the same thing or to be logically equivalent. Both in any case are thought to entail the conclusion that "each must mean something different from the other when he says what the law is". However, while it is true on a criterial semantics that two individuals who follow different rules for applying the word or concept "law" must be assigning different meanings to it, it hardly follows that two people who are using different factual criteria to decide whether a proposition of law is true or false must be assigning different meanings to the term "law", or employing different concepts of law. This simply confuses the notion of *law* as such with the notion of *the law* of a particular community.

You and I can use different factual criteria for determining whether or not something is legally binding without disagreeing about the meaning of the concept of law; and we can agree on the factual criteria without disagreeing on the application conditions of concept. This is obvious once one realizes that the factual criteria for determining whether or not a proposition of law is true or false are indexed to particular legal systems, whereas the criteria for the semantic content of the concept of law are not. So you and I can share the same concept of law, but because we practice law in different communities, we can "disagree" (in an uninteresting sense) about what the factual criteria are for determining the truth or falsity of particular propositions of law. By the same token, you and I can practice law in the same community and agree on what the criteria are in our community, and yet disagree about the general concept of law. To illustrate, we might agree that a rule that violates the equal protection clause of the 14th Amendment is not valid law, but disagree about the concept of law in the following way: you believe that the best explanation of this fact is that substantive morality is a criterion of legality whether or not such a constraint is practiced (you are a natural lawyer) and I believe that the best explanation of this fact is that there is a conventional practice of refusing to treat as binding rules that fail a test of substantive equality. I am conventionalist about the concept and you are not. What we disagree about is how best to explain the practice; we need not disagree about what the criteria of legality are.

---

[10] *Law's Empire*, 31.

Can you and I disagree about the criteria of legality in our (common) community without thereby disagreeing about the meaning of law? In other words, is criterial semantics compatible with disagreement between lawyers (or other competent and relevant language users) about the criteria of legality in their community? This, I take it, is the case Dworkin is most concerned about. Unfortunately for Dworkin, you and I can disagree about the criteria of legality in our community without our disagreeing about the criteria for application of the term "law". Suppose, for example, that we share the view that law is a contestable concept in the sense that wherever there is law, what the law is is always a matter of potential dispute, and requires an interpretive practice. Indeed our disagreement about what the criteria of legality in our community are makes perfectly good sense to us in part because such disagreement is part of what we take law to be—part of our shared understanding of the kind of thing it is. Thus, not only is dis-agreement about the criteria of legality in our community compatible with our sharing the same criteria for applying the concept law, in this case our disagreement about the criteria of legality in our community is intelligible to us just because we share the same criteria for applying the concept.

Dworkin simply misdiagnoses the situation in which we disagree about the criteria of legality in our community. That disagreement may be advanced, intelligibly, as part of an argument that positivism as a substant-ive theory of the concept of law is false—that is, as evidence for the claim that in some legal communities the criteria of legality are not exhausted by shared criteria, or that the criteria are not shared in the way in which a con-ventionalist picture requires that they must be. But the fact of disagreement over the criteria of legality tells us nothing about the proper methodology for retrieving the content of the concept of law. Dworkin constantly runs these two issues together, and the net effect is that he takes an argument about the criteria of legality in a legal system to be a knockdown argument against a semantic theory; but this is plainly a non sequitur. If—as now seems likely—Dworkin's main arguments for normative jurisprudence are actually geared to the defense of the very different thesis that retrieving the content of a community's law requires moral and political argument, then we should not be surprised to find that construing these argu-ments as a case for normative jurisprudence does not show them to their best advantage. We should consider what merit there might be in them nonetheless.[11]

As we have seen, the semantic sting argument is supposed to undermine a criterial semantics of the concept of law (as well as the substantive pos-itivist theory that Dworkin mistakenly supposes to be supported by criterial

---

[11] For an interesting argument to the same effect, see Kenneth Einar Himma, "Ambiguously Stung" *Legal Theory* 7 (2001).

semantics). The conclusion of the argument is that "law" is an interpretive concept, and therefore that in order to retrieve its content, we must engage in "constructive interpretation". In constructive interpretation, we begin by imputing a point or purpose to a thing; we then orient our interpretation of it toward the goal of revealing it in its best light—that is, as something that is the best of its kind—which in this context amounts to interpreting it as something that serves its purpose well, or expresses well the value attributed to it. This is an activity that necessarily entails substantive normative argument. Since the point or purpose that we must impute to law is that of justifying and limiting the state's exercise of coercive force, the substantive argument that we must undertake in order to retrieve the content of the concept of law will necessarily appeal to norms of political morality. This is the sense in which, for Dworkin, jurisprudence must be normative.

Let us grant that law is an "essentially contestable concept"—in the sense that competent language users do indeed disagree about its criteria of application. If true, this would be an important fact about the concept, and could well bear on the way in which one ought to go about recovering its content. As I have argued in Lecture 11, however, the dichotomy that Dworkin posits—either criterial semantics or constructive interpretation— is a false one. Constructive interpretation is hardly the only alternative to criterial semantics—and so the failure of the latter does not entail inter- pretivism. Even if, speaking broadly, some sort of interpretation is neces- sary to retrieve the content of contestable concepts, it does not follow that constructive interpretation in Dworkin's sense is the only available or appropriate alternative. It is hardly obvious, for example, that conceptual analysis of important philosophical concepts like "truth", "meaning", or "knowledge" must proceed by first imputing a point, purpose, or value to the thing the concept denotes or refers to; nor is it obvious why we should proceed differently in the case of "law". To be sure, Dworkin suggests that his interpretive model applies, in the first instance, to social practices and structures; but even if we grant that social practices must be interpreted in the light of their purpose or function, that still cannot, without additional premises, support the claim that jurisprudence must be normative in Dworkin's sense—that is, in the sense of requiring us to engage in substant- ive *moral* argument. For example, Dworkin does not claim that an inter- pretation of the concept of art (a social practice) calls for substantive moral argument. The norms appropriate to an interpretation of a practice depend on the kind of practice it is. This means that in order to anchor an interpre- tation, we need some preinterpretive account of the kind of practice we are interpreting and of its purpose or function. This is presumably the status of Dworkin's claim that law's purpose or function is to justify and limit the coercive power of the state. This pretheoretical imputation of a justificatory function to law is the premise that orients our analysis of the concept of law toward substantive political argument.

It should be noted that in maintaining that the function of law is to justify coercion, Dworkin must be claiming that this is an essential or central property of law—not just a role that law can play, or a function that some, many, or most communities happen to assign to law.[12] If the justification of coercion were not a part of our concept of law as such, then why should an analysis of the concept be oriented toward explaining law in the light of that function? A hammer, for example, can serve any number of functions—it can be a murder weapon or a paperweight—but the capacity of hammers to be used in these ways, and in that sense to serve these functions, is hardly a part of our concept of a hammer, and we would not expect an account of what hammers are to be oriented toward providing an explanation of these capacities. If the function Dworkin attributes to law is necessary in order to orient our analysis of the concept, then we have to assume that this function is a property of law as such. But that is not something that Dworkin can assume without argument; and one argument that is not available to him is that this essential feature of the concept is revealed in the process of a constructive interpretation of the concept of law. For the function must be presupposed before we can begin to apply that method, and cannot be a consequence of applying it.

The method of constructive interpretation requires, moreover, that we display the object of interpretation in its best light. To orient our analysis of law toward its imputed function means, for Dworkin, that we must recover the content of the concept of law in a way that reveals law as serving its justificatory function well—which is to say that the concept of law as such is the concept of something that succeeds, in some significant measure, in its aim of providing moral justification. Law is at least prima facie justified or legitimate. It appears to follow that in order for a form of governance to count as law, it must have features that warrant the attribution of prima-facie legitimacy. It is a question of substantive morality what those features are. Thus, an analysis of the concept of law requires us to appeal to substantive norms of political morality.

This is an argument for normative jurisprudence all right, but how seriously can we take it? At each crucial point the inferences seem to come out of thin air. We begin by imputing an essential function or purpose to law—in doing so, we do not argue that this is the only function we could impute, nor do we defend the claim that this function is essential to law; we

---

[12] Even if social practices and structures are the sorts of things that must have functions, it is not obvious that they must have essential functions, such that two institutions could not be institutions of the same kind unless they had the same function. Games are social practices, but the point of war games is different from the point of spin-the-bottle, which is in turn probably different from the purpose or function of Jeopardy.

simply assert (implicitly perhaps) that it is essential. Then we move from the claim that our analysis of the concept must be a constructive interpretation in Dworkin's stipulated sense, to the conclusion that in order to understand what law is, we must understand it as largely *succeeding* in justifying the state's police power. This move requires a specific, and rather dubious, understanding of how to apply the Davidsonian principle of charity in such a context. For Davidson, the principle of charity is motivated and defended as a precondition of understanding behavior as linguistic—that is, as conveying or having meaning. There is no apparent reason why Davidson's argument should be extended in this context to warrant applying the principle of charity as grounds for attributing *success* to law in fulfilling its function. Thus, we get to normative jurisprudence from two basic premises, neither of which is independently defended: the imputed essential function of law as justificatory-centered, and a dubious application of the principle of charity. The conclusion that an analysis of the concept of law necessarily calls for appeal to political morality appears as if by magic.

The argument for a normative jurisprudence that is supported by the text is hopeless. The groundwork for a normative jurisprudence is laid by the semantic sting, but the semantic sting—quite apart from its other infelicities—treats evidence for the claim that the content of the law of a particular community requires substantive normative argument as if it were evidence against a particular semantic theory of concepts, when it may be evidence against a particular substantive theory of the concept of law. To be sure, I have argued that even on this score, the objection to positivism can be met once we properly understand how to think about the conventionality of the rule of recognition.

The same confusion between the content of the law and the content of the concept of law that first surfaces in the semantic sting resurfaces in the positive case for a normative jurisprudence that is supposed to fall out of the fact that "law" is an interpretive concept. Instead, if anything the application of the principle of charity Dworkin invokes is better suited to an argument whose initial premise is that the content of law of a particular community depends on an interpretation of the relevant legal practice. At the end of the day—beyond the rather Disney-like defence of a normative jurisprudence that rests on an undefended imputation of a function of justifying coercion and a dubious application of the principle of charity— we are left with nothing that looks like a plausible argument for the claim that the proper method of jurisprudence must appeal to norms of political morality. Let us therefore consider whether there might be reasons available to Dworkin, or to someone sympathetic with his claims or his general approach, that could support the undefended premises of the argument I have just considered—in particular, the imputed essential function and the principle of charity.

The most direct and obvious route to a normative jurisprudence is predicated on law's having some necessary moral property that orients the analysis of the concept toward norms of political morality. If law necessarily possesses some moral property, M, then all the other features of law picked out by a theory of the concept must be at least consistent with M; and perhaps must be sufficient to explain law's having M. Thus, the elements of a jurisprudential theory must be defended on the basis of moral premises. However, setting aside the difficulties one might encounter in trying to demonstrate the existence of some essential moral property of law, there is the further worry that an argument of this sort will not support one of the claims most often made on behalf of normative jurisprudence. Proponents of the view that an analysis of the concept of law must invoke substantive moral and political considerations are—as far as I know, invariably— committed to the claim that a normative jurisprudence is compatible with the full range of important substantive theories of the concept.[13] Defenders of normative jurisprudence hold that whether one is a positivist, a legal realist, a natural lawyer, a Dworkinian interpretivist, or what have you, the substantive theory one comes to must be supported by premises drawn from substantive political morality.[14] But to argue for normative jurisprudence on the basis of some essential moral property of law may preclude several important substantive conceptual theories of law—and in particular, all positivist theories. Thus, if we proceed to a normative jurisprudence from the existence of a moral property that law necessarily possesses, we cannot hold onto the claim that a normative jurisprudence is, at least in principle, compatible with the broad range of accounts of the concept of law. Indeed, it looks like we are left with the unsurprising and familiar thesis that natural law theories of one sort or another can entail a normative jurisprudence.[15]

If we are to hold onto the claim that a defense of a normative jurisprudence should be consistent with the range of substantive theories of the concept—even those that deny that law has essential moral properties—

---

[13] This is not an entailment of the claim of normative jurisprudence—which states that in order to recover the content of the concept of law, we must engage in substantive normative argument. The point here is not that the advocates of normative jurisprudence *must* assert the independence of method and substance in jurisprudence, but that they *do* assert it. In part at least, their motivation is to suggest that their methodological claims do not turn on controversial substantive issues.

[14] Dworkin, for example, believes that a normative methodology is consistent with positivism's substantive theory of law. Dworkin, "A Reply by Ronald Dworkin" in Cohen (ed.), *Ronald Dworkin and Contemporary Jurisprudence*, 255.

[15] In fact, positivism is not obviously incompatible with there being necessary moral properties of law. Positivism is incompatible only with the existence of moral properties of law that would warrant an inference from legality to legitimacy. See the discussion of the "commendation argument" for normative jurisprudence (see below), in which I suggest that positivism might be compatible with law's having certain necessary moral properties.

then we will have to look for another route to normative jurisprudence—
one that ascribes no necessary moral property to law. What might such
an argument look like? One promising approach might begin with the
claim that an analysis of the kind of thing law is should be oriented
toward the self-conception of participants in the legal system. It is, after all,
a central claim even for legal positivism that in order for law to exist there
must be practices of identification, legislation, and adjudication that are
accepted from an internal point of view by the relevant officials. To accept
these rules from the internal point of view is to be committed to them,
to treat them as reasons for acting, as legitimate standards of conduct.
Perhaps the conception of law that informs the relevant officials' actions—
their understanding of the meaning of their actions, of what it is that they
are doing—is the lens through which we can best see the kind of thing
law is.

We can characterize the self-conception of legal participants in a variety of
different ways, but it is plausible that any adequate characterization would
emphasize the claim that law is understood by its practitioners as a special
kind of justification-centered activity—one that seeks to justify a coercive
police power. Those whose self-conception we are focusing on see the
law as a sincere attempt to track the demands of political legitimacy. It would
be hard for them to understand what they were doing if they did not
see themselves as engaged in an activity that aimed to offer a genuine
justification for the exercise of police power. This aim is only imperfectly
realizable in practice, however, since legal practice is also constrained by the
authoritative sources that constitute the distinctive identity, history, and
culture of a particular legal system. The relevant legal actors understand
law not only as justification-centered, but also as constrained by the history
of an institution—their law—that is continuous over time.

Can we get from this self-understanding to a normative jurisprudence?
Here is one argument. Were it not for the peculiar institutional history of
the law of any particular community, every participant in its legal system
would believe that she exercised power in a way that actually did track the
demands of political morality or of justice, broadly conceived. When questions of law arose, participants would simply go straight to the applicable
moral norms. The institutional history creates a potential gap between
what is morally required (or would be morally required absent any institutional history) and what the law in fact requires, because what the law
requires must "fit" the institutional history: it must be the case that the new
legal pronouncements and the old ones are seen as pronouncements of
one and the same institution—the legal system—which is continuous over
time. Law must, in this sense, display a certain integrity. Now the principle
of charity enters in the following way. In order to reconcile the necessary
belief that their practice has a justificatory aim with the necessary belief that

it is a practice that is continuous over time, participants *must* believe that the prior pronouncements were by and large morally justified. Otherwise they would have to give up either most of the prior pronouncements, or the justificatory aim—and both are necessary parts of their self-understanding as participants in a *legal* system. So the concept of law, seen through the lens of the participants of any legal institution, is the concept of something that is by and large morally justified.[16] Therefore, wherever we have law, it must be the case that the law of that community must be at least prima facie legitimate—because its practitioners necessarily see it that way. And thus we must engage in moral argument to determine whether a community has law in the relevant sense. Jurisprudence must be normative.

This line of argument is consistent with a good deal of what both Dworkin and Perry explicitly say and implicitly are committed to. It provides a defense of both the imputed justification function and the principle of charity: these elements are conceptually necessary parts of the self-conception of participants (at least of some and perhaps most key participants) in a legal system. Moreover, the self-conception argument has the distinct advantage of getting us to a normative jurisprudence from premises that do not attribute any necessary moral properties to law. Still, however seductive it may appear at first blush, the self-conception argument is inadequate to the task at hand. To be sure, we may demand as an adequacy condition of an analysis of the concept of law that it have resources adequate to explain the self-understandings of participants; but this does not mean that we must *credit* those self-understandings in the context of trying to understand what the practice is. Indeed, there are real reasons for suspicion in this context, for we might worry that participants in the practice are too close to it—that they have too much invested in seeing it in a way that legitimates their lives and actions. By crediting the internal point of view of officials in this way, we in effect preclude the possibility of false consciousness or bad faith. This disregards what would seem to be a natural psychological pressure to regard as justified one's participation in a practice that involves the use of coercive force to resolve disputes and to enforce a specific distribution of social burdens and benefits. The alternative would be for the participants to see themselves as thugs, extortionists, and racketeers. But we don't even have to assume the possibility of bad faith or false consciousness to see the problem with crediting the self-understanding of participants. All we have to do is to admit their fallibility, the possibility that they might have got it terribly wrong, and have, despite

---

[16] "By and large" is intentionally vague. We could cash out the claim in a variety of ways, any of which would be suitable to the argument under consideration. The claim could be that most legal pronouncents are justified, or that most are sufficiently justified to create real, though overridable, moral reasons, or that the legal system as a whole is capable of creating such reasons. There are other possible alternatives. Nothing here turns on this.

their good faith efforts, adopted patterns of behavior that cannot be morally justified.

It might be argued on Davidsonian grounds that there is something incoherent in the idea that the practitioners of a legal system could be systematically mistaken about the sorts of assertions that they would (indeed, must) make concerning their practice. Davidson has advanced powerful arguments for the view that in order to understand an individual's behavior as language—that is, as expressing propositions with meanings—we must regard most of the claims that she makes as true. The idea of a language user being systematically mistaken is incoherent. Perhaps something similar could be argued about the claims that practitioners in a legal system would make. We must credit most of their assertions if we want to hang onto the idea that they are practicing law. But this is surely a misapplication of the principle of charity. Let us grant that there are a priori reasons showing that the whole set of assertions that members of a culture or linguistic community would endorse must be regarded as mostly true if we are to regard them as assertions in the first place. It does not follow that the claims embedded in *specific* cultural institutions and practices must be regarded as mostly true—otherwise it looks as though we could secure a priori proof of the existence of God by applying the principle of charity to the claims that are made within the practice of religion.[17] It is simply implausible to assert that we *must* credit the self-understanding of legal practitioners in order to make sense of the claim that they are practicing law.[18]

I fear we have not solved the dilemma facing the normative jurisprudent. How can one defend the claim that an analysis of the concept of law must be normative without that argument being underwritten by a claim to the effect that law has some necessary moral property that orients an analysis of the concept to principles of political morality? The self-conception

---

[17] It might be argued that as an empirical matter, people do not adopt and maintain a practice in pursuit of a given aim unless the practice is generally reliable—that is, tends to succeed in its aim. But of course law, like religion, can have lots of different aims—even if law must always have the aim to justify and religion the aim to worship or otherwise to placate a supernatural being. But it is possible that succeeding at some of the *contingent* aims makes such an institution worth keeping and in that sense explains its persistence—even if it often or usually or even necessarily fails of its essential aim. For example, the practice of burning up animals in order to make God happy lasted (or has lasted) for quite a while, yet arguably has never made God happy (though it may have fostered group solidarity and produced the belief that God was being made happy—potential contributions to human flourishing). Even if the practice of law in some community fails systematically of its putatively essential aim to justify the use of force, it is possible that the benefits to some of being able to guide the behavior of others— or the common benefits of coordination that law provides—might enable such a misguided legal system to reproduce itself and to persist over time.

[18] The points in the previous paragraph were all made by Eric Cavallero, and I am especially grateful to him for the discussions that led to my clarifying my thinking about this line of argument for normative jurisprudence.

argument just considered is of the right sort, but is not up to the task. But perhaps we have given up too quickly on arguments that begin by attributing a necessary moral property to law. One might argue that what troubles positivists is not the claim that law has some necessary moral property, but the stronger claim that the moral property law necessarily has (or is said to have) is sufficiently strong to warrant an inference from legality to legitimacy. If that is so, then it may be possible to identify a moral property that law necessarily has and that is strong enough to orient the analysis of the concept of law toward substantive principles of political morality, yet weak enough not to warrant an inference from legality to legitimacy. In that way we might nevertheless get to a normative jurisprudence from the existence of a necessary moral property law has, while still hanging onto the claim that a normative jurisprudence is compatible in principle with the range of important substantive theories of the concept of law. One argument that might succeed in both of these aims rests on the idea that the predicate "law" functions in our normative discourse as what I will call a "predicate of weak commendation".[19] Articulating this feature of our concept of law and explaining it may prove to be the best way of understanding what drives the normative/descriptive debate.

When we speak of law, we mean a form of governance that constitutes a distinctive normative relationship between the governing individuals or institutions, and those who are governed by them. The way that law structures this relationship is different from, and in some sense morally preferable to, the relationship between, for example, the ruling powers and the subject population in the case of a military occupation. More generally, governance by law is preferable to governance by force and fear. Any plausible account of law must not only make plain the differences among these forms of governance, it must do so in a way that explains—or enables us to explain—why we believe legal governance is morally attractive. We can capture this condition by saying that law is a "predicate of commendation".

In characterizing law this way, we need not mean to imply that legal authority is always morally legitimate or justified, or even that any actual instance of it is. We certainly need not claim that the law in a particular community is justified merely in virtue of its status as law. Law is, in this sense, a predicate of *weak* commendation, and we may contrast it with a predicate of strong commendation such as "justice". A theory of justice would be implausible on its face if its extension included morally undesirable social, political, or economic arrangements. The property of moral legitimacy is an essential, or a central, feature of our concept of justice, and an argument to the effect that an analysis of justice picks out some morally illegitimate

---

[19] Strictly speaking, "law" is not a predicate; for ease of exposition I will use "law" to cover a variety of cognate predicates, including "is law", "is legal", and so on.

social arrangement is an argument for the inadequacy of that analysis. By contrast, laws—and perhaps even legal systems—can be morally illegitimate, and more often than we would care to believe, probably are. Nonetheless, we seem inclined to acknowledge that there is something commendable about law as such.

An argument for normative jurisprudence begins with this weak commendation feature of the predicate "law". If law is a predicate of weak commendation, then one could argue that the best explanation of how it is that law plays this role in our normative discourse is that law has a moral property adequate to warrant "law's" linguistic role. That is, there must be some moral property that law has that provides the explanation of the fact that "law" plays this commendation role in our normative discourse. Every instance of law must possess this moral property, M—something weaker, perhaps, than either moral legitimacy or prima-facie legitimacy. If law has such a property, an analysis of the concept of law should specify what this property M is—and in doing so, the analysis must appeal to moral argument in two ways: in specifying the content of M, the analysis must reveal how or why that property is morally attractive; and the overall analysis must be such that it picks out only things that have the property M. Thus, in selecting the other elements of the analysis of law, theorists are constrained to select a set of elements that are sufficient for, or at the very least consistent with, M. Succeeding in that is an adequacy condition for an analysis of law, and necessarily entails engaging in substantive moral argument.

This sounds like a case for normative jurisprudence, so let us consider the point more carefully. We have already granted the first premise, that law is a predicate of weak commendation. This is simply a fact about the role that law plays in our normative discourse. In acknowledging this, we leave open the question of how law plays this role. One answer is that provided in the foregoing argument, namely, that there is a moral property, M, that law necessarily has, and it is the existence of that property that explains how law could serve as a predicate of commendation in our normative discourse. Law plays a commendation role in our normative discourse because the concept of law is the concept of something with a certain morally attractive property.

Clearly, the property of being morally legitimate would suffice to explain law's commendation function, but few normative jurisprudents would wish to endorse the inference from legality to moral legitimacy. There are other values for M that might also explain the commendation feature. More importantly, it has yet to be established that the existence of an essential moral property is the only way we can make sense of the commending role "law" plays in our normative discourse.

It could be argued, for example, that the commendation feature of law is simply an induction over experience. The historical record provides us with examples of a variety of different kinds of governance, legal and otherwise, and the legal ones seem to be preferable on balance. Or perhaps it is something even less creditable: a shortsighted induction. Maybe recent legal systems have been better than their alternatives. For one reason or another, we have formed positive associations about the concept, and that is what explains the role that law plays in our normative discourse. However, this is just an accidental feature of law, and has no bearing on the content of the concept or on the proper method of jurisprudence.

The point is debatable, but I do not want to defend it here. The immediate rejoinder will be that if we have inductively based beliefs about the moral attractiveness of law, these beliefs are not to be explained by mere historical contingency—by brute facts about how various forms of governance happen to have worked out. If law is associated historically with a more humane or just form of governance than its alternatives, that fact is owing to something inherent in the nature of law. Indeed, it is not clear that we should even accept the claim that our beliefs about the attractiveness of law are inductively based in the first place. It is not obvious that the historical record—whether on a long or a short view—presents an unambiguously attractive picture of legal governance, or that the commendation feature really depends on the record's doing so. It seems likelier that the explanation of the commendation feature lies not in what laws and legal systems have actually been, but, rather, in what they can potentially be. That is to say, inherent in the nature of law is the potential for a kind of governance that we feel is more morally attractive than alternatives. Our concept of law is the concept of something that has the inherent potential to achieve, realize, or take the form of a certain ideal of governance.

The suggestion now is that the morally attractive property of law is its inherent potential to realize or to manifest an ideal of governance. As a potential, it need not be realized in every instance of law, and that explains once and for all why the argument for normative jurisprudence need not endorse the inference from legality to legitimacy. Yet at the same time, if this potential is an essential or central feature of our concept of law, an analysis of law must appeal to moral argument.

One way of distinguishing different forms of governance is in terms of the structure of the relationship between, as we might put it, "ruler" and "ruled".[20] The idea of law imposes constraints not only on the ruled, but also on the ruler. To be sure, a legal system need not be effective in constraining the exercise of the ruler's power, and may even stipulate that the law imposes no such constraints; but in so far as a ruler exercises purely

---

[20] Of course, it may be a complex relationship or set of such relationships. In speaking of a relationship, I am making an expository simplification, not advancing a naive substantive theory of governance.

arbitrary power, he or she does not govern by law. Law thus implies a kind of reciprocity between ruler and ruled. Legal rules are, as such, general in their scope and application, knowable in advance, and susceptible of compliance. These features indicate that under law, the governed are, in some perhaps very modest and limited sense, treated as autonomous agents capable of deliberating and acting on the basis of reason. This normative relationship between ruler and ruled under law is morally preferable to alternatives, and this inherent feature of law explains why it is a predicate of commendation.[21]

We can understand a range of important legal theories as alternative attempts to explicate the inherent potential of law to realize a morally attractive ideal of governance. Dworkin's assertion that law is a practice that aims to justify the state's exercise of coercive force could be seen as a way of explicating a morally attractive potential of law: certainly a state that recognizes an obligation to justify its coercive actions is capable of being better, morally, than a state that fails to recognize any such obligation. Raz's view of law as something that necessarily claims to mediate between persons and the reasons that apply to them contains similar resources. For it conceives of law's relationship to citizens as capable of serving their interest in meeting the demands of right reason, conceives of law as figuring in the deliberations of autonomous agents, and so on. Whatever their differences, Dworkin and Raz allow us to understand the moral attractiveness of a kind of governance that law has the inherent potential to realize. At the same time neither view rests on the claim that law must always realize this potential, and thus neither view succumbs to the pitfall of endorsing an inference from legality to moral legitimacy.[22]

[21] In Lecture 11 I distinguished positivism from natural law theory in terms of the social fact thesis that positivism endorses and natural law theory rejects. It is time to modify that claim and make it more precise. Some important natural lawyers, like John Finnis and perhaps Lon Fuller, could accept the claim that the criteria of legality in a community are conventional. They could even accept the claim of inclusive legal positivism that morality can but need not be a condition of legality. What, then, makes them natural law theorists? One possible answer is that they believe that law necessarily has an inherent capacity to realize a certain ideal of governance. This ideal of governance is, for them, a necessary feature of the concept and an expression of a moral ideal. That ideal, for Finnis, is expressed in a principle of reciprocity. In Fuller it is expressed in the canons representing the internal morality of law. My doubts about this line of argument are implicit in the argument below.

[22] Even Hart's analysis enables us to explain the inherent potential of law to realize an attractive form of governance. For in positing, as the function of law, the guidance of conduct by rules that are reasons, Hart posits a function that can be understood, perhaps in a variety of different ways, as morally attractive. It has the capacity to treat individuals as autonomous, to mediate between persons and the reasons that apply to them, to justify the use of coercive force, and to serve a variety of welfare-enhancing ends. The moral attractiveness of law's putative guidance function is perhaps at a higher level of generality than any of these particular accounts of what is morally attractive about legal governance, but all of these accounts are suitable to reveal that law is necessarily the sort of thing with the inherent potential of realizing a morally attractive form of governance.

The argument from commendation may now be summarized as follows. Law is a predicate of weak commendation. This is because it is a part of our concept of law that it is morally attractive as such, from which it follows that every instance of law has some morally attractive property M. That property is the inherent potential of law to realize an ideal of governance. The relevant ideal can be specified in different, perhaps competing, ways, and at different levels of generality; but any analysis of the concept of law must invoke substantive moral premises in order to explain the nature of M, and to orient the analysis toward only those practices that have M. Thus all jurisprudence must be normative.

The flaw in this argument lies in the way we are to understand the idea of the inherent potential of law. Let us grant that law does have the inherent potential to realize a variety of moral ideals that other forms of governance cannot realize, and that this distinguishes law from other forms of governance. Is this inherent potential really a part of our concept of law? We should not be led astray by the metaphysical resonance of an expression like "inherent potential". There are ways of understanding that expression that do have metaphysical implications, but the initial plausibility of the foregoing argument depends on a more straightforward and metaphysically innocent sense of law's "inherent potential".

Law just is the kind of thing that can realize some attractive ideals. That fact about law is not necessarily part of our concept of it. After all, a hammer is the kind of thing that can be a murder weapon, a paperweight, or a commodity. Religion is the kind of thing that can stir murderous passions. Medicine is the kind of thing that can form the basis of a lucrative economic sector—doing so is, in that sense, an "inherent potential" of medicine. However, the fact that a thing, by its nature, has certain capacities or can be used for various ends or as a part of various projects does not entail that all or any of those capacities, ends, or projects are a part of our concept of that thing. The only point we must grant about the "inherent potential" of law to realize an attractive moral ideal of governance is the fact that law is the kind of thing with the capacity to do so. But that alone is sufficient to explain the commendation role that "law" plays in our normative discourse. Nothing follows from this about the content of our concept of law. Thus, the commendation argument errs when it assumes that a particularly interesting capacity of law is in fact a part of our concept of it. An argument is needed to show that that is the case, and none appears to be forthcoming.

Of course, if we were to give an analysis of the concept of a hammer that did not shed light on its capacity to be used as a paperweight, that would be a prima facie inadequacy of the analysis. If we were to analyze the concept of religion in way that failed to account for the capacity of religion to stir murderous passions, we would have grounds to fault that analysis too. It does not follow that an analysis of either concept must rely on, invoke, or appeal to these capacities in identifying the central features of the concepts. By the same token, an analysis of law should help us to understand what we find morally attractive about it, and an analysis that failed to do so would be lacking. But this condition does not imply that we must appeal to moral argument in order to provide an adequate analysis of law. It is sufficient if, at the end of the day, the analysis we offer helps us to understand the morally attractive capacities of law.

In Part II of this book I have offered a theory of the concept of law that involves a variety of elements: primary and secondary rules, the rule of recognition, the internal point of view, and the conventionality thesis. These elements can be conjoined in a way that can explain why governance by law is preferable to alternative forms of governance. If one is moved by the moral ideals of autonomy and dignity, then one can see how the elements of my analysis constitute a thing (law) that has the capacity for accommodating those ideals in ways that other forms of governance cannot. If one is moved by the ways in which effective organization can enhance human welfare, then it is plain to see that law, understood in terms of the analysis I offer, can be conducive to those ends. But autonomy, dignity, and welfare do not enter at any point into the analysis that I offer, nor do any other moral properties. These ideals are external to the concept of law; law happens to be the kind of thing that can serve them well. The capacity to do so is, in a metaphysically innocent sense, an inherent potential of law. This implies nothing about how the analysis of law must proceed, and the analysis I have offered makes no appeal to any of the values that make law attractive.

Before moving on to consider Stephen Perry's very interesting interpretation of Hart as himself a normative jurisprudent, I want to consider one final way of reading Dworkin's argument that is suggested by the text, consistent with aspects of his holism, and which is in any case invited by the pragmatist approach I have been developing throughout this book. In discussing the claim that the function of law is to justify and limit the coercive authority of the state, Dworkin writes "Our discussions about law by and large assume, I suggest, that the most abstract and fundamental point of legal practice is to guide and constrain the power of government in the following way. Law insists that force be used or withheld except as licensed or required by individual rights and responsibilities flowing from past political decisions about when collective force is justified." Instead of understanding Dworkin as imputing to law a function that is an essential feature of it and thus one which demands that we orient our analysis of law around it—a function that is discernible a priori or otherwise defensible transcendentally as a precondition of our capacity to discuss and evaluate law, we can ascribe to him a somewhat different strategy of argument. On this reading Dworkin is presenting a plausible case for orienting an analysis or theory of the concept of law around a particular conception of its function. The argument for imputing this function to law is that it helps us understand discussions about law—how it is that we are talking about the same thing when we express both our agreements and disagreements about it: what it is, what value it serves, when it is justified, and so on.

Arguably, there are other ways of thinking about the point, purpose, or function of law that can be recommended on similar grounds. So we might think of law as having the function of coordinating behavior, of sustaining cooperative interaction, or as allowing for a certain realization of the self, and so on. In imputing a function or point to law in this sense, we then orient our analysis of the concept accordingly and see what picture of the kind of practice law is that emerges. Thus, instead of reading him as claiming that the function of justifying and limiting the coercive authority of the state is an essential feature of law, discernible a priori by reflection on our concept of it, we can read Dworkin as making only a provisional claim about the concept of law. This claim could be part of an account that acknowledges that there are many possible functions or values that we can associate with law. Attributing one or another function to law will orient the analysis of the concept in a particular way—identifying particular features of law as salient, while relegating others to subsidiary roles. Thus, different conceptions of the concept will fall out of different attributions of a function, purpose, or value. We then choose among the different conceptions according to appropriate criteria for assessing the theories of concept of law.

I couldn't agree more with such an approach. The problem is that applying it hardly yields a normative jurisprudence. If anything, we would choose among such theories of the concept in the light of the role the concept plays in our general theories of the world. Does thinking about law as oriented primarily toward the guidance of conduct, the relationship between agents and reasons, for example, fit better with other concepts cognate to law and with other human practices in, so to speak, the immediate social neighborhood of law? Or does thinking about law in terms of political power and obligation provide a better fit? Here, the norms for evaluating the theories are pragmatic, theoretical, epistemic, and most importantly, discursive.

It is very clear that, understood in this way, there is no reason at all why all jurisprudential theories would necessarily invoke moral argument. It is clearer still, I hope, that the choice among conflicting conceptions of the concept is not made on grounds of political morality. The grounds are broadly speaking epistemic and discursive. We are choosing a theory of the concept—the best theory of the concept—as part of a construction of a general theory of the world and the concepts we employ to structure it. Different theories of the concept allow us to nest law and the concept of it differently: some emphasizing its centrality to the guidance of conduct; others to the theory of political obligation; others to an ideal of the person that can be realized only given certain social forms and institutions.

If we pursue this tack, we are not in the business of carving the universe at its joints; we are not trying to gain access to or pick out metaphysically essential properties of law that are prior to our analysis of the concept, and that serve to orient it. Rather, this project of conceptual analysis is committed roughly to an ontology of law that follows from the relevant epistemology of it. And while it is natural to read Dworkin, for one, as having a constructivist ontology of law, I doubt that pursuing this project along the lines I have just described can warrant a normative jurisprudence. For even if interpretivism is a normative epistemology in Dworkin's sense, it falls short of requiring moral and political argument.

In an extremely interesting and important series of papers Stephen Perry advances yet a different argument on behalf of normative jurisprudence. Instead of a general argument of the sort I have considered to this point, Perry has pursued a strategy of developing a critique of Hart's analysis of the concept of law. In stark contrast to Dworkin—who imputes a criterial semantics to Hart—Perry's stated aim is to establish that Hart was engaged in normative jurisprudence. Specifically, Perry maintains that Hart relies on substantive grounds of political morality to identify the features of law that figure most prominently in his account—such features as rules, the internal point of view, law's guidance function, and so on.

We can read Perry's discussion of Hart in either of two ways: as a surprising and counterintuitive interpretation of Hart or as part of a defence of a normative jurisprudence. Perry clearly believes that his interpretation of Hart is support for his general defence of the normativity of jurisprudence. If that is so, then we need to formulate a version of the claims of normative jurisprudence that would lend credence to his understanding of his project. If normative jurisprudence is understood as the claim that to retrieve the content of the concept of law one necessarily has to invoke substantive principles of political morality, then Perry's arguments against Hart's conception of his own project would have no bearing on normative jurisprudence one way or the other. Perry's being right about Hart is compatible both with normative jurisprudence, so conceived, and with its denial.

What then is the underlying or implicit conception of the project of conceptual analysis that animates Perry's critique? Does some view about the nature of conceptual analysis itself make the kind of argument Perry offers relevant to a general methodological claim about the analysis of the concept of law (rather than being just a series of critical observations about the way in which Hart carries out his project)? I think we can provide an understanding of the project of conceptual analysis that we can impute to Perry

that in addition to rendering his arguments against Hart intrinsically interesting make them part of a potential defence of normative jurisprudence,
and thus a proper object of scrutiny in this lecture. For the pragmatist
who is skeptical about traditional conceptual analysis and its emphasis on
uncovering important analytic truths about concepts, the question is not
whether there are interesting analytic truths connecting law and morality,
but how central moral and political argument is to retrieving the content of
our concept of law. We can read Perry as claiming that such arguments are
far more prominent in retrieving the content of the concept of law than one
might suspect. As evidence for that claim, Perry invites us, in effect, to look
at the actual efforts to determine the content of the concept in Hart.[23]
Understood within the pragmatist approach this is a perfectly fair and
reasonable strategy of argument.

If Hart actually did rely on moral principles in picking out the elements
of his positivist account, that might be evidence for the claim that a priori
reflection on our concept of law cannot by itself yield a theoretically satisfying range of analytic truths about its instances. This need not be because
the concept of law is intrinsically indeterminate, but simply be because,
though determinate, the content of law is not sufficiently discernible a
priori. Whereas Hart thought *the law of a particular community* was not likely
to be fully determinate, he did believe that the concept of law itself was
sufficiently determinate for all theoretical and practical purposes. Thus,
implicit in the strategy of argument Perry pursues is the view that something in the nature of *the concept* of law, or of conceptual analysis, entails
that conceptual analysis of law must be normative—and that is why Hart
appeals to substantive moral argument in his analysis of the concept of law.
To determine its content it is not only possible but necessary to engage
in substantive moral and political argument. For whatever reason, we
need substantive arguments to establish the centrality or prominence of
various features of our concept of law; and Perry's critique of Hart suggests that substantive moral arguments are required in order to identify
what the salient features of our concept of law are. The appeal to morality
need not be dictated by any analytic truth discernible by a priori reflection on the essential features of the concept; rather, we turn to moral
argument in order to get a fix on what the prominent or central features of
the concept are. This is, in any case, an interesting way in which we can
understand Perry's critique of Hart as providing an argument for normative jurisprudence.

We can distinguish among three related but distinct arguments that
Perry advances in support of his claim that Hart appeals to substantive

---

[23] He tentatively suggests that much the same is true of Raz's work, but does not pursue it
in detail.

moral and political argument early, often, and prominently in developing his theory of the concept of law. These are: (1) the "subject-matter" argument, (2) the "internal point of view" argument, and (3) the "function of law" argument. Let us consider each in turn.

The claim that jurisprudence is normative could be understood as the claim that before conceptual analysis can even begin we need to appeal to some norm or standard in order to pick out the features of law to which the concept of law must answer. We need to identify, if only in a provisional and revisable form, which features of law are central to the concept.[24] We need reasons for including law's claim to authority and its institutional nature while excluding the fact that judges usually wear robes. This process of selecting the salient features of the concept is inevitably normative. It reflects not only different and distinct philosophical interests, but may reflect different and distinct conceptions of the point or purpose of law as well.

It is one thing to claim that normative considerations figure in the project of identifying the features of law the theory of the concept must account for; quite another to claim that the norms to which one must appeal are those of political morality. Hart quite clearly appeals to epistemic norms in identifying those features of law the concept must answer to. This is clear from chapter 1 of *The Concept of Law*, where Hart tells us that an adequate theory of law will enable us to see the connections and differences between law and systems of sanctioning on the one hand, and between law and morality on the other, and that such an account will reveal as well the relationship between law and rules. For if we want to understand the role of law in our deliberative lives, then we need better to understand the way rules govern conduct. In effect, Hart is claiming that a range of theoretical norms, such as consilience and unification, govern theory construction in law. A theory of law must explain law's relationship to a range of cognate concepts in the normative and practical domains. This is why the concepts of coercion, rule, institutionality, deliberation, and agency are important for a philosophical theory of law, whereas the wearing of robes by judges is not. Thus, although it is clear that Hart appeals to norms in developing his theory, this is no reason to conclude that he appeals to moral or political norms.

It may be worthwhile in this context to revisit for a moment Hart's provocative claim that analytic jurisprudence is a kind of "descriptive sociology". We can understand this self-characterization in a way that also enables us to discern, at least in part, what might motivate Hart's critics to read him as engaged in a project of reporting on usage. The investigation of

---

[24] See Stephen R. Perry, "Interpretation and Methodology in Legal Theory" in Andrei Marmor (ed.), *Law and Interpretation: Essays in Legal Philosophy* (Oxford: Clarendon Press, 1995), 97–135.

usage is not, as some have claimed, oriented toward identifying some fixed set of shared criteria sufficient to determine the application conditions of the predicate "law". Rather, the investigation of usage serves to provide us, in a provisional and revisable way, with certain paradigm cases of law, as well as helping us to single out what features of law need to be explained. Descriptive sociology enters not at the stage of providing the theory of the concept, but at the preliminary stage of providing the raw materials about which one is to theorize.

Investigating common usage may allow a theorist to construct a "folk theory" of the concept of law, a more or less comprehensive (if incompletely articulated or rationalized) understanding of law's important features: rules, adjudicatory machinery, coercion, and the like. Conceptual analysis should be responsive to the folk theory—sometimes by vindicating its claims, by showing the connection among the elements and their relationships to one another, and other times by requiring revisions in it.[25]

Hart's reference to descriptive sociology may convey a bolder and more interesting claim as well, one that calls to mind Hilary Putnam's important discussion of the division of linguistic labor. In any culture characterized by expert discourses, what ordinary speakers mean by a given expression may just be whatever the relevant experts mean; indeed, the majority of ordinary speakers can even be wrong, if they tend to make false assumptions about what the experts mean by words like "beech", "lymphoma", or "operating system". In other words, it may turn out that ordinary use lacks the resources for constructing anything like a folk theory of the concept of law—usage may instead reveal only broad disagreement and confusion about the extension of the term "law". This would not mean that the philosopher has no choice but to substitute a contestable conception of law defensible only by appeal to substantive moral and political judgments. Rather, conceptual analysis can take its bearings from expert discourses such as social-scientific inquiry.

Economists, historians, sociologists, political scientists, and anthropologists all study law—both from the internal and from external points of

[25] There is no doubt that this is the role that Hart had in mind for the investigation of usage; he was not engaged in the criterial semantic project that Dworkin attributes to him. Instead, by consulting ordinary use we identify some of the salient features of law that a theory of the concept of it needs to explain, for example, the difference between systems of constraint that impose obligations and those that do not; as well as the difference between those that govern conduct in virtue of their content and those that purport to provide content-independent reasons for acting. This appeal to ordinary use in turn underwrites the appeal to epistemic or theoretical norms as regulating the analysis of the concept of law. This is, we are looking for a theory of the concept that explains—elegantly, simply, and in as comprehensive a way as possible—the differences between legal practice and other sanctioning systems on the one hand, and between legal practice and moral rules on the other.

view. In doing so, they work with their own paradigms of law, which they may revise in the light of the theories they construct and in ways that are responsive to the interests that motivate their inquiries. By attending to these inquiries outside of or beyond philosophy, we can obtain a rich and valuable picture of the forms of governance and organization that have been characterized as constituting law in different times and places, and under very different circumstances. A philosophical inquiry into the concept of law should be able to illuminate something about the practices that have been picked out as law in the social sciences, while explaining the importance of and the connections between the features that have figured prominently in the accounts of various social scientists of law. In the end the purposes of philosophical inquiry need not, and probably will not, fully coincide with all of the purposes of the social sciences; but a satisfactory philosophical account should be continuous with these more naturalistic inquiries. Thus, Hart appears to have ample normative resources for identifying the features of law for which an adequate jurisprudential theory should account: he appeals to the epistemic norms of unification, consilience, systematicity, and the like; and he may also appeal to the social sciences as independent theoretical inquiries that a philosophical theory of law should heed. With this rich set of normative resources available to Hart as explicit parts of his project, it is unclear what reason we might have to impute to him an appeal to moral and political norms as well. He does not seem to need them, and he denies appealing to them in the ways that Perry claims he does.

According to Perry, Hart's arguments against Holmes and Dworkin rely on the view that law has a proper function—specifically, the guidance of conduct through rules that are reasons for acting. As a shorthand notation, we will say that according to Perry, Hart thought that the function of law was the guidance of conduct. This commitment in turn shaped Hart's view about how to think about what law is, the importance of rules to law, and so on. In contrast, Dworkin attributes no guidance function to law. Instead, he claims that the function of law is to limit and justify the coercive authority of the state. Holmes probably agreed with Hart that law served a guidance function, but he emphasized law's use of sanctions, rather than its commitment to rules, as central to its fulfilling that function. It is clear, according to Perry, that Hart's arguments against Holmes and Dworkin must depend on sorting out these disputes in a particular way: by establishing, contra Dworkin, that the proper function of law is guidance; and, contra Holmes, that the function of law is to guide by rules that are in principle capable of being standards, and not by sanctions that are not. On Perry's reading, then, Hart's account of what needs to be explained about law depends on his substantive view about the proper function of law, a conception that must be defended by substantive political argument.

Perry's claims about Hart are most clear in his interpretation of Hart's objection to Holmes.[26] Any theory of law will have to account for the role it plays in the lives of individuals who relate to law from both the first- and the third-person perspectives. The first-person perspective is that of the individual who is a participant in the legal practice. An account of law that seeks to employ the methods of the natural sciences will miss the role legal standards play in the deliberative and practical lives of those governed by law. It will look for regularities of behavior, associating various incentives or sanctions with changes in behavior. Such approaches to the study of law are typically reductive. They take a concept like "legal rule" and give it content in terms of statistical regularities associating the probability of sanctions and the likelihood of certain behavior. Thus, to say that there is a legal rule that people ought not do X is to say that if individuals do X, there is a probability, P, that they will have some legal sanction, S, visited upon them.

Hart's complaint about such formulations of law is not that they are unilluminating or inapt: they may be useful for a range of scientific purposes, including formulating hypotheses about how behavior will be affected by changes in the frequency or quality of sanctions, and so on. Rather, Hart's complaint is that, whatever their virtues may be, these accounts lack the resources to explain various aspects of the first-person perspective on law. For in reducing rules to probabilities of sanctions, they leave no room for understanding compliance with law for the reason that the law requires it. To borrow his phrase, they define the internal point of view out of existence.[27]

Hart's primary target was the Scandinavian realists, like Alf Ross. The Scandinavians were not just reductionists; they were also moral or evaluative skeptics, and their skepticism about the content of evaluative judgments grew out of their logical, and not their legal, positivism. As they understood, it, the only meaningful propositions were those with empirical content and thus those testable before the tribunal of experience. Moral and normative language generally lacks cognitive content, and were instead to be analyzed non-cognitively as prescriptions, or as expressions of attitudes. To scientize the law and its normative discourse, they found it necessary to reinterpret the language of the law in a way that attributed cognitive

[26] The discussion here follows the structure of the debate between Perry and Shapiro in their essays that appear in Stephen J. Burton (ed.), *The Path of the Law* (Cambridge: Cambridge University Press, 2000). Many of the objections I offer to Perry's account appeared first in Shapiro's critique of Perry, and are more fully developed there.

[27] It is worth noting that Hart's criticism of the reductionists does not apply to Austin's account. There is an important difference between analyzing legal rules as predictions of sanctions and analyzing legal rules as commands *backed by* sanctions. The latter is compatible with compliance for the reason the law requires it, whereas the former is not. I am grateful to Ken Himma for this point.

content to it. Thus, legal norms were viewed as elliptical ways of expressing the likelihood that certain conduct would meet with certain unhappy results. Instead of expressing anything fundamental about law, the legal language of rights, duties, privileges, and liberties is reducible to probabilities of sanction. Hart argued that such an analysis of law lacks the resources necessary to account for the fact that at least some individuals comply with the law for the reason that the law requires it. Law has an internal dimension that these analyses simply cannot capture, and it is in that sense that they define the internal point of view out of existence. To understand law is to understand the way in which it can and often does figure in one's deliberations about what one ought to do, and not merely as shorthand for predictions that are accessible to external observers about what judges and other officials will do.

The jurisprudence of Oliver Wendell Holmes, as Hart understands it, is limited by the same meager resources—sanction and behavior—as those available to the Scandinavian realists. Holmes, however, is not driven by skepticism about the cognitive content of moral expressions; and unlike the Scandinavian realists, who seek merely to uncover causal connections and lawlike regularities suitable to a scientific inquiry, Holmes looks to unmask the role law plays in the deliberative process of those who see the law from the first-person perspective. To this end, Holmes introduces the concept of the "bad man". The bad man's concern is not to identify the reasons that law provides, but rather to avoid the sanctions with which the law threatens him. Thus, although legal statements remain reducible to predictions of sanctions, the sanctions themselves are understood as entering into the deliberative processes of the "bad man".

Despite this first-person element in Holmes's account, Hart levels against him the same objection with which he criticizes the Scandinavian realists—he takes Holmes to task for defining the internal point of view out of existence. Perry finds this to be puzzling at best. After all, the Scandinavians seek to uncover lawlike regularities in behavior that are available to the external, social-scientific observer. Holmes, in contrast, seeks to understand the law from the perspective of those governed by it. Indeed, Holmes's entire project would seem to be aimed at giving a distinctive content to the internal point of view. Perry concludes that Hart's objection isn't really that Holmes defines the internal point of view out of existence; rather, Holmes has "the wrong kind" of internal point of view. On Hart's account, the legal rule itself—which represents a social judgment about what ought to be done—is the reason for acting; whereas Holmes locates the reason law provides in the threat of sanction. The former account captures a morally more attractive form of guidance—a form that presupposes a conception of the person as an autonomous agent capable of acting on the basis of rules that are reasons, and not merely as a calculating animal, responsive to threats.[28]

Perry's critique of Hart mistakes a conceptual argument for a moral one. Hart has two main conceptual motivations for rejecting sanction accounts. In the first place, it cannot be denied that individuals sometimes act for the reason that the law requires it, and Holmes lacks the conceptual resources to account for that. If legal rules are defined as predictions of sanctions, then legal rules cannot be reasons in virtue of their being law: predictions are not reasons for action.[29] Yet the internal point of view, as Hart understands it, is the point of view of one who takes the law as a reason. Hart is not faulting Holmes for having a morally unattractive account of the internal point of view; he is quite justifiably faulting Holmes for not being able to account for obvious facts about the way in which the law sometimes figures in human deliberation and action.[30]

Moreover, for Hart, the theoretical role of the internal point of view goes beyond the need to make conceptual room for an obvious empirical fact about the experience of living under law; the internal point of view is also necessary in order to explain the very possibility of law—for Hart maintains that law depends on the existence of criteria of legality that are practiced from the internal point of view. All sanction and predictive theories lack the resources to explain the possibility of legal authority, for they cannot explain the existence conditions of legal rules authorizing sanctions, or the existence of rules specifying the rules to which sanctions can attach. Sanction theories are not merely undesirable or incomplete; they are incoherent. They depend on the claim that laws are sanctions, but cannot explain how sanctioning is possible.

In sum, whereas Perry claims that Hart must be defending a particular conception of the internal point of view against Holmes on substantive moral or political grounds, the fact is that moral and political

[28] In fact, Hart does not presuppose any more than Holmes does about the nature of the person or of human motivation. Hart assumes only that persons are capable of acting on the basis of reasons. If Holmes's bad man is a deliberative agent—as he must be on Perry's account—then Holmes assumes as much about the nature of the person as Hart does. Nor, of course, does Hart deny that individuals living under the law sometimes act for the purpose of avoiding sanction.

[29] You predict that I will do X. I may act for the reason that you made a prediction; but your prediction itself is logically not the sort of thing that could be my reason for acting.

[30] Perry's argument goes astray because of a certain ambiguity in the phrase "the internal point of view". We might mean by that expression, roughly, "the insider's point of view" or "the first-person point of view". On the other hand, we might mean "the committed point of view", or the point of view of one who adopts the rule as a reason for action. There is nothing more clear in *The Concept of Law* than that Hart means by the internal point of view the second of these senses. There are many points of view that are internal in the first sense. The point of view of Holmes's bad man is internal in the first sense, but not in the second. In accusing both the Scandinavian realists and Holmes of defining the internal point of view out of existence, he has this second sense in mind. The argument to this point follows Scott Shapiro's critique of Perry.

considerations have nothing to do with either the argument Hart makes or the arguments a positivist would need or want to make against Holmes. If Hart actually relies on the claim that law has a proper function in order to derive the elements of his substantive theory of law, then we will have to look elsewhere to find evidence of it.

To this end, Perry introduces what I call the "function of law" argument.[31] Hart explicitly claims that it is futile to search for any function of law more specific than the guidance of conduct. By contrast, Dworkin maintains that law has the function of employing and constraining the use of the coercive authority of the state in a way that at least prima facie justifies the law's claim to legitimacy. This difference between Hart and Dworkin can shed light on their respective theories of the concept of law and their differing views about legal content. For Dworkin any interpretation of legal practice must operate within the parameters of trying to show the law in its best light; the positivist is committed to no such claim. On the other hand, the disagreement between inclusive and exclusive legal positivists makes sense only within the context of the claim that legal norms must be capable of making a practical difference in terms of guidance, that is, a difference in the reasons the law provides to those subject to its demands. We cannot choose between positivism and Dworkin's interpretivism without determining who is right about law's proper function. Yet that dispute is not itself factual. If the disagreement between Hart and Dworkin is not a factual one about law's actual function, then it must be a normative one about law's proper function. Thus, the substantive considerations that support one or another conception of law's proper function are part of every theory of the concept of law and determine its content.[32]

Law is a human construction capable of satisfying a variety of human interests and needs (though it can serve evil as well as desirable or valuable ends). It is one thing, however, to claim that law can bring about certain desirable states of affairs, or that it can achieve certain ends—and something else altogether to claim that law has a function. Not every goal or end

---

[31] See Perry, "The Varieties of Legal Positivism."

[32] Even if Hart's theory of law is based on a contestable conception of law's proper function—and in a moment I will argue that it is not—it is important to note that not every jurisprudential theory must or does impute a proper function to law. Not only does my theory of the concept of law not rely in any way on ascribing a proper function to law, it does not even rely on the claim that law has a function. In fact, I deny that law has a function in the traditional philosophic sense. Particular laws may have functions or purposes; and a community may construct a legal system for a purpose. But there is no function that is inherent in law itself. On my reading of him, Raz is similarly dubious of law's having a function in this sense. On the other hand, Shapiro may well be right in thinking that Hart thought of law as having a guidance function. That function is supposed to figure in certain kinds of social-scientific explanations of law's existence, persistence, and shape, and so on. While I think Shapiro is right about Hart, he is, as I argue in Lecture 10, probably wrong in thinking that functionalism is adequate to ground a certain reading of the practical difference thesis, according to which no norm can be law if it is not capable of making a practical difference.

or product of a process is its function. The idea of a thing's function can be specified in a variety of ways; we can assign functions to things, as when the hammer on my desk functions as a paperweight. We can design things or kinds of things to have functions—for example, hammers have the function of driving nails. These are stories in which things get their functions from the uses we intend for them. However, things can have functions that are not related to intentions in that way—for example, the hand has the function of grasping, or of enabling us to grasp things. The story that connects hands with their function can invoke intentions (divine design); but we can also tell a causal story that explains how a certain outcome—the capacity to grasp things—is part of a causal–evolutionary explanation of the existence and shape of the hand.

In ascribing to law the function of guiding conduct, Shapiro suggests (and I concur) that we should not read Hart as advancing any sort of moral argument about law's proper function. Instead, we should understand him to be offering a certain kind of functional explanation of law. This type of explanation is familiar in the social sciences, and is a sort of hybrid incorporating both intentional and non-intentional elements. Hart never elaborated the formal structure of the explanation, but the basic idea is that law's capacity to guide conduct effectively is part of the explanation of its existence and persistence, as well as of the shape law takes in its mature forms.

The elements of such an explanatory appeal to law's guidance function are all present in chapter 5 of *The Concept of Law*. If law consisted only of primary rules imposing obligations—rules that guide epistemically by marking certain standards as those to which one must comply—then guidance would be "inefficient" in at least three ways. First, there would be uncertainty about which rules had the authoritative marking; a more effective scheme of guidance would have a reliable way of identifying which standards bore the relevant mark. Second, legal guidance would be static and unresponsive to changing circumstances and interests; the capacity to amend, alter, and abandon certain rules and introduce new ones allows for a more effective form of guidance. Finally, it would be unclear in some circumstance what the rules required of us; it would be more effective if disputes about law's requirements could be resolved authoritatively. It is plausible to think that the effectiveness of these elements for guiding conduct is part of the explanation of why they are widespread and enduring features of mature legal systems. Individuals acting over time have developed the structures of law in order to serve those various ends— morally worthy ones as well as morally worthless ones—because law can serve those ends more effectively than other forms of governance. Societies that can function effectively in various ways have tended to endure, and their institutions have spread through various processes of diffusion. Thus, ascribing to law the function of guiding conduct enables us to understand why mature legal systems take the form of a union of primary and secondary rules.

Hart's argument in chapter 5 of *The Concept of Law* is thus a kind of social-scientific functionalist explanation of law. This explanation reinforces the philosophical analysis of law as a union of primary and secondary rules, and makes the philosophical theory continuous with a standard social-scientific explanation. Wherever law arises, no matter the historical and cultural differences, no matter the particular human ends it may serve, we can expect it to acquire roughly the same structure in its mature form. This generality is among the notable strengths of Hart's account. Contrary to Perry, there is nothing in Hart's argument to suggest that the moral attractiveness of guiding conduct through rules is the basis for his view that such guidance is the function of law.[33]

Whatever their general interest, none of Perry's arguments actual establish that Hart engaged in substantive moral and political argument in identifying the salient features of his theory of the concept of law. Hart identifies in a preliminary way those features of law that an analysis of the concept must be responsive to by applying familiar norms of theory construction, not by applying those of political morality. His conception of the centrality of the internal point of view rests on conceptual claims about the possibility of legal authority and logic of reasons. Again, there is nothing in his argument that suggests a moral or political foundation for the internal point of view. Finally, his claim is not that law has a proper guidance function that must be defended by its moral or political attractiveness; rather by attributing to law a guidance function, we can more adequately understand why law arises, persists over time, and takes the shape it does in its mature forms. If Perry's arguments fail to capture the actual arguments that underwrite Hart's commitments to these salient features of law—its commitment to rules, the internal point of view, and the guidance function—they cannot support a claim for a more general normative jurisprudence.

Whatever the proper methodology of legal theory, significant substantive differences remain. Even allowing for the fact that different theorists may have somewhat different projects in mind, the field is fraught with apparently intractable disputes. Strong arguments are advanced all

---

[33] The claim that Hart relies on a moral argument fails to take seriously his explicitly positivist commitments. It is ironic that commentators who embrace a Dworkinian interpretivist project sometimes appear unwilling to apply the charitable principles that govern such a project to their reading of Hart. One would think that those principles would require us to read Hart in a way that strengthens and deepens his consistently positivist themes. Though positivists may be mere Agatha Christies to Dworkin's Shakespeare, it is uncharitable to interpret a positivist project as a second-rate production of *Hamlet* when it could be interpreted as a perfectly satisfying murder mystery.

around, and there appears to be little prospect of an imminent consensus. Do we have any reason to suppose that increasingly sophisticated conceptual analysis will ultimately yield conclusive answers to the kinds of questions with which this book is concerned—or is each seeming advance simply more grist for the mill of philosophical controversy? At its best, conceptual analysis helps us clarify the nature of the underlying disagreements that we have; at its worst, it can be little more than a contest of poorly fathomed intuitions dressed up in fancy philosophical attire. Or so one might argue.

We can in fact distinguish between two different challenges to the project of this book that draw upon the idea that conceptual analysis is of limited usefulness. Both challenges draw upon the claim that the concept of law is itself indeterminate. The claim need not be that all contestable concepts are indeterminate, thus rendering conceptual analysis in any domain of philosophy of only limited value—though it is clearly compatible with such a view. For our purposes, the central claim is that the concept of law is indeterminate. The more modest challenge holds that because the concept of law is indeterminate, conceptual analysis of it must be augmented. The more ambitious challenge to the project of this book is the claim that a priori conceptual analysis needs to be replaced by a social- or natural-scientific inquiry generally; or, minimally, that the model for philosophical inquiry needs to be changed from armchair reflection to something more akin to, and continuous with, the methods of scientific inquiry. Let us consider challenges of both sorts beginning with the first. Here the claim is not that the concept of law is inaccessible or inapt for conceptual analysis; rather the claim is that conceptual analysis reveals the concept of law to be indeterminate and in need of conceptual "legislation" or "engineering".

Underwriting the engineering or legislative project is the view that the disputes among jurisprudential theses about, for example, the role of morality in legal argument cannot be resolved by reflection on the concept of law. No amount of reflection on the concept of law (or presumably no substantive argument from premises of political morality) will yield a determinate concept: one that answers the fundamental questions of jurisprudence that have been the concern of this book—in particular, the ways in which morality is implicated in our concept of law. It then claims that we need to complete or fill out the concept to precisify it. We cannot appeal to the tools of conceptual analysis—mere a priori reflection or substantive normative argument—to do that. Instead, we are left to engineer or discipline the concept so that it may serve best the practical political aims for which it may be best suited.[34]

---

[34] Cf. Liam Murphy, "The Political Question of the Concept of Law" in Jules Coleman (ed.), *Hart's Postscript: Essays on the Postscript to "The Concept of Law"* (Oxford: Oxford University Press, 2001).

There are several things that need to be said about this line of challenge. First, we should note that we do not aim for precise, disciplined, complete concepts all the time. We recognize that many of our ordinary concepts— such as "bread", "wood", "table", or "chair"—are vague and ambiguous. But that is fine for the purposes to which we put them. We do not in general feel it important to be able to analyze them much beyond identifying so-called family resemblances. We typically do not believe that much of theoretical or practical importance hangs on more precise analyses or formulations of these concepts. If unanticipated problems arise, we feel they can be dealt with adequately without the construction of a full-blown precise theory of the concept. This is not true of all concepts; and the very existence of jurisprudence is evidence that we do not believe it is true of our concept of law (in much the same way that philosophy of language invites the suggestion that we do not think it true of our concepts of truth and meaning). Those who advance this line of argument then are committed to two claims about our concept of law. The first is that there are compelling reasons for a disciplined, precise concept of law; and second, that the tools available to conceptual analysis are inadequate to that task.

It is also important to note similarities and differences between this approach to constructing a theory of our concept of law and what we may call the Benthamite approach. Both accept that there are compelling practical reasons for having a precise concept of law—one that removes vagueness and ambiguity—but they disagree about the role ordinary philosophical analysis is to play in constructing it. The Benthamite project is an engineering project from the outset. Our concepts—like our beliefs, intentions, character traits, and actions—are subject to evaluation in light of their consequences. We should have only those concepts that have the best consequences.[35] Likely the concepts we should have will have much in common with the ones we do have—for a variety of obvious reasons—so we will need to determine what the content of our concepts really is to figure out what they ought to be. But philosophical analysis is no more than contingently and instrumentally connected to the engineering project. This is not true in the case of the approach currently under discussion. In this view, conceptual analysis is the appropriate philosophical method. If it yields a complete and precise concept, that's great. Only if it fails to yield a determinate concept should it be supplemented or disciplined by political considerations. The limitations or incompleteness of conceptual analysis frees us to complete and discipline the concept by appealing to the practical political consequences (if any) of alternative conceptions. This is in stark

---

[35] This is why I am not inclined to characterize Bentham as a normative jurisprudent. Bentham adopts a normative stance on the concepts we *should* have, and not a normative account of the concepts we have.

contrast with the Benthamite project, in which conceptual analysis is no more than a tool in a practical political agenda.

Having made all this clear, there are two points to make about the practical–political challenge to conceptual analysis. First, what is the evidence—beyond the existence of disagreement—that the concept of law is indeterminate in any interesting or important way? Certainly Dworkin and I would both contend that the tools available to us generate precise and compelling answers to all the fundamental questions about the role of morality in law. We may disagree with one another about what the correct answers are, but we do not doubt for a second that our theories provide complete and persuasive answers to those questions. If the challenge is that the concept is incomplete if there remains disagreement about its content, then no philosophically interesting concept is precise or adequately analyzed. To be sure, part of the difficulty comes from disagreements about what the criteria for a theory of a concept are or should be.

More importantly, from the pragmatist perspective defended throughout this book, the challenge we are considering to conceptual analysis of the concept of law is no real challenge at all. For on my view there is no reason to suppose that conceptual analysis is not responsive to practical considerations.[36] My objection to such projects is not that its advocates allow appeal to practical considerations; rather, they do not understand that conceptual analysis—at least when it is of the pragmatist variety that I have defended—is always responsive to such considerations. Those who level this charge against conceptual analysis underestimate the extent of the resources available to it. They have in mind a picture of conceptual analysis that is immune from practical or political considerations. What they offer as an alternative to conceptual analysis is already a part of it.

In a recent series of papers expressing skepticism about the potential of conceptual analysis to resolve these substantive disputes about the nature of law that have been the focus of the second half of this book, Brian Leiter has been developing and defending a project of what he calls "naturalized jurisprudence".[37] His work presents a challenge not only to my project, but

---

[36] If this book stands for anything, it stands for the claim that we do not determine the content of our concepts from a priori reflection alone. Rather we construct theories of our concepts, and those theories answer to the full range of norms—theoretical, epistemic, discursive, political, and practical. If the present challenge to conceptual analysis is to be read as the claim that the sole or paramount criterion for evaluating theories of our concepts is that of practical–political theory, then this position simply collapses into the Benthamite project, which is one not of conceptual analysis but of conceptual engineering. This is not a challenge to my project or to any project in analytic jurisprudence; it is just another kind of project altogether. On the other hand, if the claim is that a theory of the concept of law should in principle answer to practical–political considerations, then this is no challenge to my thesis either; for nowhere do I deny that an analysis of the concept answers to such concerns.

[37] See Brian Leiter, "Rethinking Legal Realism: Toward a Naturalized Jurisprudence" *Texas Law Review* 76/2 (Dec. 1997) 267–315.

to all of contemporary analytic jurisprudence. Naturalized jurisprudence is interesting and valuable in its own right, but Leiter gives us no reason to abandon the fundamental methodology of analytic jurisprudence. For the project of naturalized jurisprudence itself requires so much in the way of conceptual analysis that there is no meaningful sense in which it could be said to replace it; at most, it can support conceptual analysis in a narrowly circumscribed, but perhaps important, way.

It is important to distinguish between more and less ambitious versions of the claims that can be made on behalf of naturalized jurisprudence. An ambitious form of naturalism asserts that a priori conceptual analysis of law is a fruitless activity in which progress is illusory at best. A more modest naturalism denies only that certain important aspects of legal theory can be fruitfully addressed by a priori analysis. Ambitious naturalists would have us abandon philosophical jurisprudence altogether in favor of a social science of law; modest naturalism claims that analytic jurisprudence need not be abandoned, for it may play a secondary role within an overall naturalistic project. Leiter's project is decidedly of the more modest variety.[38] He does not believe that conceptual analysis in general, or of law in particular, is a fruitless activity.

Within the province of jurisprudence proper, Leiter's focus is on the theory of adjudication; and more specifically, on the issue of determinacy with regard to adjudicatory content. A theory of adjudication seeks to identify the procedural (and possibly also substantive) norms that, if correctly followed by judges, will yield all and only those outcomes that are warranted by the set of authoritative legal standards binding on them. For every dispute, there are three possible outcomes warranted by law. These are: "plaintiff wins", "defendant wins", or "indeterminate"—that is, the law does not determine who wins.[39] A theory of adjudication, then, aims to identify the function, if it exists, that takes as inputs the set of authoritative or binding standards and yields as its output the right answer to each legal

[38] Certainly, the mere fact that there is disagreement about what the conceptual truths of law are—and even about whether there are such truths—does not mean that conceptual analysis of law is fruitless. If that were the case, we should have to conclude the same about philosophy generally. (This may be a popular view outside philosophy, but should be advanced by a philosopher only with great care and other employment options.) Serious and fundamental disagreement is the mark of philosophy, not the end of it. The history of philosophy just is the history of important, apparently irresolvable disputes about important philosophical concepts. Nonetheless, there can be no denying that philosophical inquiry has contributed to our capacity to understand ourselves and our relationship to the world around us. Replacing philosophical inquiry with social science, philosophical method with the methods of the natural and social sciences, would hardly put an end to disputes about the nature of law or anything else for that matter; only those with no real experience of the social or natural sciences and their controversies would believe any such thing.

[39] This last possibility is denied by those who maintain that there are always right answers as a matter of law.

dispute for which there is a right answer as a matter of law. The theory should give the answer "plaintiff wins" to all and only those cases in which the plaintiff does have the best argument as a matter of law; the answer "defendant wins" when the same is true of the defendant; and the answer "indeterminate" when the available legal materials fail to compel either result.

Leiter claims that no amount of philosophical reflection on the concepts of law and adjudication, or on the idea of a right answer, will reveal that function—if indeed such a unique function exists in ours or any other legal practice. If there are norms determining when particular answers are right, they are not accessible by reflection on concepts; if such norms exist, they are instead internal to the practice of adjudication itself.

Much of Leiter's argument draws upon an analogy with Quine's work in epistemology. It may enable us better to understand Leiter's arguments if we remind ourselves of the core of Quine's argument against "armchair, a priori epistemology". Like a theory of adjudication, epistemology is "justification-centered"; it is the philosophical study of epistemic justification, and its aim is to identify those norms of evidence and reasoning which, if followed, would warrant beliefs, theories, world-views, and the like. Consider our sense experience as constituting the set of epistemic inputs, and our beliefs, theories, or world-views the set of epistemic outputs. The question is, under what conditions do the epistemic inputs warrant or justify particular epistemic outputs, such as beliefs? Those conditions constitute the norms of epistemic reasoning.

In his groundbreaking essay "Epistemology Naturalized" Quine rejects the peculiar philosophical project of seeking to discover the norms governing epistemic reasoning a priori. The most famous and easiest to grasp of his objections relies on the Duhem–Quine under-determination thesis. Roughly, it holds that the same evidentiary base is consistent with an infinite number of diverse and incompatible hypotheses or predictions, and therefore no evidentiary base uniquely determines an epistemic output; or, put the other way around, no epistemic output is uniquely warranted by any evidentiary base. We can see the same point in terms of Quine's confirmation holism, which is in effect a corollary of the under-determination thesis. According to confirmation holism, the relationship between evidence and belief (or theory) is holistic, in the sense that all evidence tests—that is, confirms or disconfirms—a set of beliefs as a whole, and not an individual belief or hypothesis. That is because by making adjustments or revisions elsewhere in one's stock or web of beliefs, any evidence can be reconciled with the belief or hypothesis it might otherwise be thought to disconfirm. How willing one is to abandon any particular belief in the face of recalcitrant evidence is a function of how central the belief is to one's web of beliefs—that is, how many other beliefs it supports and to what extent it does so—and of the relative advantages of the new theory in enabling one to make one's way through the world.

Considerations like these suggest that there is no point in looking a priori for norms regulating proper reasoning. Rather than employing armchair reflection to determine the test of justified belief, we should investigate the processes by which cognizers come to hold the beliefs they have. The analytic philosophical project of epistemology is replaced by a (social) scientific (in this case, psychological) project. The analogy with the theory of adjudication is reasonably straightforward. The theory of adjudication is the philosophical activity of trying to determine, by reflection on the concepts of law, content, interpretation, and the like, the set of norms of proper adjudication. Applying them will yield uniquely warranted outcomes when such outcomes exist. The claim of naturalized jurisprudence is that a conceptual analytic theory of adjudication encounters the same difficulties as those that doom analytic epistemology. Any number of inconsistent outputs are compatible with the set of adjudicatory inputs, and there are a large number of interpretive principles or ways of organizing the inputs that are themselves internally consistent and that warrant different outcomes. There are no unique interpretive principles and there is no philosophically respectable way of picking one out as correct.

Leiter concludes that we need to replace or supplement legal philosophy with sociology, psychology, anthropology, or economics of law. We should turn away from philosophy to an appropriate social-scientific inquiry— one that looks to uncovering lawlike regularities in decision making, or one which seeks to identify which norms, if any, are internal to the practice of adjudication. Leiter does not deny that there may be such norms—only that philosophy has a role to play in determining what they are or in justifying them.

There is nothing objectionable about a sociological, psychological, or a psychosocial jurisprudence. No philosopher of law could quarrel with a project of trying to uncover lawlike regularities in judicial decision-making. Such social-scientific laws of judging—if any could be discovered—might render judgment more predictable, which could have the salutary effect of facilitating coordination and planning; a social science of adjudication would also be valuable on purely theoretical grounds, as a way of making law and legal practice more rationally intelligible. The problem is that there is no reason to think that such a social-scientific project can be a substitute for the philosophical methodology of analytic jurisprudence. In fact the naturalized project can proceed only after a good deal of philosophical spadework has been done.

Leiter is himself aware that the project of a naturalized jurisprudence requires an analytic jurisprudential component, but he underestimates its extent. The very idea of an adjudicatory function operating on authoritative legal standards presupposes that we have criteria for determining what the authoritative legal standards are. Thus, the naturalist is committed as a conceptual matter to the existence of a test of legality. Moreover, not every view about the nature of the test of legality is consistent with the naturalist project. He cannot, for example, accept the Dworkinian theory of the criteria of legality, for that account falls out of Dworkin's theory of legal content.[40] If Dworkin is right that the content of the law is fully determinate, then the naturalist cannot possibly be right. This encumbers the naturalist with the burden of presenting a philosophical argument against Dworkin's entire jurisprudential project. The naturalist is thus in the same boat with every other analytic philosopher of law—his project requires analytic legal philosophy as much as Raz's or mine does.

These considerations suggest—though they do not demonstrate—that naturalized jurisprudence presupposes a positivist conception of how to think about the criteria of legality. But that places naturalism within positivism, and positivism, however attractive, is of course, a controversial substantive jurisprudential view. More importantly, these considerations suggest that naturalism will be plausible only if positivism is. And thus, rather than escaping the work of traditional analytic jurisprudence, naturalism again is shown to rely upon it. In that case, naturalism could not be entertained as a serious alternative to analytic jurisprudence.

It is a further question, of course, whether the naturalist must defend a particular view about the content of the criteria of legality, and in doing so come out on one or the other side of the inclusive–exclusive legal positivism divide.[41] In one of his essays Leiter suggests that the American legal realists —prescient naturalists on his reading—were implicitly exclusive, or what he called "hard" positivists.[42] It is not obvious to me why legal realists or any other putative naturalist would have to come out in favor of exclusive legal positivism. But if Leiter is right, then his defense of naturalism presupposes a specific resolution to another, in this case quite subtle and specialized, debate in analytic jurisprudence between inclusive and exclusive legal positivism: one that implicates particular views about how to understand legal normativity. This strikes me as presupposing quite a lot of analytic legal philosophy for a view that is supposed to be an alternative to analytic legal philosophy.

However the naturalist comes out on the inclusive–exclusive legal positivism question, he is committed to the claim that the rule of recognition (or, more generally conceived, the test of legality) has determinate content. If the rule of recognition did not have determinate content, then it would be impossible to identify the set of adjudicatory inputs. But if the rule of

[40] See Lecture 11.   [41] See Lectures 8–10.
[42] Brian Leiter, "Realism, Hard Positivism and Conceptual Analysis" *Legal Theory* 4/4 (Dec. 1998) 533–47.

recognition has determinate legal content, how is it that the rules that are valid under it do not? If the rule of recognition can pick out certain standards of conduct as official or legally authorized, why is it that legal rules valid under the rule of recognition cannot pick out acts as legally mandatory, prohibited, or permissible?[43] It is no help to say that while the rule of recognition and rules valid under it all have determinate legal content, the law has no determinate content. That would involve defending a claim about the nature of legal content that would be on its face controversial, if not implausible. Indeed, if particular legal rules are extremely indeterminate, then we could infer perhaps that legal guidance content is often indeterminate—that is, the rules would not offer adequate guidance to citizens and others whose behavior is regulated by the rules. But this would tell us nothing about legal *adjudicatory* content.[44] For there may be very well-entrenched practices in communities for resolving disputes in the face of guidance indeterminacy.[45] To be sure, those practices or norms are not discerned by a priori reflection on the nature of content or adjudication. But that is just what a positivist theory of adjudicatory content already tells us: that the "function" that takes as its inputs "official legal pronouncements" and gives as its outputs "decisions in particular cases as a matter of law" will depend on the particular practices of different legal systems. Positivism entails the view that we cannot determine adjudicatory content a priori. In this sense, naturalism is no replacement for legal positivism; a limited form of naturalism is if anything a corollary of a positivist theory of legal content.

[43] I first heard this objection pressed against Leiter by both Scott Shapiro and Roberta Romano. In response, Leiter could argue that there is nothing implausible in the suggestion that the rule of recognition has determinate content while rules valid under it do not—after all, they are different kinds of rules. One kind picks out rules, the other picks out behavior as conforming to or failing to conform to the rules. So the former picks out propositional objects while the latter picks out actions. That might explain how the former can be determinate while the latter not. It is not obvious a priori why picking out rules should be easier than picking out acts that fall under rules—in part because in the legal context the rules that are being picked out are created by actions, and so what one is really picking out are rule-making acts; so there is no real difference.

Still, Leiter could respond that it isn't in the nature of rules in general or legal rules in particular that if any are determinate, all must be. Some rules can be determinate and others not. Indeed; but the burden is clearly shifted to Leiter to explain why the rule of recognition should be determinate while rules subordinate to it not. The burden is great, since Leiter's argument for the indeterminacy of rules subordinate to the rule of recognition is based on the range of available non-unique interpretive principles. That issue applies equally to the rule of recognition.

[44] See Lecture 11 for this important distinction.

[45] In other words, indeterminate particular legal inputs may mean that ordinary folk cannot reliably determine what actions a particular legal rule requires of them or what liberties and rights it confers on them. From their perspective, the rules are inadequate guides to action. But this tells us nothing at all about whether the adjudicatory content of the law is indeterminate, for it tells us nothing about how disputes under the rules are to be resolved by officials. A great deal of guidance indeterminacy is compatible with adjudicatory determinacy. Leiter's thesis concerns the latter, not the former, kind of indeterminacy.

Whatever the function might be that, in a particular community, yields adjudicatory outputs from legal inputs, we cannot discover or present a theory of that function unless we first have a theory of law telling us what is true of law as such.[46] Thus, the naturalist does cannot, simply by focusing on adjudication, avoid the fundamental question of analytic jurisprudence: what, if anything, is essential to our concept of law; or what are the elements of that concept on our best theory of it? In short, at every turn naturalism has to confront the most vexing issues in analytic jurisprudence, and must defend a particular view about how each of those issues ought to be resolved. At best, naturalism is not an alternative but a supplemental element of a positivistic picture of adjudicatory content.

These considerations seem to me to undermine any strong claims that can be made on behalf of a naturalized jurisprudence. The very possibility of naturalism depends on resolving nearly all of the substantive issues in analytic jurisprudence that have been the focus of the last two parts of this book. Strong naturalism—the claim that the philosophy of law must give way to a social science of law—is ambitious but implausible. Modest naturalism is at once both less ambitious and more plausible. Properly understood, however, it is simply an element of a positivistic conception of adjudicatory legal content; it relies so much on a positivistic theory of the concept of law that it can hardly be seen as a threat to it, let alone to analytic legal philosophy generally.

In this book I have done my best to set out and defend a variety of substantive views in law: some in the philosophy of tort law, the majority in analytic jurisprudence. In doing so, I have also tried to defend, in some places by example and elsewhere by substantive argument, a certain pragmatist approach to philosophic method: focusing largely on the relationships among concept, principle, and practice, and on the nature of conceptual analysis. My goal has been to contribute to progress in our understanding of law and legal practice, not simply to win arguments. I have tried not only to note the weaknesses, but also to acknowledge the strengths, of the views that I have criticized—and I reiterate here the high esteem in which I hold the theorists who have contributed those views to our field. If, as a result of this book, the issues are more sharply focused than

---

[46] In other words, as I pointed out in Lecture 11, we cannot infer from "adjudicatory content" to "legal adjudicatory content". There is a premise missing, namely that whatever judges are required to decide in a case—or whatever they do decide in a case—states or expresses the law. We can have good reasons for reserving the category of law to a subset of official acts— even those mandated by legal sources. Raz, for one, claims that only those acts, rules, or authoritative pronouncements that can be practical authorities can be law. Not every authoritative pronouncement is for that reason alone law. Thus, we need a theory of what law is before we can have a theory about the determinacy or indeterminacy of adjudication. Therefore, before the naturalist gets to claim that analytic legal philosophy has to be replaced by a naturalist project, he has to do as much analytic legal philosophy as do the rest of us.

before; if the debates have been renewed and the resources with which we can address them augmented, then I have accomplished all that I set out to do. If, beyond that, some of the arguments I have advanced prove persuasive, I have exceeded my expectations. Finally, I hope that in engaging my contemporaries I have also managed to convey the respect and gratitude I feel toward our predecessors in legal philosophy, this field we are so fortunate to call ours.

Index